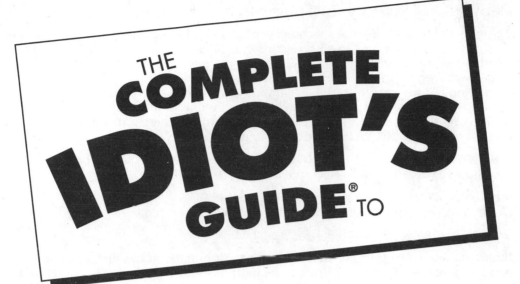

THE COMPLETE IDIOT'S GUIDE® TO

Mothers and Daughters

by Rosanne Rosen

alpha books

201 West 103rd Street
Indianapolis, IN 46290

A Pearson Education Company

Publisher
Marie Butler-Knight

Product Manager
Phil Kitchel

Managing Editor
Jennifer Chisholm

Senior Acquisitions Editor
Randy Ladenheim-Gil

Development Editor
Deborah S. Romaine

Senior Production Editor
Christy Wagner

Copy Editor
Catherine Schwenk

Illustrator
Jody Schaeffer

Cover Designers
Mike Freeland
Kevin Spear

Book Designers
Scott Cook and Amy Adams of DesignLab

Indexer
Lisa Wilson

Layout/Proofreading
Angela Calvert
Mary Hunt
Natashia Rardin

Contents at a Glance

Contents

Foreword

The moment I received the news from my doctor that I was actually going to become a mother, I was filled with an unbelievable mixture of joy and exhilaration. I could barely contain my excitement as I feverishly charted my course to becoming the best mother in the universe.

Then all of a sudden, right in the middle of all my planning, I became engulfed in a huge wave of anxiety that made me feel like I was drowning. "Wait a minute! What am I thinking? I can't do this myself! Where's the manual that is magically supposed to appear with all the answers and instructions I so desperately need?" Running around in a cold sweat, I read everything I could get my hands on to try to prepare myself for one of the most profound miraculous relationships in anyone's life—that of a mother and child. And if you add to the mix that your child is a daughter, the intricacies woven into the exquisite tapestry you weave together become even more significant.

A mother-daughter relationship is always complex, to say the least. Having almost a mirror of yourself that you love more than anything in life, yet knowing you must ultimately push her out of the nest is always painful and difficult. That is, of course, until your precious little girl becomes a teenager. Then suddenly, both of you discover horns, cloven hooves, and a suspicious-looking tail whenever you look at each other. You think your daughter treats you like you just escaped from a leper colony, and she thinks if she solved the riddle of the sphinx it wouldn't be enough to please you. Both of you begin to wonder if there's any help in sight!

Well let me assure you that help has finally arrived. Remember when I first became a mother, frantically wishing a manual would appear with the answers I needed? Amazing though it may seem, the elusive manual has just been located. It's called *The Complete Idiot's Guide to Mothers and Daughters*.

In it you will finds the tools you'll need, tools that will be invaluable to you as a mother, daughter, and even grandmother. With the wisdom contained in this book, your journey together throughout these transitions will become smoother, easier, and much less frustrating. There's no reason why loving each other and growing together can't bring you happiness, joy, and even fun!

This book contains a wealth of information to show you how. So read it, learn from it, and enjoy!

Jaid Barrymore

Jaid Barrymore has appeared in numerous films, including *Night Shift, Doppelganger, Me, Myself and I, Inevitable Grace,* and *The Last Days of Disco*. She has often been a guest on *Howard Stern, Ricki Lake,* and *Gordon Elliott* and has been seen for over a year in the smash Off-Broadway comedy hit *Grandma Sylvia's Funeral*. She is the mother of actress Drew Barrymore.

Introduction

I am a mother, a daughter, and a writer. The combination has allowed me to provide you with a highly informative book to the mother-daughter relationship that is tempered by the realities of sitting in each of your shoes.

No one can boast of reaping all of the joys of this relationship without incurring any of the exasperation or pain. Indeed that may be what makes a good relationship so highly prized.

The point of view shifts back and forth between mother and daughter in this book because it takes two to make this relationship work at the most treasured level. Yours need not be a troubled relationship to benefit from the contents. This book certainly has been written to assist and repair damaged relationships, but it is also meant to add improvements to darn good ones and celebrate those that are at a peak of richness, too.

If one moves slowly through the contents of the book, there is much to learn. I think that the unique way we grow into maturity as women is worthy of your attention. It enables all of us to appreciate who and what we, our daughters, and our mothers are all about. In this world where family relationships are dissolving quickly, there is no better friend one can look for than in a mother and a daughter.

How This Book Is Organized

The Complete Idiot's Guide to Mothers and Daughters is organized into six parts. It is best if you read them in order. However, on any given page there is worthwhile information that should benefit your exploration.

Part 1, "Growing Up Female," takes you through a woman's unique cycle of life out from under a man's shadow. Gender differences that affect us as women, mothers, and daughters are brought to the fore. Exploring and defining how a woman's identity is formed, the forces that shape her life, and the stages she passes through serve as a solid foundation from which to explore the mother-daughter relationship.

Part 2, "Raising Daughters," gets right to the issue of nurturing girls and following them through stages of growth until they are well into adulthood. Two chapters are devoted to the period of adolescence because it is so complex, impacts a young girl's life so greatly, and is regularly noted as the most difficult time for mother and daughter. Without addressing this stage of development, a mother or daughter may miss keys to unlock significant problems. Nonetheless, necessary attention is given to daughters moving out on their own, finding love, and maintaining economic self-sufficiency and the most beneficial ways in which moms can support them during these times.

Part 3, "Establishing Patterns and Legacies," is a crash course in the complexities of the mother-daughter relationship and builds upon the knowledge of mothers and daughters gained in the two previous parts of the guide. You will read about a slew of varying mother types, the infamous mother-daughter dilemma, why mothers and daughters drive each other crazy, and how they function with the larger family circle.

Each of these critical areas helps determine how a mother and daughter feel about each other and the kind of relationship they share.

Part 4, "The Age of Discovery," takes the reader through several insightful journeys meant to increase empathy and garner support. First daughters are asked to evaluate themselves and their intergenerational partner. Then both are taken by the hand through a mother's advancing years. The purpose is to prepare mom and daughter for these changes in their lives and to assist them to find happiness, peace, and contentment at that time. Other valuable discoveries include mothers and daughters who don't fit the traditional mold and need greater understanding between themselves and the general public. There is much to be gained by reading about adopted or lesbian daughters and their moms.

Part 5, "Sharing Revelations, Making Adjustments," gets the reader to work on their mother-daughter relationship. Issues of attachment, expectations, and mother-blame are resolved through communication techniques, repair and improvement exercises, and outside expert advice.

Part 6, "A Celebration of Mothers and Daughters," makes all of your reading, work, worries, tears, and efforts worthwhile. This section is the pot of gold at the end of the rainbow. Unwrapping the prize package of friendship between mothers and daughters should motivate you to go back and work harder or congratulate yourself for a job well done. Meeting role models who have overcome a variety of motherly obstacles not only allows us to applaud them but serve to guide others who don't yet have a lot to celebrate. This section is full of delights, like those afforded grandmothers and granddaughters, and savored moments and memories exclusive to mother and daughter.

The two appendixes supply additional information. Appendix A has a suggested list of reference books on early childhood development. Appendix B provides a glossary of words introduced throughout the guide in the "building blocks" boxes. The index at the back of the book will conveniently enable you to put your finger on specific subject matter and show you where every particle of information on a particular topic can be found.

Woman to Woman

These boxes offer advice, food for thought, and tidbits of information that are pertinent to mothers and daughters.

Pearls of Wisdom

These boxes present thoughts about mothering daughters contributed by women around the world.

Explosives

These boxes provide facts, figures, or findings that are worthy of immediate attention.

Building Blocks

These boxes present definitions and vocabulary words.

Acknowledgments

No book is ever complete without thanking those who have helped the writer. In my case I am indebted to my agent Jeff Herman, who has given me his unrelenting support over the past eight years, and my friend and editor, T. R. Fitchko, for her sustained encouragement. I have benefited greatly from the help, acceptance, and enthusiasm of acquisitions editor Randy Ladenheim-Gil, whom it has been my pleasure to work with on two *Complete Idiot's Guides*. And to the other editors who put their mark on this book, your time is appreciated.

I owe a special debt of gratitude to the mothers and daughters who shared their thoughts, experiences and wisdom with me. To my daughters, Sara Jane and Halley, and my mother, Lillian, I say thank you for being a part of my life and allowing me to be such a big part of yours!

Trademarks

All terms mentioned in this book that are known to be or are suspected of being trademarks or service marks have been appropriately capitalized. Alpha Books and Pearson Education cannot attest to the accuracy of this information. Use of a term in this book should not be regarded as affecting the validity of any trademark or service mark.

Part 1

Growing Up Female

A woman's journey as both mother and daughter must be seen in light of her biological makeup, unique experiences, and social milieu. Who a woman is when she enters the world and what paths are open to her are essential to understand before we can successfully comprehend the complexities of mothers, daughters or their relationships.

Obviously this discourse could fill volumes. The information handily provided for you has been sifted and sorted, bringing you the most important elements. Chapter 1, "A Woman's Unique Cycle of Life," draws upon the elements that separate women from men. Gender is in. Gender differences are politically correct and certifiably measured. They give women a vantage point that is all their own.

Without knowledge of a woman's life cycle, you can't possibly begin to recognize how one achieves the female identity described in Chapter 2, "Sprouting an Identity." And without acknowledging the forces that shape a woman's life in Chapter 3, "Forces That Shape Women's Lives," or the passages she transverses in Chapter 4, "Passages Through a Lifetime of Motherhood," it would be fruitless to try and grasp how women relate to the world around them, interact with their mothers, or love their daughters.

The four chapters that comprise "Growing Up Female" give you the necessary foundation to begin your exploration into the wonders, trials, tribulations, joys, fears, recriminations, and satisfactions that characterize the mother-daughter relationship.

Chapter 1

A Woman's Unique Cycle of Life

> ### In This Chapter
>
> ➤ Drawing the inside blueprint of a woman
>
> ➤ Figuring out what *is* female
>
> ➤ Proving women are unique
>
> ➤ Peeking inside the female brain
>
> ➤ Laying the groundwork for female relationships

There is no way to deny it. Men and women belong to the same species. We're all humans. However, there is no doubt any longer that women are vastly different from men. As women we've always known this—even if some of us temporarily bought the "unisex theories" of the past. It is just within the last decade that scientists have begun to fastidiously prove that women and men are distinctly different creatures from the inside out.

The factors that make women unique critically affect their relationships in the world. One cannot possibly begin to understand how a woman thinks, feels, and behaves as an independent person—let alone a mother or a daughter—without uncovering her internal and external blueprint. This is the only way to begin to comprehend exactly who she is.

In this chapter I will look at the inner recesses of the female being. The only problem with this initial investigation is that it's ongoing and still in the scientific works. Nonetheless, there is plenty of interesting, accessible information to get us started on our way.

Moving Out of Man's Shadow

A warning to the reader. Let's face facts here without throwing a feminist hissy fit, no matter how well justified it may initially appear to be!

"Women's differences have been seen as deviations from the norm, rather than as essentially different and worthwhile in their own right, in large part by taking men as the benchmark for human development," Joan Borysenko, Ph.D., tells us in her book, *A Woman's Book of Life: The Biology, Psychology and Spirituality of the Feminine Life Cycle* (Penguin Putnam, 1992). "In fact, there has never been a theoretical framework for understanding women's development that wasn't based on a comparison to men."

Writers, theorists, scientists, and philosophers have tried to relegate women to a secondary position socially, religiously, and biologically for centuries. Fortunately times are changing. In the medical realm more attention is now paid to female physiology, development, and diseases. *Evolutionary biology* and *evolutionary psychology,* relatively new disciplines, don't make sense without acknowledging significant gender differences, notes Deborah Blum, author of *Sex on the Brain: The Biological Differences Between Men and Women* (Viking Press, 1997) and professor of journalism at the University of Wisconsin-Madison.

Explosives

"Woman is an unfinished man, left standing on a lower step in the scale of development."

—Aristotle, Greek philosopher

Building Blocks

Evolutionary biology is the scientific study of the development of a physical organ or organism over time. **Evolutionary psychology** is the study and reconstruction of the past and how it has influenced contemporary behavior.

The Ever-Present Maternal Genetic Factor

Your family tree, according to genetic studies, is carried along the matrilineal (mother's) line because specific genes that aid in the development of an embryo are contributed solely by the female's egg. It is the presence of this unbroken lineage of genetic information that Borysenko cites as evidence to refute the old-fashioned notion that women are merely "unfinished men."

It Takes Two to Tango

Deborah Blum in her book, *Sex on the Brain,* maintains that reproduction and sex are wired into our mental, emotional, and physical being. Although some species do not include two sexes, humans do for the sole purpose of reproduction. Furthermore, where reproduction is involved, Blum says biology's rule prevails—there must be two whether banana plants, hummingbirds, or humans.

Men and women have evolved to efficiently carry out the mating game. In order to accomplish this, men and women have varying reproductive organs, gender predispositions, and amounts of the same sex hormones that encourage them to mate and nurture.

Our genetic predisposition—emotional and physical—can be altered by interacting with the environment. Scientists say *genes* have been programmed that way. Consequently, understanding yourself, your mother, and your daughter requires more than a simple story of the birds and the bees. It is a complex story that begins with a woman's life cycle from conception on.

Building Blocks

Genes are the matter within the male and female chromosomes that determine the inherited characteristics when a new life is created. They spell out how the body's amino acids, which turn into proteins and then muscle or other attributes of our physical being, are to be assembled.

FYI, Discovering More Gender Differences

Try this true/false test based on traits that many experts now believe are gender related or influenced. See how current you are on your understanding of what separates women from men:

1. Girls experience and express more emotional highs.
   True   False

2. Little boys act more impulsively than girls.
   True   False

3. Male fetuses are more active in utero (among fetuses that have the same weight).
   True   False

4. Girl babies exhibit a slightly greater reaction to human faces after six months of life than boy babies do.
   True   False

5. Preschool-age girls play in less competitive and smaller groups than boys do.
   True   False

Building Blocks

In chemical terms, **testosterone** is a cholesterol derivative with four carbon rings and a specific ratio of oxygen and hydrogen along the edges. Larger amounts are found in men, although women too have some amount of the hormone. Testosterone is attributed with making primary distinctions between the male and female bodies.

Woman to Woman

A neuroscientist at Yale University, Patricia Goldman-Rakie, discovered that the anatomical differences in male and female brains explained why girls show strength in communication skills while boys demonstrate greater strengths in spatial and motor skills.

6. Girls age three to four tend to resolve conflicts more by accepting a compromise while boys of the same age use verbal and physical threats.
   True   False

7. Aggressive behavior can be traced to the *testosterone* hormone levels in boys and men.
   True   False

8. Women relieve stress by talking and men by private downtime.
   True   False

9. Hormonal differences account for the variation in female-male responses to the previous eight points.
   True   False

The purpose of this quick quiz is simply to give you something more to think about when it comes to pondering how you, your mother, or your daughter got to be the person you are today. By the way, the correct answer for all the questions is "True."

Examining the Female Brain

Scientists are beginning to assert differences between the male and female brains that are determined by genetic mapping that occurs at the time life is created.

The difference in the size of male and female brains—men average nearly a 15 percent larger brain—has nothing to do with greater or lesser intelligence. It is the effect male and female hormones have on the lobes of the brain that has much to do with how the two sexes behave and whether or not these areas of the brain grow larger in men or women.

Other gender theories defer to specific sides of the brain that handle such things as emotions and language. There has been some scientific supposition that the connections made and transverse between the right and left side of the brain in women are more highly developed and, therefore, explain why women are more adept at verbally expressing their emotions.

Answering the Million-Dollar Question

Is it Mother Nature or Mother Nurturer that makes the difference? Can you blame everything on genetic composition rather than external circumstances? But then how could you complain or boast about how your mothers, friends, experiences, achievements, and overall environment shape you in positive or negative ways? The truth is that it is a combination of all of the above that makes you who you are. Scientists are still debating and researching the actual mix.

By most estimates genes do not determine 100 percent of human behavior. For example, Michael Lewis, director for the Study of Child Development in New Jersey, believes that experience changes and shapes 90 percent of our personality traits and that only 10 percent of the temperament an infant is born with shows up in his or her adult personality.

No doubt whatever the ratio of interplay of nature and nurture, there is plenty of room for mothers and other forces to affect a daughter's persona. In the next chapter I will delve deeper into how you and your daughters or mothers developed your female gender identity.

Another Factor in the Mix

The only problem with each discipline or body of research is that it tends to push its own point of view to the exclusion of others. In the past *sociologists* were prone to explain human behavior only in terms of social factors. They pointed out specific conditions that affect behavior like population density; the greater the density of a population, they found, the greater the competition and the less altruism among individuals.

There is, of course, validity to the notion that our social milieu affects our development. However, just as genes cannot take the full blame or credit for human behavior, most experts today agree neither can sociological explanations.

A sociological exploration of the affect of feminism on women's behavior is worthwhile. However, the

Building Blocks

Sociologists study human behavior based on how relationships come into being, what social forces maintain and change them, and why they dissolve.

Woman to Woman

As recently as 1992, a report by the American Association of University Women found bias in textbooks and teacher attitudes. Another study uncovered that teachers called on boys in the preschool setting more often than girls despite the latter's greater frequency to raise their hands. This is where mothers and daughters need to affect some needed change and unload some nurturing.

atmosphere created by feminism cannot singularly explain women's behavior toward their mothers, daughters, romantic partners, or even their professional colleagues.

Pearls of Wisdom

"Being pregnant is such a time of anticipation and optimism and dreaming ... and fear and insecurity and self-doubt."

—Vicki Lovine, author of *The Girlfriends' Guide to Pregnancy (or everything your doctor won't tell you)*

The Case for Nurturing

Kyle D. Pruett, clinical professor of psychiatry at Yale University's Child Study Center and author of *Me, Myself and I* (Goddard Press, 1999) said that healthy development of a child requires the cooperation of nature and nurture. "What matters most is the way we nurture nature .... Biology and genetics alone, without the profound contribution of care and nurture in a trusting relationship, falls short again and again ...."

As an example of his claim, Pruett cites a Harvard study that looked at the behavior of children with the genetic predisposition to be shy, wary, or distrustful. Children whose parents were generally overprotective and who did not encourage them to move out into the world remained on the sidelines. However, mothers and fathers who encouraged, nudged, and supported exploration of the larger world considerably reduced their child's shyness.

Estimates of Genetic Influence

It is helpful and interesting to see where interplay of forces occurs and which traits have greater influence. Keep in mind, some of this is still hashed around in heated debates.

Trait	Percent Genetic Influence	Percent Environmental Influence
Eye color	100	0
Intelligence	70	30
Shy	50	50
Extrovert	50	50
Self-esteem	10	90

Determining the Mating Cycle

Surprise. Falling in love, having sex, and getting pregnant may not accurately be attributed to the mysteriously romantic notions revered in the past. Our romantic bubbles may just about to be burst. Listen to what those who are studying the anatomy of love and sex have to say.

Ellen Berschied, a professor of psychology at the University of Minnesota, wrote that if she were forced to give a definition of romantic love, she would whisper, "It's about 90 percent sexual desire." To boot, sexual desire is now being explained in terms of our biological origins, hormones, and our need to reproduce.

The Urge to Merge

Helen E. Fisher, a research associate at the American Museum of History and author of *Anatomy of Love* (Fawcett Books, 1995), claims that women begin flirtations that lead to sexual liaisons. Eye contact starts the sexual juices (hormones) flowing, she notes. Smiles come second. Especially provocative and welcoming to the male are wide, full smiles with clenched teeth.

Sounds a little like our cousins, the female apes? That's intentional. Fisher explains the growth and demise of human love through brain physiology and how it relates to our primordial mating pattern. This diagram shows the cycle that Fisher describes. The duration of this reproductive cycle is approximately four years.

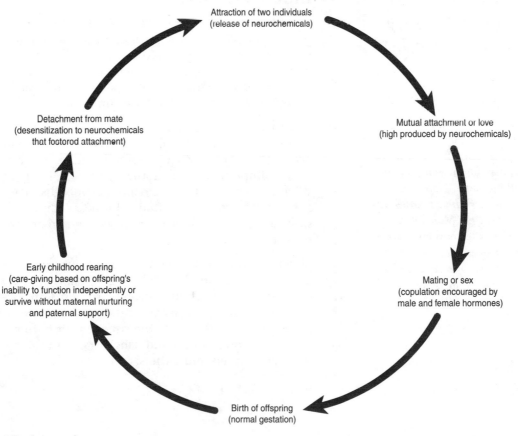

The love cycle.

Explosives

Don't panic. Love and attachment don't have to wane. Sexual attraction isn't the only thing that keeps two partners of the opposite sex together, although Blum (*Sex on the Brain*) warns it isn't wise to ignore sex in a relationship or put it on hold for very long. Love may no longer be a mysterious elixir, but you still need to stir the brew and keep it on a low simmer to outlast Fisher's four-year cycle.

Woman to Woman

To further your understanding of fathers and children, let me suggest the work of Dr. Kyle Pruett. You may find it worthwhile to read his earlier work, *The Nurturing Father: Journey Toward the Complete Man* (Warner Books, 1988) and his more recent release, *Fatherneed: Why Father Care Is as Essential as Mother Care for Your Child* (The Free Press, 2000).

Motherly Love

A mother's love for her child has been used by many psychologists as a jumping-off point to explain other types of love. They believe that a normal personality must be nurtured by love—specifically, the kind of love extended through a mother's touch and warmth, fostering security, trust, and attachment.

Whether or not this love is prompted by genetic composition, hormones, biological evolution, societal expectations, or individual personality differences won't alter its importance or a mother's effusive display of it. What is primary is that women do exude this maternal love. The sheer magnitude of it often comes as a surprise to the new mother, as does her own attachment to her child.

Because of the physical connection of birth mother and child, there are those who argue that a mother's attachment to her child is stronger than paternal attachment and more resistant to separation. However, there is no need to debate the issue for our purposes. My focus is on mothers and daughters, not a contest between mothers and fathers.

The Least You Need to Know

➤ Women and men are two different and distinct animals, both of great value.

➤ The female brain, genetic composition, environmental factors, and levels of both sex and reproductive hormones all play a part of girls' development.

➤ Most experts agree that nurturing can temper nature.

➤ Evolutionary psychologists define a mother's love for her child as an innate or chemical attachment to offspring as a result of biological evolution.

Chapter 2

Sprouting an Identity

In This Chapter

➤ The seeds of individual identity

➤ The unique aspects of the mother–daughter attachment

➤ The normal pains of separation

➤ How we become autonomous women

➤ Where our emotions come from

➤ How mothers and fathers look at little girls

Whether the relationship is good or bad, the bond between mother and daughter is so strong, so intense that it always remains a critical factor throughout life. The health of the mother-daughter relationship, however, requires acceptance of the existence of this natural bond and, just as important, the need for separation and growth of individual identities.

This chapter describes the beginning stages of individual growth and identity. To understand your mother-daughter relationship or affect change in it, you must begin here.

As you read this chapter, stop and pause. There should be a number of places where you say to yourself, "So that's why she does (I do) what she does (I do)."

The Strength of Attachment

Babies do not come into the world with a blank mind as people believed in the 1940s, says Sarah Blaffer Hrdy, professor emeritus of anthropology at the University of California and author of *Mother Nature: A History of Mothers, Infants, and Natural Selection* (Pantheon Books, 1999). Hrdy says infants are, in fact, programmed to reach out for warmth and closeness.

It is widely accepted that human infants enter the world with a need for a primary attachment to a human figure, most notably the mother. The German psychologist John Bowlby introduced the concept of Environment and Evolutionary Adaptation. His ideas help explain why infants became attached to mothers—notably physical contact with their mother's skin, stomach, heartbeat, body heat, smell, and movement. By flailing their arms and crying looking for comfort, infants could achieve what Bowlby called "the set-goal of proximity to mother." This proximity then made them feel sufficiently secure.

Building Blocks

Bonding is the attachment mothers rapidly form with their infants after birth. It is a positive emotional attachment that stimulates desire for rewarding interaction, initiates lactation, and changes the psychological state of a mother.

Bonding, the Contemporary Version of Attachment

Paula J. Caplan, Ph.D., author of *The New Don't Blame Mother* (Routledge, 2000) espouses another opinion on attachment and does not believe that mothers innately bond with or love their child immediately after childbirth. Rather *bonding* occurs sometime after birth.

While theories go in and out of vogue, as is evidenced by a thorough reading of the collective information on motherhood, so do practices that are spawned from these new ideas. Today in delivery or post-delivery rooms a nurse is likely to place the child (once the infant is cleaned off) on top of the mother, explaining that she needs time to bond with her offspring. In turn the child is supposedly introduced to his or her mother's scent.

Not all pairs of mothers and daughters have had this post-birth experience. But do not panic! Studies show that if mother and child did not have the opportunity to "bond" immediately after childbirth, there are no ill consequences.

Emotional Development, the Value of Attachment

Feeling the attachment of a child isn't just something that makes mama feel good. There is a real purpose for it in terms of the child's development. And, in fact, attachment is not solely focused on mothers. The attachment that encourages healthy emotional development can be for multiple caregivers.

Secure attachments are created from reliable, consistent, and pleasurable patterns for comfort that are fixed in a baby's brain through smell, touch, and sound, explains Kyle D. Pruett, M.D., psychiatrist at the Yale Child Study Center.

Kids who form secure attachments exhibit more self-control and ability to self-regulate emotions later in life. Furthermore, children who achieve attachment to at least one caregiver feel more secure and are more comfortable venturing out into the world and exploring it.

Attachment, Mother–Daughter Style

Those who have studied this complex relationship under a microscope say that mothers readily identify with children of the same sex and consciously or unconsciously expect their daughters to become replicas of themselves. This includes values, tastes, and lifestyles. Caplan warns us not to get carried away with this concept and its ramifications. It seems too much of this has already been done and has fueled the notion of "mother blame" that we will investigate in Chapter 5, "Nurturing a Murphy Brown."

The Teeter-Totter Between Attachment and Separation

If attachment is so beneficial, why is separation so important? Because every woman needs to become her own self! Separation doesn't occur rapidly or in a straight line. It fluctuates between forays from attachment to tests of independence. Separation teeters up and down when Rebecca attempts mastery over her world. As Rebecca becomes more proficient in areas of development, she wants to assume more control.

For instance, once Rebecca is able to pick up little pieces of solid food, she wants to feed herself and determine her own intake apart from what Mom thinks she should eat. Or, she may want to climb the steps of her backyard slide all by herself, although Mom may be skeptical that she can

Woman to Woman

Moms, this ought to make you feel better about leaving the nest for work or play. According to Hrdy, "A securely attached infant is an infant secure about his world in general, present and *future*. A secure infant is far more comfortable, even in his mother's absence, than an infant in doubt about his mother's commitment."

Explosives

Overprotective moms could be considered "too-good mothers." They are eager to take control and protect their children from real or imagined harm. The problem is they may interfere with normal development. For a complete picture of these women, refer to Chapter 6, "What's Happened to My Sweet Little Girl?"

accomplish this on her own. There are times she will run back to Mommy's arms, relying on that old feeling of safety associated with attachment.

The Proper Balance of Safety and Exploration

By 18 to 36 months of age, Rebecca becomes more unwieldy and much more determined to do things herself. The stage can pose difficulties for well-meaning, caring moms, who in the name of safety, inadvertently tamper with the growth of autonomy and the development of self-esteem.

Child psychiatrist Dr. Hisako M. Koizumi, professor at Ohio State University, thinks it is helpful for mothers to think in terms of balance. The proper role during this stage of development is depicted in the following diagram. Koizumi says Mom's goal should be that of providing a safe environment in which the child can explore, grow, and master tasks that will help her achieve confidence in her own ability to function independently in the world.

Balancing safety and confidence.

Danger signs

Separation at this early stage of life is critical for future development, Koizumi explains. This is true because development is best viewed as climbing a set of stairs. One cannot reach the next step until they have successfully climbed the step below. In order to understand exactly what those steps encompass, Koizumi thinks it is imperative moms educate themselves about each development step of their child. Appendix A, "Suggested Reference Books on Early Childhood Development," provides a beginning list of suggested reading.

Autonomy, the Prize for Separation

Autonomy, the right and ability to make decisions, govern oneself, and become self-sufficient, occurs on three fronts—mind, body, and emotions. The child who achieves autonomy appropriate within each stage of development feels satisfaction with herself, gains self-confidence and develops a strength of self that will serve her well through subsequent periods of growth and adult life.

If the early months on the road to self-recognition prove to be a challenge for mother and child, just wait until your daughter turns 10 or 11. That's when she really begins to define who "she" wants to be and asserts herself in that direction.

Tangled Vines

Lives of mothers and daughters are intertwined in a way that is different than mothers and sons. The authors of *The Motherhood Report: How Women Feel About Being Mothers* (Louis Genevie, Ph.D., and Eva Margolies, McGraw Hill, 1988) wrote that the mother-daughter bond may be closer than mother-son because there is a greater expectation of permanency. There is no reason that young women have to give their mothers up as the number one woman in their life like men do.

Terri Apter, a psychologist who studied mothers and daughters and wrote the well-respected book, *Altered Loves: Mothers and Daughters During Adolescence* (Ballantine Books, 1991), believes that boys work to sever relationships in order to achieve autonomy; girls, on the other hand, struggle to redefine them. The distinction, Apter says, is significant. Autonomy means to be able to take care of oneself and at the same time remain emotionally connected. Despite the difference or the presence of a continued emotional connection, achieving this type of separation can be difficult and full of stress and strain.

A variety of other experts say here's why it gets sticky:

➤ The mother-daughter relationship is dynamic and always changing.

➤ The normal growth process is an ongoing pattern of pulling and pushing in and out of dependence and independence.

Pearls of Wisdom

"It is hard for parents to do less and less and still feel they are doing a good job."

—Janis Keyser, specialist in human development and author of *Becoming the Parent You Want to Be* (Broadway Books, 1997)

Pearls of Wisdom

"Vines are thickly rooted, hard to disengage, and become entangled as they grow. The same is true with mothers and daughters."

—Linda Randall, Chicago psychotherapist

➤ The way the youthful struggle is handled, particularly during teen years, may extend through the college years and provide the future basis for adult interaction.

➤ A mother's own sense of self is critical to being able to successfully and healthily separate from her daughter and free herself to achieve her own identity.

➤ The biological connection between mother and child affects the process of separation. A child's bid for autonomy can cause a twinge in a mother's mind and body and feel like a pound of flesh being taken away.

➤ Autonomy can be bittersweet for the mother.

Woman to Woman

Experts say that a child's growth into an autonomous being is less traumatic for fathers because they are less riveted to their physical separation than moms. Fathers can provide support and help for mothers to separate from their children, particularly in good marriages. Dr. Koizumi has called upon fathers to perform this function among women and children under her therapeutic care. Nonetheless, there is no substitute for a mother's personal, mental, and emotional good health and fulfilled identity.

Pearls of Wisdom

"With a son you only have to worry about one boy, but with a daughter you have to worry about all of the boys."

—Brian Harris, age 31, Washington, D.C.

Gender Identity

The divide in gender identity between girls and boys normally occurs between 20 and 24 months. Pruett believes that emotionally and sexually the brain is wired around this time to think in terms of specific gender. The child has a concept of himself or herself as a boy or girl. You may want to refer back to Chapter 1, "A Woman's Unique Cycle of Life," to review a more thorough coverage of gender and gender differences.

Mom, Dad, and Baby Gender

If you don't believe that moms and dads look at their male and female children differently, get a load of this:

➤ A 1993 Gallup poll of more than 1,000 adults reported in *USA Today* found that among those who responded to each question, 43 percent think it is easier to raise a boy; 27 percent a girl; and 23 percent felt no difference.

➤ A study reported in *Family Circle* in 2000 conducted by allowancenet.com uncovered a gender gap in how kids are paid for work within the family. Of the top 10 chores, cleaning, making bed, doing homework, picking up clothes, cleaning bathroom, doing dishes, doing laundry, loading or emptying dishwasher, brushing and flossing teeth, and vacuuming, boys got anywhere from 10¢ to $8.00 more per job. They averaged $1.50 more per chore than girls.

➤ A nationwide study reported in *USA Today* magazine in 1994 revealed that girls living in the same home as their biological father had less intellectual opportunities than their brothers, were more likely to receive discipline, and were given more responsibility for chores.

➤ According to Ohio State University researcher, Frank Moot, when fathers aren't in the home intellectual opportunities improve for girls. Mothers on the other hand do not diminish the atmosphere for their sons at that time, but they do generally try to improve the environment for their daughters.

Explosives

There are also cultural influences that affect female identity. An extreme is the devaluation of female infants in some societies. Female infanticide has been a long-standing practice in China, says Hrdy. The rate is higher today than in previous years, although not as high as earlier centuries.

The ABCs of Female Emotional Development

Along with gender identity comes emotional development and expression, which many researchers today believe are uniquely female. The "emotional foundations" of growth are more crucial than the physical, says child expert Kyle D. Pruett, M.D. The impact of emotional development is far reaching. Pruett and others believe it affects a child's ability to …

➤ Trust, share, cooperate, and love.

➤ Express contentment, pleasure, exuberance, and joy.

Explosives

Be careful not to step on a child's sense of growing independence. Independence goes hand in hand with emotional development, particularly from 18 to 24 months old.

➤ Cope, solve problems, and restrain from anger.

➤ Give help when needed.

➤ Process information.

Empathy: Learning to Relate Human Style

An infant expresses empathy before he or she has any notion of self. Empathy is primary to development and helps infants develop trust of their caretakers. Behaviorists explain that caretakers mimic an infant's smiles, pouts, and gurgles. This provides infants with a mirrored image of their feelings and sets up a connection in their brains of visual signs that help them learn to read moods.

Building Blocks

Empathy is the ability to project one's own intellect and feelings into another person's life, situation, or experience in order to understand that person better. If one possesses empathy, he or she has greater means by which to assess, comprehend, sympathize, and react to others.

Empathy, Studying the Female Response

Empathy is one of those nature and nurture issues brought up in Chapter 1. Female developmental theorists claim that girls develop relationally, whereas boys develop more in the direction of autonomy and independence. The reason, some say, has to do with same-sex identification.

Now don't get up in arms and argue that we have gone way beyond teaching girls just to be girls. You are out of touch these days if you don't believe in gender differences. What has changed is that the negative assessment of what is female has been thrown out the window. Now that I have clarified this, you can proceed without resistance.

Daughters, unlike sons, do not repress or hide characteristics they see in their mothers, and readily accept and display *empathy* and tenderness. These two emotions can provide another meaningful connection for mother and daughter.

Relationships with a Female Point of View

Research at the Stone Center for Women's Research at Wellesley College found that women are more relational by nature and incur greater stress than men when they feel isolated. Hence, women are more likely to maintain social relationships. Furthermore, they seek out relationships for support and comfort. The hormone oxytocin might be the key, thinks Pennsylvania State University researcher Laura Cousino. It seems that under stress women produce more of this hormone, which is thought to be a mood regulator. Consequently during periods of stress they prefer patterns of be-friending and talking. Engaging in being close to others has an anti-anxiety affect and calms women down. To achieve this, women …

➤ Nurture and talk with their children.

➤ Talk with friends and family members.

➤ Engage in basic interaction with others, even strangers.

A Plus for Female Sociability

Dr. Joan Borysenko, Ph.D., a mind and body psychologist and biologist educated at Harvard Medical School, believes that women's social connectedness keeps them healthier than men and confers longevity. This is particularly true, she notes, in wid-owhood where men do not fair as well as women. The proof, she thinks, is reflected in males' higher rate of mortality after becoming widowed.

Prepped for Meaningful Adult Relationships

Contemporary researchers claim that women's relationships are founded on creativity, compassion, autonomy, and wisdom. Women, it seems, are prepped for meaningful connections and relationships—that could include your mother or your daughter.

Women see themselves as part of the world around them, not separate from it. Their primary experience of self is relational. That self is organized and developed within the context of important relationships. This phenomenon is called "self-in-relation" and pertains to the way women see themselves in the context of other people and their environment. Key to this concept is the belief that women are interdependent and that relationships provide a valuable context within which to grow and become empowered.

It is precisely this concept—that women become greater through relationships—that encompasses the "very soul of the feminine world view," says Borysenko.

Explosives

Although past theorists viewed relationality a female weakness and male autonomy a show of strength, that view no longer holds true.

> ### The Least You Need to Know
>
> ➤ Mothers form a particular attachment to their female children that affects their long-term interactions.
>
> ➤ A child will not develop autonomy and adjust well to the outside world without separation and a feeling of accomplishment.
>
> ➤ Separation is more difficult and ongoing for mothers and daughters.
>
> ➤ Nature, nurture, culture, and parental attitudes contribute to gender identity.
>
> ➤ Women view themselves in relationship to others and their environment. In this way they develop a greater sense of relationships that are core to their very understanding of themselves.

Chapter 3

Feminism ?
Adolescence

Your
Mom

Motherhood

?   ?

Forces That Shape Women's Lives

In This Chapter

➤ More on the feminine gender

➤ A new name for aging, transitional rejuvenation

➤ Options that change women's lives

➤ Mothers and daughters, different options and different viewpoints

---

Women are shaped by much more than genetic composition. How they approach or are lead into each stage of development, the social milieu of the time, the cultural climate, and the mindset of nurturers account for a large part of the adult female. No wonder mothers and daughters encompass great similarities ... and considerable differences.

We're moving forward in this chapter, building understanding of the generations of women that we interact with intimately. There is no shortcut to our quest. Without such information, neither mothers nor daughters can fully comprehend one another nor create the satisfying and harmonious relationships they seek.

From Childhood Through Adolescence

Growing up, as I acknowledged in the previous chapter, means becoming one's own person. With that come differing opinions, rebellion, and loss of complete parental control. The humorous thing is that when daughters begin to exhibit this perfectly natural behavior, many of us cringe! Life was simpler when they didn't question our authority.

Preadolescence, a Preview of What's to Come

Somewhere between 10 and 11 years old, Sally develops the ability to see things from different points of view—hers included. More and more she will begin evaluating Mom's opinions and how they stack up with her own. This ability to begin to see things from different points and return to the original is called "reversibility thinking."

It may be comforting to keep in mind that much of that original opinion may be made up of the values and ideals little Sally has been raised to believe in before this new era of independent analysis.

Adolescence, Agony, and Ambivalence

The onset of puberty, adolescence, and moral independence is a particularly precarious time for daughters and an era of trauma for their mothers. Once this phase sprouts into full bloom an outgoing, productive Sally can turn into a frustrating, sulky, self-centered young teenager.

Matrophobia, or the fear of becoming like one's mother, is particularly prevalent in adolescence. In fact, it is so common in Western culture that many experts consider it normative behavior.

The Adolescent Self

All of the sudden sociological (magazine and media ads) and biological (hormonal) forces are demanding that Sally focus on a physical presence that is attractive to the opposite sex. According to Joan Borysenko, Ph.D., author of *A Woman's Book of Life,* these forces are so powerful that a happy, well-adjusted young girl may become confused and ambivalent over who she was and who she is supposed to be. The pushes and pulls to strengthen "the power to be or the power to please" can, Borysenko claims, exacerbate the onset of depression.

Building Blocks

Matrophobia is the fear of becoming like one's mother or emulating her basic characteristics. If the fear is particularly potent, a woman may estrange herself from her mother in order to establish her own identity.

The whole idea of "self versus others" makes the young woman in transition feel conflicted by family pressures, the influence of friends, and pride in her own independence. If she feels guilty for the pride and satisfaction she feels in her own independence, there is a risk she might forego her own attitudes, desires, and opinions in favor of the posture of peacekeeper. Borysenko warns that the role of peacekeeper is performed by connecting with others but excluding oneself. She says that society reinforces this because we grow up with the belief that a good woman is not selfish.

Woman to Woman

Approximately 95 percent of those who suffer bulimia or anorexia are females. Only 5 to 10 percent are males. A study by the American Association of University Women reported some disturbing findings that clearly show how self-image diminishes as girls grow. Sixty percent of elementary school girls in the study said they felt happy with themselves. This number fell to half of that, 30 percent, by high school. Sadly enough, 10 percent of American women are reported to starve, binge, or purge themselves. This number doubles to 20 percent during adolescence. And as if that weren't troubling enough, nearly 15 percent of anorexic women die.

Women who grow up and deny their own identities to win favor of others miss out on the cornerstone of intimacy and mature love, a hearty dose of self-respect. (For mothers and daughters looking for more information and answers about the teen years, check out Part 2, "Raising Daughters.")

Transitions and Periods of Rejuvenation

Advertising has told us that women aren't getting older, they're getting better. Now social psychologists and a host of other behavioral professionals are putting aging into more positive terms as well. Hence the new lingo, transitions and periods of rejuvenation.

The Youthful Twenties and Thirties

Adulthood is all about acting out who you are and emulating your role models. The first go at this for many is after leaving home in their late teens or early 20s. It is the time when individual dreams formulated in earlier years for adulthood are sought for fulfillment of love and life.

It is around 30 when women begin to re-evaluate these goals and the reality in which they find themselves. It is unlikely that they were able to anticipate what adulthood would really be like, notes Yale psychologist Daniel J. Levinson. Consequently women undergo an important transition between 28 and 32. It is promoted by "the exploration of new possibilities and the finishing up of old business that may be getting in the way of a woman's continued growth," Levinson explains.

The Power-Packed Forties

The middle years, Borysenko says, can provide women with authenticity and power. A new round of thinking and planning begins between ages 40 to 45.

Woman to Woman

During the perimenopausal years, women experience a decline in female hormones and a slight increase in male hormones. The increase in testosterone may account for this wonderful resurgence of assertiveness.

Woman to Woman

Cornell University sociologist Phyllis Moen studied 427 wives and mothers for 30 years. She found women with multiple roles and larger social networks had more self-esteem, greater concern for the larger world, stayed healthier, and lived longer. Now if that isn't proof that "having your own life" is essential, I don't know what evidence could possibly be more convincing.

"When a woman is emotionally mature and psychologically healthy this new boldness is channeled into personal, family, and social causes that further the feminine values of relationality and interdependence," Borysenko notes. It is no wonder, she adds, that the psychiatrist Carl Jung associated this period of a woman's life frequently with her deepened sense of social responsibility.

Unfortunately the opposite is true for women who are emotionally immature. "Her fierceness may express itself instead as increased self-hatred, fear of aging, or an unfortunate need to control other people," says Borysenko.

The Empty Nest Years

The number of empty nests in the United States is growing with the population of baby boomers reaching this stage. Contrary to a popularly voiced sentiment, this isn't necessarily the devastating state of affairs we have been lead to believe it is. Nor is it a sudden break, but a gradual transition.

There are studies that show the current generation of emerging adults is five years behind their parents in marrying and achieving total financial self-sufficiency. A generation ago, men married at age 23 and women at age 21; today men marry at age 28 or 29 and women at age 26. They move in and out of their bedrooms in the process, and maintain emotional ties to parents and family.

Once the nest is empty, however, the door is open for Mom's renewed sexual interest, freedom, and search for new endeavors. With it may also come satisfaction and appreciation of a woman's experiences and mature persona. It is the latter that feminist Jane O'Reilly says is the most important aspect to consider when entering your fifties. "Let there be less marveling at our wonderful preservation and more respect for the maturity of our minds and spirit."

Opened Doors and Unlimited Choices

The first wave of feminism in 1830 was the struggle by white, middle-class American females to abolish female servitude and secondary status for women. The advent of the second wave of feminism in the 1960s and 1970s, introduced by Betty Friedan and her 1960 treatise *The Feminine Mystique,* called for liberation of the American housewife, an end to sexual objectification, equity in marriage, and equal entree into the workforce. The third and more recent as well as inclusive wave of the 1990s, fostered by books such as *To Be Real: Telling the Truth and Changing the Face of Feminism* (Anchor Books, 1995), was intended to break down all stereotypes, promote empowerment among women, and to sanction the pursuit of a full range of options.

Each wave, however, engendered enough of a difference to theoretically separate the generations that carried the banners of feminism. The current generation of youthful grandmothers and older moms most likely coveted feminism in a way their offspring did not. In fact, many of our daughters initially rejected or resisted feminism because it sounded radical, angry, and out-of-date.

Rose L. Glickman, author of *Daughters of Feminists* (St. Martin's Press, 1995), said that in 1993 she expected her daughter to grow up to be the same kind of feminist as she. However, that was not the case. Her daughter had surpassed her "strength and confidence as a women" and accepted unequivocally that women should assume equal roles in society. Other issues such as university departments of women's studies, women professionals, and attention to women's issues in the courts seemed relatively irrelevant because they were commonplace.

Explosives

Just in case you have forgotten how monthly periods got dubbed "the curse" here is a reminder. Eve got "the curse" as punishment for her sins. This was supposedly to signify the degenerate nature of women according to ancient beliefs. In the sixteenth century people believed demons came out of menstrual flow.

The Younger Generation Says Nay to Victim Feminism

I recall a heated debate with my high-school-age daughter who was being educated in an all-girls school to maximize the quality of her education and her future opportunities. I took her to the Woman's Museum in Washington, D.C., where she proceeded to verbally attack me and a volunteer that she found it ridiculous and offensive to separate women's art from that of the larger art world. It wasn't until several years later that she came to me and told me she appreciated the existence of a museum dedicated solely to art produced by women.

Nonetheless our visions of feminism are distinctly different. My daughter's generation is more likely to embrace a feminism that promotes female power and sexuality. This is different from the earlier feminism, that mothers of my generation may have adopted, which engaged in male bashing and preferred to shrug off the throes of sexuality.

A Mom's Feminist Legacy

Despite discrepancies in feminist ideologies, Glickman says a mom's legacy affects her daughter's ...

➤ Personal relationships with women and men.

➤ Commitment to social influences.

➤ Choice of occupation.

➤ Political orientation. (Although Glickman found that the daughters of feminist moms won't vote for a woman simply because she is of the same gender. To gain political support, a candidate must pledge to uphold women's rights, minority rights, or gay and lesbian rights.)

Today's young women, wrote Glickman, see value in a movement that triumphantly elevated the female experience from a relatively trivial level to one of importance in today's culture. These daughters appreciate that their mothers made this happen.

Winds of Social Change

Several other major winds of social change have blown women in new directions. Some are as a result of feminism and some can be attributed to the change in our industrialized and rapidly altered technological world. For our purpose, how they came about is not nearly as important as their presence and affect on women's lives.

The changes we should be most concerned about as women—mothers and daughters—are ...

➤ The increase in life spans.

➤ The economic independence of women.

➤ The rise of women in the labor force.

➤ The high divorce rate.

➤ The increase in the number of unmarried couples who live together.

➤ The changing definition of family.

➤ The partial acceptance of motherhood outside of marriage.

➤ New fertilization techniques.

➤ The rights and social acceptance of a lesbian lifestyle.

Hi Ho, Hi Ho, It's Off to Work We Go

Sixty-three percent of women with preschool-age children and 77 percent of moms of school-age kids worked outside the home in 1998. There has been a groundswell of daughter successors in father-headed family businesses and 25 percent of future Chief

Economic Officers in family businesses are expected to be taken over by women in the twenty-first century. Approximately 50 percent of medical and law school enrollment is filled by women applicants.

Torn Between Home and Work

Economic necessity, self-fulfillment, and single parenthood have all prompted the change. However, it hasn't occurred without debate or hard-felt decisions. According to a survey in the Columbus Dispatch on April 24, 1998, titled "Detour Ahead," of 1,500 mothers found that one third of working moms would rather stay at home. That figure is higher among younger mothers (between ages 18 and 29), 80 percent of whom would prefer to be at home than work, found a survey by Public Agenda, a nonpartisan policy group, in August 2000.

What universal researchers have noted is how con-flicted mothers feel today over working. They are damned if they work and damned if they don't work—sacrificing themselves or sacrificing their children. (When we discuss motherhood in the Chapter 4, "Passages Through a Lifetime of Motherhood," interesting new information should bring some sense of relief to the dilemma.)

Although it is politically correct to approve of stay-at-home moms these days, the devaluation of mother's unpaid labor and the high stakes of pay outside the home affect perception of one's self. A September 2000 article in *USA Today* noted that support groups and Internet cites for stay-at-home moms are making a notable arrival on the scene.

Joan K. Peters, author of *When Mothers Work* (Addison-Wesley, 1997), thinks that the only way for women to preserve their identity is, in fact, to work outside the home. "In short, equality means that women can no longer use motherhood as an excuse to drop out of public life and men simply cannot have it all," she says.

Woman to Woman

Matilde Salganicoff runs work-shops for the Wharton School of business in Philadelphia, Pennsyl-vania. She observes, "Women are taught to be more nurturing and are socialized to express more concern with helping the fami-ly." Because of this observation, Salganicoff thinks women have the potential to better fulfill the demands of management re-sponsibilities in the workplace.

The Rap, Rigors, and Rights of Lone Motherhood

One fourth of all families worldwide are headed by single women. However, one third of all families in the Caribbean, sub-Saharan Africa, and Latin America are headed solely by women. Furthermore, that number is rising. Some experts see this as an in-dication of the decline of responsible fatherhood.

Woman to Woman

According to a report in *Time* magazine, "The Changing Family: Couples/The Lesbians Next Door," the lesbian population in the United States is anywhere from 6 to 13 million. However, they are relatively invisible and overlooked. Approximately 1.5 million lesbians in the United States are moms. Professor of family relationships and human development at Ohio State University Patrick C. McKenry asserts that family composition such as two lesbian moms is not what makes the importance of successful or unsuccessful mothering. Rather, he says, it is providing a loving environment for children where they can develop a good sense of self-esteem that counts.

But, it is unfair in light of new social attitudes to blame these figures completely on abandonment rather than attribute them to choice—the choice of divorce or the choice of giving birth singularly. Motherhood has become a choice as a result of scientifically sound measures of birth control and value given to the determination of one's personal future. Additional medical discoveries and social acceptance of diversity have allowed for different kinds of choices, including partnership.

Many women are making these kinds of choices. A *Newsday* magazine article stated that in 1999, 60 percent of women having children outside of matrimony were 30 years of age or older. We can assume these women were familiar with the birds and the bees, and, therefore, willingly gave birth to a child. The overall number of those born to mothers who are not wed stand at around 6.3 million, up from 3.7 million in 1983.

A New Definition of Family

The title of Ms. and hyphenated names aren't forming the headline news in the realm of family sociology today. The new definition of family is two or more people who not only share a common residence and economy, but also affection. Researchers tell us that no one can be certain exactly when or how the family started. But they all know there is not one set formula that has gone unchanged over the centuries.

Anthropologists explain that some form of family is found in all societies, although their structures may be very different from ours. Families were forged early on to protect sex bonds, support the social patterns of hunters and gatherers, assist prolonged child care, and advance the division of family labor.

Dr. Kyle Pruett of Yale University says that there is evidence that despite the variation produced in culture, families, ethnic background, or religious preferences, happy kids can be raised in all of these settings. The critical ingredient of good family life is nourishing the individual to meet challenges.

Experts say the bond among individuals that promotes an atmosphere in which there is a ready exchange of love, the forum to share hopes, address fears, relax together, and solve problems is the essence of good family life.

The Female Agenda

Given all of the options open to women, mothers and daughters included, just what do they want to include in their lifetime agendas? Susan Maushart, author of *The Mask of Motherhood* (The New Press, 1999), states that it isn't always what we thought we wanted. In fact, while our mothers may have had too few choices, the contemporary young woman now faces the need to "juggle" the varied elements of her adult life.

Most women want love and family companionship. Along with that they want to find personal satisfaction, individual fulfillment, and some semblance of peace and order. How they can do that after stepping into the role of mother will be discussed in Chapter 4.

Pearls of Wisdom

"Whether they are responding to a biological imperative or a desire to nurture children as their mothers nurtured them, nothing can finally deter or destroy the power of their love. Since the first woman, Eve, bore the first child, Cain, most women have willingly borne children and cared for them with great joy ...."

—Brenda Hunter, Ph.D., author *The Power of Mother Love* (Waterbrook Press, 1997)

Ties That Bind or Cracks That Divide

Before closing the door on Chapter 3 and the forces that shape our lives as women, it is a valuable exercise to stop and compare mother and daughter. If you are the woman between a younger daughter and an older mother, extend the exploration to both. Take the quiz below to discover if there are ties that bind or cracks that divide.

1. Was your upbringing similar to that of your daughter or your mother?
   No   Somewhat   Mostly

2. Do you have the same ability to engage in reversibility thinking as your mother or daughter and do you?
   No   Somewhat   Mostly

3. Do your like who your mother is and would you want to be like her?
   No   Somewhat   Mostly

4. Have you and your mother or daughter achieved the ability to act independently of one another?

No   Somewhat   Mostly

5. Are you and your mother or daughter productive, happy, satisfied individuals?

No   Somewhat   Mostly

6. Have you and your mother or daughter reached emotional maturity?

No   Somewhat   Mostly

7. Do you and your mother or daughter respect differences of opinion on work, sexual orientation, women's rights, family, and feminism?

No   Somewhat   Mostly

8. Did your mother and are you now providing a nourishing environment in which your daughters can meet and overcome life's challenges?

No   Somewhat   Mostly

If you were able to answer "Mostly" to nearly all of these questions, chances are you and your mother or daughter are standing on one patch of solid ground. Your responses should have signified the ability to approach your relationship with mutual understanding, history, appreciation, respect, and self-confidence.

The wise mother or daughter would set out to improve this plot of ground in the presence of too many negative answers. Some good talking could help to begin a continuing discourse that might create some ties that bind. In the event you do not know how to initiate or engage in this kind of mother-daughter exchange, you may want to take a peek at Chapter 20, "It's Time to Learn How to Talk."

The Least You Need to Know

➤ It is part of the normal growth pattern to seek and evaluate one's own opinion separate from that of one's mother.

➤ It is common for women to have some feelings of conflict and guilt when going through the process of self-discovery.

➤ Like our daughters and our mothers, our lives as women are always changing and calling for reevaluation and rejuvenation.

➤ There are many social forces that cast our daughters with a different dye. To want to nurture them in our own image is unfair and unjust.

Chapter 4

Passages Through a Lifetime of Motherhood

In this chapter we will sound our trumpets for motherhood, admit our fears, and define our conflicts. The reason is threefold: to let our female contemporaries know what others are experiencing; to prepare our daughters for enlightened motherhood; and, to unveil more of ourselves to our mothers and our daughters.

In doing so, we are offering courage and solace to other women, extending a helping hand to our daughters, and strengthening the bonds of mother-daughter understanding.

Anita Diamant in *The Red Tent* (Picador USA, 1998), a beautiful work of fiction that details the lives of matriarchs in the Bible, wrote, "If you want to understand any woman you must ask about her mother and then listen carefully. The more a daughter knows the details of her mother's life—without flinching or whining—the stronger the daughter."

Pearls of Wisdom

"Motherhood is fearsome because it is so intensely powerful, entailing acts of creation before which all other human endeavors wither into shadow. In the creation stakes, motherhood is the big league, and everything else—art, science, technology—is a farm team. Is it really any wonder that (as the evidence suggests) at some subconscious level all men are terrified, awestruck, and deeply envious of the gender-specific miracle of creation?"

—Susan Maushart, from *The Mask of Motherhood* (New Press, 1999)

Uncovering the Realities of Motherhood

There is a general consensus among mothers, researchers, feminists, and nonfeminists that women and literature have dwelled on the fuzzy side of motherhood, keeping the negatives under cover. The problem is, the other stuff is what women need to know. In fact, a national study reported that only one out of four women had a realistic idea of what motherhood would entail.

Consequently, a new genre of books is coming to the surface that recounts the trials, tribulations, and tensions of motherhood. The purpose is to let women of childbearing age in on the secrets before going through the initiation rites, and to alleviate the guilt one might incur reconciling the image of motherhood with the reality of it.

Susan Jeffers, Ph.D., in her book, *"I'm Okay, You're a Brat!"* (Renaissance Books, 1999) touts the idea that women deliberately have been kept in the dark about how hard it is to be a mother. When one confronts her own misery or ambivalence towards the task, she becomes confused and silent, ashamed of her own feelings.

Now it is out in the open! You're okay. It's okay to feel frustrated, confused, and angry. Motherhood isn't always a sunny picnic; but in most cases, the just dessert eventually makes up for the stormy days and rained-out celebrations.

Pearls of Wisdom

"Every mother alive knows all about feeling overwhelmed by the enormity of the task. And every mother alive has her bad days when she longs to flee home for a desert island or a convent, the mall, or a deserted movie theater."

—Brenda Hunter, Ph.D., psychologist and mother of two adult daughters, and author of *The Power of Mother Love* (Waterbrook Press, 1997)

In Anticipation of Motherhood

The problem may start as far back as what women say they anticipate about motherhood:

➤ Nurturing a living being

➤ Creating the ideal family unit

➤ Intensifying a love relationship with a partner

➤ Gaining pleasure and satisfaction in being needed

➤ Cuddling that cute bundle and smelling that wonderful baby smell

➤ Producing a biological being that will love you forever

"It is impossible to describe how big the whole thing is—it is all-consuming," says Sara Jane Harris, a 30-year-old mother of an 18-month-old child living in Bethesda, Maryland. "It is the most enigmatic sequence of events. It has brought me to tears of both genuine elation and panicked horror. It is an almost tortuous job because my focus in life is to make this new person the happiest, strongest person alive—even if it drains my own soul to the core."

"But knowing that I am the mother, the MOMMY, and that I am the only one that baby wants when truly in need, is the most satisfying, fulfilling, overwhelming gift that God could give anyone. As many times as I have nearly pulled entire sections of hair from my head or cried until there were no more tears, I wouldn't trade my life with my baby for anything—not even for all of the answers to the questions that make this journey so convoluted. I want to be where I am. The nighttime hugs and squeals of sheer delight at rushing down the slide into my arms move the earth for me."

Pearls of Wisdom

"My grandmother used to tell me, 'A mother is only as happy as her least happy child.'"

—Fran Rothman, mother and grandmother, Breckinridge, Colorado

The Shock of Motherhood

We've all heard and probably said it: "Why didn't someone tell me being a mother was like this?" The shock of what we got was amplified by the discrepancy between what we had expected. Here's what most moms say surprised them about motherhood:

➤ The extent of nurturing required

➤ The overwhelming sense of responsibility

➤ The deprivation of sleep and personal time

➤ A disorganized household frenzy

➤ The feelings of alienation from the outside world

➤ The guilt over not being able to perform up to the standards of a supermom

➤ The physical exhaustion

➤ The disruption in marital interest and harmony

➤ How much they love and focus on this tiny new being in their lives

A Reality Checklist

Jeffers is deeply concerned over the myths and realities of motherhood. She admits, "There are some of us who adore our children but don't adore the process of raising them." Jeffers lists some of the reasons mothers find this to be true:

1. Life changes after you become a mother and it is never the same again.

2. You regret the loss of career opportunities and may become depressed over loss of sleep, mobility, privacy, and freedom.

3. You love your children so much that you will worry about them all the rest of your life.

4. You bear the blame for everything that goes right or wrong in your children's lives.

5. It is common for you to have some negative feelings about childrearing.

Woman to Woman

It has been generally found and concluded by various researchers that women with the most positive attitudes towards motherhood described themselves as loving, patient moms with supportive spouses. Those with the most negative attitudes had children with more problems, unsupportive spouses, and less loving children. These women described themselves as impatient and shorter on love.

What Moms Really Feel on the Inside

When National Family Opinion Incorporated polled 1,100 moms between the ages of 18 to 80 in the 1980s, it found …

➤ One in four women with very positive feelings about motherhood.

➤ One in five women with mostly negative feelings about motherhood.

➤ The majority of women with primarily ambivalent feelings on motherhood.

However, what is important is the final outcome. Despite the frequency of negative feelings, distress, or anguish, a mother's moments of joy with her children carried more psychic weight into her evaluation. In everyday living, the positives of motherhood are more powerful than the negatives.

A Mother's Love Isn't Always Unconditional

A mother's love has been characterized as different from all other forms of love. Women have expressed a mother's love using such words as the following:

➤ Intense

➤ Stronger

➤ Biological

➤ Protective

➤ Giving

➤ Forgiving

➤ Responsible

Although it seems to be widely acknowledged that mothers say love for a child is unconditional, numerous accounts offer opposite testimony.

Ingredients for Extreme Motherly Love

There are, in fact, reasons why some mothers are able to love more, love less, and love unconditionally. According to research, the factors that allow a mother to feel overwhelmingly positive about her children and love them despite any or all negative inferences include …

➤ Her ability and desire to put her children's needs before her own.

➤ Her unending and unselfish desire to give.

➤ The support and participation of the child's father.

➤ Her ability to tolerate and appreciate gender differences and independence.

➤ Her personal satisfaction with life.

➤ Her willingness to allow the child to grow into his or her own being.

All of this is a lot to ask of a mom these days, especially on a daily basis. Practically speaking, it is an overriding combination of these activities that is present most of the time but not all of the time in moms who love their kids the most.

Explosives

Too much of a good thing can turn sour if a mother loves blindly in a way that keeps the child from growing, developing, and dealing with frustration. A mother's love must incorporate and accept the separate identity of a child with all of the human frailties and disappointments from which no one is exempt.

The Reciprocity of a Mother's Love

There is no doubt that a child's reaching out for her mother, showing affection, whispering "I love you, Mommy," or demonstrating some form of love and need at any stage provides great happiness for Mom. As we continue to unravel the complexities of mother-daughter relationships we will delve more into a mother's need to feel a daughter's love and approval in Chapters 16, "Who Is This Woman I Call Mother?" and 17, "Mom's Getting Older."

Balancing Motherhood and Self

Women have been getting mixed messages about the shoulds and shouldn'ts of motherhood. What this has succeeded in doing is …

➤ Putting undue pressure on women to work or not to work or be supermoms.

➤ Making moms feel guilty about being stay-at-home moms or feel guilty for being working moms.

➤ Causing self-conscious embarrassment if they aren't pursuing a career outside the home and self-doubt for pursing a lifetime career outside the home.

Explosives

According to *The Motherhood Report,* a study reported in 1988 by Louis Genevie, Ph.D., and Eva Margolies, the greatest satisfaction expressed by mothers in childrearing was in the early stages through the toddler years. Following that stage there was a decline in satisfaction that bottomed out (not to anyone's great surprise) during adolescence. Satisfaction began to steadily climb after puberty had been reached.

Get the message? You are damned if you do and damned if you don't. And that is precisely how a large number of younger moms feel.

We all know the history lesson here. Before the 1960s, Mom stayed home. The working woman was the deviant. Now that anything goes, the natural conflict of mothers' needs and children's needs should be addressed. Only then can the weight of stress and guilt building on motherhood's "shoulds and shouldn'ts" be thrown off.

Finding a Balance: The Conflict of Motherhood and Self

Scientific findings of researchers may shed new light on the topic. Key among these findings are …

1. The happiest women are the busiest women.

2. Those moms who are the most harried do not have a negative feeling about motherhood.

3. The choice to stay at home can mean a loss of self, believes Sally Placksin, author of *Mothering the New Mother* (Newmarket Press, 1994). In

order to avoid that loss, women have created networks, support groups, and publications to reassure them that it is okay to stay home.

4. Children in households with working mothers did not have more problems than in households with stay-at-home moms.

5. More important to a child's overall sense of happiness is whether or not her mother is happy and satisfied with her lifestyle, whether this meant she stayed at home or worked.

6. Twenty-five percent of couples in the United States today are choosing not to have a family.

7. As Madeleine Albright, former U.S. secretary of state, observed, "Women's careers don't go in straight lines. They zigzag all over the place."

Woman to Woman

Many women make career choices that accommodate their mothering interests. For example, Susan Molinari, former New York Congresswoman gave up her seat in the legislature to work for CBS news because it would allow more time with her daughter. Molinari said she didn't want to miss watching her child grow up. And, Geraldine Ferraro, the first woman to run for vice president of the United States stayed home for 14 years to raise her children before pursuing a full-time career.

It's All About Sequencing: The Tale of Dr. Beech

Amy Beech graduated medical school at age 23, got married to a fellow doctor, and looked forward to a promising career. The second year of her residency she became pregnant, although she had not planned on having children until she was established and almost 40.

What she did then was to begin a process of sequencing—looking at her life as mother and doctor in steps or stages—but not doing everything all at once. She interrupted her training, had her first child, and stayed at home for 18 months before she resumed her medical training. After the birth of her second child, she took nine months off from work to concentrate on the care of her child, then started a master's program in public health and a residency in preventive medicine. She finished her degree and residency just before the birth of her third child.

In order to accommodate her growing family, her personal need for achievement and appease her sense of parental duty, Beech stayed at home for one year doing part-time medical consulting and teaching. It wasn't easy. Each time Beech returned to work she felt torn between professional and family responsibilities. "No matter what you choose, you feel you didn't choose the right thing," she said.

However, finding a role model helped Beech become more comfortable with sequencing and reconcile to the fact that she could have it all, but not all at once. Her role model, Dr. Tony Easton, president of the Association of American Family Medicine, managed a full life of varied roles that Beech admired. Beech said that Dr. Eaton, a mother and grandmother, worked part-time, baked cookies, drove carpools, and tended to four children before resuming full-time work outside the home.

Pearls of Wisdom

"My mother was just diagnosed with breast cancer and I don't know what I would do without her. I see how attached you are to a young daughter and how later in life you can become great friends. She still does things that drive me crazy—like being a buttinsky, but I think I am doing the same things to my two-year-old daughter."

—Karen Rogers, travel agent, Columbus, Ohio

Women and Their Solutions

Nationwide, women are finding ways to fulfill their desire for family and careers. Here's a sample of how some of them are doing it:

➤ Sixty-seven percent of pediatric residencies are being filled by women because they allow more time for family and children.

➤ Women are opening their own businesses that accommodate the time crunch of family and work. More than one third of female business owners are between the ages of 35 and 54.

➤ Women are taking advantage of new industries where they can create policies that are good for moms and children. Take for example the large number of women-owned computer businesses in Silicon Valley.

Passage to Adulthood and a Lessening of Motherhood

After years of struggling and figuring it out, let's face it—the kids grow up, leave home and Mom is left with residual, minor responsibilities of motherhood. This passage makes some moms notably distressed, feeling hurt or not needed. But according to *The Motherhood Report* ...

➤ A majority of mothers agreed they look forward to the time when the kids will leave home.

➤ The adulthood stage of children was preferred by more than one in four mothers.

➤ Many moms felt relief with a lessening of motherhood responsibilities.

➤ Moms reported an improvement in their marital relationship.

I have always maintained that the overall grand design of mothering—full of conflict, squabbles, heartache, pain, joy, and worry—makes this eventual departure from home bearable and desirable. It seemed appropriate that I couldn't wait for my daughters to leave home. What I hadn't thought about was that one day I would want them to come back.

Reminiscing with Mothers: A Heartfelt Story

Of six women sitting around a table at an outdoor restaurant, only one had a child living nearby. Prospects appeared bleak for any more returning to the roost within the same area code. The rest of our offspring—16 young men and women—reside on each coast and dot cities in between. The lures of casual mountain life, advanced academic pursuits, and high-powered career tracks meant that fame and fortune would be found far from their original home bases.

As always, before we settled into other conversation we nostalgically discussed our children. A twinge of bitterness and loneliness mixed with equal amount of seriousness and jest invariably accompanied the proverbial inquiry: Did we do too well preparing our kids for life? Our agreed-upon mission was to shape sons and daughters into adults who would be self-sufficient enough to meet all challenges and live life to its fullest. We wonder now whether we foolishly encouraged them to seek new horizons, ignoring the inevitable and unforeseen consequences that would leave us with children living thousands of miles away.

Woman to Woman

Karen Payne, in compiling her book *Between Ourselves, Letters Between Mothers and Daughters* (Houghton Mifflin Co., 1984) found women in the past and present who reciprocated love, friendship, and support. These mothers and daughters "encouraged each other to go far beyond the conventional definitions of good mothers and dutiful daughters, and have given each other crucial support in creating alternatives to values which tend to limit women's lives," wrote Payne.

I never thought that would be a problem. Unlike my husband, I did not cry when our two daughters went off to summer camp. The thought of an eight-week reprieve from motherhood's responsibilities, arguments, and decisions brought a smile to my face as they boarded the plane for Maine. Later, bedrooms replaced by college dorms were hardly cause for sorrow but were instead opportunities for cleaning and redecorating.

I thought I would always be eager, ready, and prepared for each new phase, just as I had been when the girls gave up playing Candy Land with me and sought their own friends. In fact, my daughters' temporary whereabouts—no matter how troublesome or on what faraway continent—never left me with a lingering lump in my throat. Nonetheless, just like an older and more experienced friend had warned, that changed when I realized my child-centered universe had not just been altered but was forever evacuated.

What redeeming attribute was I supposed to apply to the fact that Sara Jane was living with her husband and Halley had carted off her life's belongings to Boston? After some thought and solitude, I realized that age and maturity engender reciprocal love, respect, and support. The distance between us fosters and necessitates our verbal expression and demands constant communication—hallmarks of our relationships.

Absence denies spontaneous lunch dates but makes us cherish the days we can spend together. And acceptance of each other's path enables us to be true and equal friends. My girls' adventures are not my loss. They are my gain. Their pursuits, achievements, perspectives, and insights challenge, teach, and encourage me to make and meet new goals. I am energized by their praise for every small success, and I am determined to work hard to maintain their admiration. Yes, I have indeed entered a new era.

The Least You Need to Know

➤ Nothing is wrong with you if you are overwhelmed and temporarily disillusioned by motherhood.

➤ Motherhood is as hard as it is wonderful.

➤ Most women don't have it all. They have a lot but at different times.

➤ Motherhood does interfere with or put on hold your individual goals and pursuits.

➤ A good mother is a woman who is happy with her own place in life.

Part 2

Raising Daughters

Raising children is no simple task. Rearing daughters poses extra challenges, especially during adolescence. Whether you are a mom in the midst of this tumultuous time period or one who has survived it, understanding adolescence is imperative. It is a major stage in your daughter's development that will affect the woman she becomes or has become. And, how you get through it together is critical to your relationship as well as to her health and well-being.

However, focusing on adolescence alone isn't the only issue contemporary moms face. Many of these mothers are at odds with the milieu, goals, and dreams that comprise their daughters' world. It takes a world of understanding to bridge the gap with daughters these days.

The essential mindset for moms who accept the responsibility of motherhood as nurturing her daughter into productive, self-sufficient, and autonomous adulthood is thoroughly explored in these chapters. Daughters will have instructions and guidance on how to raise Mother later in the book.

Chapter 5

Nurturing a Murphy Brown

In This Chapter

➤ Mothering your daughter for stardom

➤ Knowing how your daughter looks at you

➤ Defining a mother's role

➤ Thirty critical mothering tips

➤ Discovering the level of dad's influence

The information in this chapter is vital and revealing. Researchers contend that an overwhelming majority of women never held a baby before becoming mothers; nonetheless, it is my observation that most women are quick learners. I think the same is true at every stage of motherhood. For the most part, mothers are intuitive about their children, attuned to their innermost feelings, devoutly interested, and extremely caring.

Mothering a daughter isn't a mystical experience, the forces of which are beyond your control. But it is almost always a complicated process. Having someone simplify that process, offer direction, and provide food for thought educates you in this journey, supports your own good common sense, and may encourage you to evaluate other options you are unaware of.

Naturally, your daughter is unique. It is not my purpose to help you all turn out carbon copies of Murphy Brown—the 1990s television sitcom reporter who mothered a

child alone, opted for full-time, high-profiled employment, and was confronted with breast cancer. What is admirable about this popular figure who caused a ruckus in real life political circles was her ability to meet challenges, follow her dreams, and victoriously wrestle with contemporary issues.

Four Essential Ingredients of Mothering a Daughter

Although volumes have been written on the subject of mothering a daughter, the four ingredients that follow are absolutely essential to her happy and healthy growth into adulthood. This introduction into Chapter 5 is just the beginning. Each will be thoroughly discussed and developed as the book progresses.

Essential Ingredient #1

The first one is easy, or least it ought to be: Be a loving, accepting presence.

Essential Ingredient #2

The second one is a little more difficult: Trust your educated intuition.

Moms have every right to believe in themselves. So-called experts aren't the only ones who know a thing or two about raising daughters. Paula J. Caplan, Ph.D., author of *The New Don't Blame Mother,* says that the whole notion that experts are the only ones with sound reasoning here intensifies a mother's unfounded sense of inadequacy.

So trust in your own "educated opinions." This book is in no way meant to encourage mothers to relinquish their creative thought or authority in favor of the printed word. The information provided needs to be consumed, digested, and applied by your special brand of mothering to your very unique daughter. "Mother knows best," is, as far as I am concerned, a valid statement.

Essential Ingredient #3

The third one requires thinking outside oneself: Maintain an open-minded vision.

Without this ingredient it will be difficult to see your daughter's point of view, accept her dreams, or recognize her special gifts.

Essential Ingredient #4

This ingredient poses a singular challenge to the woman called mother: Never lose sight of yourself.

As we progress through this chapter, you will see how important who you are and the image you project is to your developing daughter.

Pearls of Wisdom

"Yet my mother's life provides me with a good road map into the next generation, if for no other reason than that the detours and dead ends are marked for me .... She had great expectations ... she also taught me ... a child needs a shove in the right direction sometimes."

—Writer Faye Moskowitz, author of *A Leak in the Heart* (David R. Godine, 1987), speaking about her mother who immigrated to the United States and died in 1948

Your Daughter's Burgeoning Image

Simply put, girls initially learn from their mothers. They mimic the persona their mothers project for them, according to *imitation theories*. In a study of 1,000 successful women conducted by Dr. Sylvia Rimm, Ph.D., and described in her book *See Jane Win* (Crown Publishers, 1999), half of the women identified with their mothers. One quarter identified with their fathers.

You, moms, are who they have their eyes on, even down to how they eat. A September 2000 *Elle* magazine article reported on a survey taken by the National Dairy Council. Sixty-four percent of the women polled said they follow what their mothers do when it comes to exercise and eating.

Building Blocks

Imitation theories are theories that describe a child's early identification with and modeling after the same sex parent. These theories contend that children imitate through mimicking what they see, hear, and perceive their same-sex parent doing.

Under Your Daughter's Watchful Eye

Being under your daughter's constant scrutiny puts a big responsibility on a mother's shoulder. With every tick of the clock it's impossible to present your tip-top self and be the best role model. Nor can you control her interpretation of your actions, words, and deeds. Nonetheless, here is what you should be aware of.

Research shows:

➤ It is more important what you show your daughter than what you say. In other words, actions speak louder than words.

➤ Your daughter sees a very limited you in which there is room for misinterpretation.

➤ A mother's influence is indelibly etched into her daughter's being.

The Need for Honest Role Modeling

Mothers, you are setting a bad example when you try to make things look too easy or curtail your singular aspirations to make life simpler, says Caplan.

Not showing the entire picture of yourself shortchanges your daughter and sets up unfair or unrealistic expectations. If you try to protect her from the realities of girlhood or womanhood, you won't be preparing her for life. You might, however, inadvertently engender her frustration or plant the seeds for anger and blame that may later be directed at you.

Woman to Woman

Honesty is at the core of a good mother–daughter relationship. The only way to understand each other and to head off future heartache is by allowing your mother and daughter to see your true intentions and feelings. Honesty is the doorway into another individual. It should be open on both sides of the relationship.

Here is an example from my life. My older daughter told me not long ago that she only remembers me crying once in all the years she lived at home. The rest of the crying I did in the privacy of my bedroom. However, she said had I not tried to put forward such an unrealistic example of strength and fortitude in front of her, she would have been more comfortable with her own volatile emotional state and with me. It wasn't until later, after an adult heart-to-heart, that she understood that our emotional makeups were quite similar.

To get this lesson right, you might find it helpful to take a moment to stop here. Consider how your mother's persona differed from the one she projected and which you later wished she had been more forthright in showing.

Your mother's persona (give examples of hidden emotional behaviors or feelings you have since found out your mother hid from you):

1. _____
2. _____
3. _____
4. _____

Now, see if you can think of some of the ways in which you hide your real identity or feelings from your daughter.

Your persona (list feelings that you hide from your mom and the times you hide them):

1. _____
2. _____
3. _____
4. _____

The Impact of Mom's Actions

Whether we like it or not, watching us teaches our daughters how to conduct their lives as working women, daughters, moms, aunts, granddaughters, wives, lovers, hostesses, cooks, and friends. The Ms. Foundation for Women created "Take Our Daughters to Work Day" in the United States because its leaders know girls learn from their mothers. The feedback the foundation received from daughters who participated in the project demonstrated that the girls developed a greater understanding of their mothers. They expressed admiration and amazement that their mothers worked so hard during the day and appreciation of the fact that they assumed the largest part of work in the household as well.

It is the same the worldwide. Lasenua Madanguda, a teacher and native African, lives in a rural area outside of Machakos, Kenya. Her role modeling is twofold. First, "African mothers must show their daughters what a wife does," she said. "One of the challenges of being an African woman is to bring up a daughter that can establish her home and please her husband and in-laws and produce a daughter who will also do this. It's one big circle."

Second, Lasenua sets the standard for her daughters to follow in terms of education and career. Lasenua's example is being followed by her daughters, one already a college graduate and the other who attends her alma mater, the University of Nairobi.

A Tasty Morsel of Mother-Daughter Mimicry

I was peeling potatoes at my daughter's sink when, much to my surprise, I realized I was ankle-deep in water. Instructed not to disturb my daughter for anything other than an emergency, I waded and wondered whether this situation qualified. Probably not. She was busy at her computer completing a graduate paper due before the holiday.

Actually, nothing in the kitchen could have presented much of an emergency for my younger daughter. At that point in her life, the tiny alcove reflected the lingering effects of her Peace Corps experience. Water anywhere was welcome. Conventional can openers were banned. And the mortar and pestle I was given to chop nuts for my pie was standard equipment.

It all goes to show that the kitchen is a place where even a feminist mom like me can assess her daughter's growth and personality. After all, Martha Stewart demonstrated the compatibility of domestic mastery and feminism when she became the billionaire chief executive of an empire promoting artful entertaining, flower arranging, scrumptious recipes, and household hints.

Like everything else in your mature daughter's life, her kitchen reflects her tastes, interests, and priorities. In an ideal world, experts say, all are off-limits to a mother's criticism. It is imperative that moms respect and accept their offspring's individuality if they wish to foster intimate, egalitarian, and lasting relationships.

Therefore, I did everything within my power to control my laughter. But when I discovered the wad of plastic bags—waiting to be reused or recycled—underneath the sink had dislodged a pipe, I let the hysteria rip. My laughter was uncontrollable by the time I patched the pipe with a dishtowel and unearthed a garbage disposal my daughter didn't even know she had.

Curiously, when our family sat down to eat the pilgrim-style meal made on an oven that posed a temperature guessing game, there were signs of holidays past. A table neatly set by my daughter and a floral centerpiece emulated the home she grew up in. Evidently, nuances of accomplished, refined domesticity that I emulated from my grandmother and mother's festive meals do eventually surface—however unique their expression.

My other daughter is, on the other hand, entirely taken by the presentation she remembers. The first holiday meal my husband and I attended in her home we found a table elegantly displayed with wedding china, a towering floral arrangement, silver trays, and

Explosives

Mom, be nurturing, but do not be intrusive. Be extremely cautious not to encourage your child to live out your aspirations, fulfill your needs, or imitate your style in place of hers. Rather, observe your daughter so that you are aware of how she is growing and developing her own tastes and fulfilling her own dreams.

Pearls of Wisdom

"Almost everyone thinks of their life as a rough draft and their child's life as an edited version—and they will be the editor. But it's a shock when you discover you're not working from the same manuscript. In these times we live in, when the pace of change is so rapid, the kid's manuscript changes very often."

—Sumru Erkut, Ph.D., associate director, Center for Research on Women, Wellesley College

perfectly arranged fancy desserts. In fact, so much time was given to the presentation and the beauty of the setting that the turkey, late to land in the oven, was served as our dessert.

If my daughters continue to follow my lead, in another dozen or so years, their husbands will be donning aprons and making the pumpkin pies.

A Mother's Role

What you must reconcile yourself to is the fact that you cannot be a perfect mom. Do the best that you can and enjoy your daughter.

Remember how fortunate you are to have your daughter. Frances, an 83-year-old mother from North Port, Florida, believes that an aunt had spoken the truth to her when she said years ago, "You haven't lived until you have a daughter." At the time Frances was the mother of a son and didn't conceive her second child, a daughter, until eleven years later.

Remember you aren't the only influence in your daughter's life. There are plenty of others. Even the famed Dr. Spock admitted later in his life that we can't be entirely certain how or why a child turns out like he or she does. Susan Jeffers—psychologist, parent, and author—notes a long and varied list of contributing factors that influence an individual during their growth years. They encompass what she calls a "child's circle of being." The circle includes such things as the following:

➤ Genetic makeup

➤ Circumstances of delivery and birth

➤ Number of siblings

➤ Presence of grandparents

➤ Finances

➤ Friends

➤ School experiences

➤ General health

➤ Physical attributes

Pearls of Wisdom

"You are your daughters' best supporter. Remind them you're their ally and definitely not their enemy."

—Sylvia Rimm, Ph.D., psychologist and author

Explosives

Here's a piece of information that may surprise you. More women who attended all-female colleges graduated and ended up in *Who's Who of American Women* than women who attended co-ed colleges.

➤ Cultural surroundings

➤ Choice of food, books, and music

➤ Intelligence

➤ Personality

➤ Geographic location

➤ Religion

➤ Societal customs

Remember you are there to guide your daughter to develop her best potential for happiness and self-sufficiency. You can do that by being a sounding board, supporter, and a friend. You must show her that you are consistently in her corner. And you must respect and discipline her in a way that establishes fair and realistic expectations.

Prescriptives for Mothers

Let's be a little more definitive on what moms can do to raise women who will achieve self-sufficiency in adulthood. The following list is compiled from research studies conducted by Dr. Sylvia Rimm (based on 1,000 successful women) and information from Sondra Forsyth, author of *Girls Seen and Heard* (Putnam, 1998).

You might be interested to know that in Dr. Rimm's study, 83 percent of the mothers of these high achievers were home full-time when their daughters were of preschool age. By the time they entered high school, 67 percent of these girls' mothers had established careers outside the home.

Based on Dr. Rimm's findings and those reported by Forsyth in her book, here is a comprehensive list of things you should do to nurture high achieving women:

1. Provide a healthy example.

2. Allow your daughter to see fully who you are.

3. Show your daughter that you are proud to be a woman.

4. Make sure you give your daughter as much direction and time as are given to sons.

5. Help your daughter to discover the things she likes to do, wants to try to do, and doesn't like to do.

6. Reinforce how wonderful and worthy your daughter is of her own life.

7. Allow your daughter to be her own person.

8. Let your daughter be free to make her own solid choices.

9. Help your daughter to remain strong and happy through the period of adolescence by holding onto a strong self-image.

10. Try to focus on her strengths, intelligence, and problem-solving ability; don't dwell on her inadequacies.

11. Encourage your daughter to develop dreams, focusing primarily on those that are obtainable.

12. Help her to develop traits that are considered primarily masculine traits—assertiveness and proficiency in math and science—that will help her in life.

13. Make sure your daughter stays productive, not idle and wasteful of time.

14. Encourage your daughter to speak up for herself and not let her back off from difficulties.

15. Encourage your daughter to be realistic about her strengths and weaknesses.

16. Help her to bounce back after the unexpected.

17. Teach your daughter to find the value in qualities that separate her from others or make her different.

18. Teach your daughter to familiarize herself with women who are active, productive contributors.

19. Encourage her to seek leadership opportunities.

20. Be determined for both of you to think outside the box.

21. Set high educational expectations.

22. Make education a high priority and stress the need for her to stay academically challenged.

23. Teach your daughter it's possible to be smart without being the smartest.

24. Introduce many and varied activities into your daughter's life and help her learn to balance them.

25. Encourage competitive activities.

26. Broaden your daughter's horizons through travel.

Pearls of Wisdom

"I didn't belong as a kid and that always bothered me. If only I'd known that one day my differences would be an asset, then my early life would have been much easier."

—Bette Midler, actress and singer

Woman to Woman

Competition has the potential to be a very constructive experience. Among high-achieving women, one third of those studied mentioned that they could recall positive experiences centered around competition.

27. Stress the unimportance of popularity and the value of independence from peers.

28. Help your daughter to see the value in creativity, challenges, and contributions.

29. Be opened-minded about your daughter's career path, whether it is traditional or nontraditional.

30. Encourage your daughter to select a mate who will respect her choices.

Seeing the Glass as Half Full

When it comes to single parenting, women are the majority gender assuming the majority of child rearing and custodial care. Approximately 40 percent of fathers in the United States do not live with their own children.

Only one in three women receive court-mandated child support and fewer than half continue to receive post-divorce financial support. One third to one half of the children in one study had no contact with dad. The findings in a California study were more heartening. Sixty-four percent of divorced children in the study who were living with their mothers saw their fathers during the previous month.

In light of these findings and the absence of daddy, it might be reassuring for single moms raising daughters to know that there is ample evidence that they …

➤ Are more effective as parents than one normally assumes.

➤ Feel just as great a sense of well-being as women with spouses.

➤ Appear just as loving and patient as other moms.

➤ Devote more time to their children in an effort to try to make up for being a single parent.

➤ Report improvement in their relationships with their children after becoming single and reducing the conflict in the home.

Explosives

One of the biggest mistakes single parents make is trying so hard to compensate for the absence of the other parent that they are overindulgent and overly permissive. Studies show that this can lead to serious discipline problems down the road.

Understanding What Dads Can Do for Daughters

Here's what the collective research has found about the role dads play with daughters:

➤ Fathers influence their daughters' lives more as the girls age.

➤ A girl's relationships with males are influenced by her early relationship with her father.

➤ Daughters who have high involvement with their fathers show greater non-gender-role typing and less sex stereotyping.

➤ Daughters view their dads as heroes and protectors who embody order and authority.

➤ A father validates his daughter's dreams and desires.

➤ A father helps form a daughter's perception of femininity.

➤ Dads help girls to feel valued.

➤ Fathers affect in positive ways their daughters' inclinations to achieve.

➤ Daughters are nurtured by love from both parents.

➤ Fathers contribute to the development of self-esteem and self-confidence in daughters.

➤ Dads help their daughters develop a sexual and personal identity that affects their eventual achievements, parenting skills, and marriage.

➤ Dads convey beliefs and values that are adopted by their daughters.

Mom, this information is not given to intensify grief or mourning over the absence of your daughter's father. It is provided so that you are able to understand her better and make up for what is missing in her life.

Woman to Woman

In an interview with *Cosmopolitan* magazine (February 1, 1994) Barbra Streisand said she always had a longing to know her father. He had died shortly after she was born. She didn't feel connected to her mother, who discouraged her singing and never said, "You're smart, you're pretty ... you can do what you want." Her mother never told her that her father was interested in drama, moving to California, and becoming a writer.

Learning Some Extra Steps

To ensure the healthy development of your daughter in the event she does not have contact with her father, Dr. Rimm and other psychologists suggest that you ...

➤ Be both mother and father. Rimm explains this means double duty for moms. It is their responsibility to partake in activities that a dad who is present in the home would engage in, and provide male and female role modeling.

➤ Be cautious not to include your daughter in too many of your adult activities, lest she feel and act like an adult and you lose that vital ability to guide her.

➤ Stop short of having intimate conversations with her about her father's or your dates.

➤ Be a role model of self-sufficiency.

➤ Maintain confidence in your parenting abilities even though you are going it alone.

➤ Provide a reliable, participating male surrogate.

➤ If your daughter's father has died, discuss good and positive memories of him with your daughter.

Woman to Woman

Helen Gurley Brown, former editor in chief of *Cosmopolitan* magazine and more recently editor in chief of *Cosmopolitan International Editions,* said she identified with her mother, a smart, intelligent woman of elegant taste who gave up her job as a teacher to conform to her husband's wishes. Helen's dad died when Helen turned 10, and her mother had to find employment. Helen says she admired and appreciated her mother for trying not to make her take on adult responsibility too early despite serious financial need. This woman, who through determination and talent took *Cosmopolitan* to unprecedented heights, started in the workforce as a secretary.

The Least You Need to Know

➤ A good mother is one who provides a valid, healthy role model for her daughter.

➤ A daughter looks to her mother for an image of herself.

➤ A mother's actions speak louder than her words.

➤ Mothers are only one influence in their daughters' lives.

➤ Mothers must take extra steps to raise a daughter to be the best achiever she can be.

➤ Mothers should not overlook the roles fathers play in their daughters' lives.

Chapter 6

What's Happened to My Sweet Little Girl?

In This Chapter

➤ The heart of adolescence

➤ Mom's role in her daughter's adolescence

➤ Signs of adolescent trouble

➤ Adolescent battles

➤ The aftereffects of adolescence

Your preadolescent darling—the one who liked you to help pick out her clothes, chat with her friends, and share meals with her—has suddenly disappeared. In her place at the dinner table is a young, silent, sulking girl with budding breasts. What's she thinking about as she studies you under lowered lids? You will soon find out.

A lot of work has been done for you. This chapter represents a consolidation of the most valid, up-to-date research that is available on your adolescent, teenage daughter. Read very carefully. I guarantee you will begin to look at things differently after you do so.

Gleaning a better awareness of the changes your daughter is facing at this stage is important. It will increase your sympathy and help you understand what Sally, Tina, or Rebecca needs from you to more peacefully and successfully traverse this hazardous landscape.

A Time of Terror Doesn't Cover It: Defining Adolescence

The dictionary definition of adolescence doesn't begin to give you the information you need—nor does describing it to your friends as "being stuck in a horror film with your daughter." Getting to the heart of adolescence in a meaningful way requires impassioned, intelligent, and objective investigating.

Adolescence is technically defined as the years between the onset of puberty and the arrival of maturity—more specifically, the ability to reproduce. Nonetheless, Terri Apter, author of a revolutionary study reported in her book, *Altered Lives: Mothers and Daughters During Adolescence* (St. Martin's Press, 1990), extends this time period to include those years between ages 11 and 21. A more complete definition of adolescence requires cultural, physical, and psychological qualifications.

Cultural Connections Between Prolonged Adolescence and Mood Swings

Interestingly the prolonged length of adolescence in highly developed countries such as the United States contrasts with other countries. In less-developed regions around the world, the beginning of a young woman's reproductive years still dictates the end of adolescence.

However, anthropologists suggest that more skills are needed to enter adulthood in advanced societies, hence the prolonged time attached to adolescence. In their studies of societies where women assume adult responsibilities earlier, anthropologist have noted the absence of infamous mood swings or rebellious argumentative behavior so characteristic of adolescence as we think of it.

Explosives

Girls have not gotten their fair due from psychologists and academics who study adolescence. It is only recently that time and attention has been focused specifically on them during this period of their lives. However, now that they are the subjects of study don't expect simple, pat answers. Girls are quiet and secretive. Getting to the bottom of their feelings at this age isn't easy.

Physical Changes—More Than Meets the Eye

Aside from the obvious changes such as the appearance of breasts, body hair, and *menarche,* Joan Borysenko, Ph.D., notes that new pathways in the brain that account for logical, abstract, and symbolic thinking during adolescence begin to develop. This contributes to a young women's ability to think in a *self-reflective* manner.

Building Blocks

A girl's first menstrual period is called **menarche.** In the last century the mean age decreased to around 12 years of age at the onset of menarche in the United States. Better nutrition is one of the contributing factors.

Self-reflective is a term that developmental psychologist Jean Piaget used to describe the ongoing thought process whereby an individual stands back from herself and using another voice evaluates her behavior.

The "heart of the brain," or more technically the frontal lobes, continue to grow during the adolescent years, Borysenko says. In lay terms, part of their function is to collect and store information on what are considered socially acceptable behaviors and inhibit those that are not.

Much of this stored data comes from the adolescent's conscious and unconscious determination of how far she will travel on the path of "niceness" or "selfishness" which further develops her ability to empathize. The decisions and actions she takes are indelibly imprinted or recorded in this part of the brain.

"To Be Me or Not To Be Me?" That Is the Question

Adolescence is marked by an internal struggle between one's true self and a false projection of self, contends Mary Pipher, Ph.D., and author of *Reviving Ophelia, Saving the Selves of Adolescent Girls* (G.P. Putnam, 1994). "Adolescence is when girls experience social pressure to put aside their authentic selves and to display only a small portion of their gifts," Pipher says.

Unfortunately the social pressures Pipher says your daughter is hitting head on work to her detriment. Pipher advocates serious cultural change that would alleviate these undue pressures that disorient and depress your girls. Without such alteration, she sees a continuation of the process whereby young girls bury themselves and submit to the social pressures at hand.

Knowing the Pressures Adolescent Girls Face

There are numerous elements that make up the complex, complicated, and ambiguous wall that adolescents are bumping into. No wonder it disorients and depresses them, Pipher and a host of others say. Here are some of those elements:

➤ A culture full of sexism and violence against women.

➤ Judgments based solely on appearance.

➤ The expectation for girls to be beautiful and sexy.

➤ Demands to be honest, but not honest enough to hurt someone's feelings.

➤ Values to be smart, but not so smart as to make males feel less important.

➤ Promotion of independence, but not complete independence.

➤ Pressures to have casual sex and abuse substances.

➤ A milieu full of teen violence.

➤ The belief that growing up means growing apart from Mom.

Explosives

The pressure of self-criticism and negative perceptions that Pipher talks about are apparent in the results of research. Surveys show that 40 percent of girls in one Midwestern community thought about suicide. Another study reported by the *American Journal of Family Therapy* in 1999 found that adolescents thought the way they looked affected their romantic appeal and happiness.

The wall made up of these overwhelming factors puts young women in a defensive rather than an offensive position during critical years of growth and emotional development.

Making a Choice

Girls have two choices, to try to fit in or remain true to who they are. If they choose the former they may be on the outside. If they choose the latter they could very well betray their own values and identity to fit in.

A bright young woman, sensitive and alert to the sexual innuendoes of her cultural surroundings, may have even more trouble reconciling with the outside world, Pipher believes. Despite her preciousness she isn't equipped to emotionally or cognitively handle what she sees. She may become frustrated trying to make sense out of the world that greets her—a world that Pipher says does not make sense in its mixed messages to women.

Deciding What to Do

A girl can respond to all the changes and pressures by conforming to them, withdrawing, becoming depressed, and becoming angry. Most often the course is for girls to respond in all four ways and opt primarily for social acceptance by allowing themselves to split into two selves—an *authentic self* and a *culturally scripted self*. For the average girl that translates into a public persona that is the image of who they are supposed to be, Pipher said.

The concern is that young girls are pressured to deny their authentic self, which contributes to their self-esteem, relationships to men, future achievement, and self-satisfaction.

Building Blocks

The **authentic self** accepts all of her experiences, even those emotions and thoughts that aren't necessarily deemed socially acceptable. And, she is comfortable with all of them. She is true to her real self and accepts responsibility for who she is. The **culturally scripted self** is the part of an individual that is designed to respond to and reflect socially acceptable behavior and values designated by peers, adults, family members, and teachers among others. The culturally scripted self does not necessarily correspond freely to the authentic self.

Getting the Short End of the Gender Stick

No one is making this stuff up. Not even the era of bra burning, voting in 13 women U.S. senators, or even the fight for equal rights tells the whole story! The American Association of University Women conducted a major study on gender and adolescence among 3,000 boys and girls, ages 9 to 15. The title of the report, "Shortchanging Girls, Shortchanging America" tells the other side of the story.

The results:

1. Girls demonstrated a greater loss of *self-esteem* than boys.
2. Girls showed a loss of confidence in math and science.
3. Boys said they were good at something more often than girls who dwelled more on their shortcomings.

Building Blocks

The expression of how much one values herself is her **self-esteem.** People derive self-esteem based upon how they measure up to the image they have of themselves, their level of performance, and how much others appear to value them.

Pearls of Wisdom

"Girls with healthy self-esteem have an appropriate sense of their potential, their competence, and their innate value as individuals. They feel a sense of entitlement; license to take up space in the world, a right to be heard and to express the full spectrum of human emotions."

—Peggy Orenstein, *School Girls: Young Women Self-Esteem, and the Confidence Gap* (Doubleday, 1994)

4. Teachers encouraged boys to be more assertive in the classroom than girls.

5. There was a big gap in the confidence level of boys and girls. Boys exhibited a higher degree of confidence than girls.

Your Rebel Has a Cause

The whole notion of rebelling should be taking on a new light as you read through this chapter. This isn't to say that girls don't rebel against authority, social forces, or their moms. But much of what we loosely termed rebellion before, may, in fact, be something else.

Adolescence is a time of idealism and soul searching for young women. Where and how they fit into the cosmos is very much on their minds. Some experts describe adolescent rebellion as a rebellion against the "archaic aspects of childhood."

Often when daughters do things their moms find objectionable, they are rebelling against being treated like a child who doesn't have any right to their own judgment. These girls are not, in fact, rebelling against parental authority but showing confidence in themselves and making decisions to determine what fits into their adult value system.

However, some acts that are fueled to get your goat, unceasingly defy limits, and are based on poor decision making qualify as good old-fashioned, unqualified acts of rebellion. Now that you know there are different kinds of rebellious actions, try to figure out where your daughter fits in.

Fingerprinting Your Adolescent Daughter

See if these prints don't conform to your daughter's adolescent profile. They are typical, natural aspects of this period of growth and need mother's full understanding, sympathy, help, and acceptance.

➤ She lets emotions guide her thinking.

➤ She relies on her emotional feelings to determine what is true, despite reasons to think otherwise.

➤ She has less self-confidence than in her preadolescent days.

➤ She shows a loss of sense over who she was before puberty.

➤ She is self-absorbed.

➤ She feels embarrassment over physical changes.

➤ She is critical of herself.

➤ She is extremely self-conscious.

➤ She shows confusion between her past and emerging self.

➤ She is frightened by leaving childhood behind.

➤ She shows emotional upheaval and uncertainty.

➤ She feels isolated.

➤ She thinks no one understands her.

➤ She is susceptible to peer influence and approval.

➤ She is secretive.

➤ She is more sensitive to parental comments.

➤ She thinks in extremes—she is completely happy or devastatingly sad, beautiful or ugly, smart or stupid.

Woman to Woman

An experienced middle school teacher said that the embarrassment over bodily changes in her young female students is glaring! They will go to all lengths to hide in the locker room before gym class so that no one will see their bras when they change clothes. To alleviate the anxiety and fear that their peers will discover they have gotten that dreaded period, this teacher has given several of the girls the key to an unused teacher's lounge where they can change and dispose of their pads beyond the watchful eye of others. She remembers her not-too-distant past when she would rather wear the same pad all day than risk discovery.

Is it any wonder that girls with this typical fingerprint go through such inner turmoil during adolescence! Moms, commit this M.O. to memory, then figure out what else is going on inside your daughter's head.

What's Going on Inside Your Daughter's Adolescent Head?

A lot! Here's where the surprises come into the picture. Your adolescent is groping for connectedness and individuality, not separation! Apter's revolutionary study mentioned earlier in the chapter found that your daughter isn't trying to break away from you as was previously thought. The essentials of her theory are of inordinate importance to adolescent moms and have been widely accepted by other experts. The key concepts are …

1. Separation is more accurately expressed as autonomy, and autonomy does not necessarily include rejection.

2. A girl going through adolescence does not look for attributes that distinguish her from her mother.

3. Even in adolescence, a daughter is continuously bound to her mother by love, gender, and feeling.

4. A daughter going through adolescence fights for survival of her new self and particularly wants her mother to see and love her for who she is.

5. Validation from Mom is all the more important because of the natural connection between a mother and her daughter.

6. Adolescent girls see themselves in relationship to others (discussed in Chapter 2, "Sprouting an Identity"). They want to stay connected to friends, family, and Mom, and to fulfill the demands placed upon them.

Battles Are Part of It

You aren't imagining it. Battle days are increased during adolescence. And most experts will tell you that Mom is the favorite target of her daughter's anger and frustration. Why? You will forgive and forget. But Apter believes there is a silver lining to these battles. Young girls actually seek arguments. They can be productive in defining and developing individuality. Of course, that doesn't make them any easier to tolerate.

Watch Out: It's Battle Time!

Researchers actually found a rhythm for the fights between moms and adolescent daughters. Battles normally occur when a mom and daughter come home at the end of the day. Mom tries to assert her control and daughter tries to maintain her free, out-of-sight independence. Mom asks questions, perhaps too many questions. Daughter reacts in that singular-minded way adolescent girls do. She feels like she is suspected of doing something wrong and doesn't stop to think logically that her mom may simply be interested in her life. Tensions arise on both sides and an erupting battlefield is inevitable.

Some of the most common battles at this stage are over …

➤ A lack of neatness, particularly in her room.

➤ Clashes over what she should wear.

➤ Curfews.

➤ Boys and dating.

➤ Selection of friends.

➤ A variety of liberties.

Loading the Cannons: A Daughter's Arsenal

Other sources of contention between moms and daughters at this stage that erupt into battles have to do with …

➤ Turning down Mom's advice.

➤ A daughter's attitude that she knows it all and Mom knows nothing.

➤ Frustration when Mom doesn't validate her daughter's budding new identity.

➤ A mom who forgives and forgets—her favorite target.

➤ Disappointment or frustration when a daughter feels as if she hasn't won Mom's approval.

➤ Blaming Mom for her unhappiness.

➤ What she is or isn't allowed to do.

➤ A daughter's desire to prove she can do something Mom doesn't think she can.

➤ A daughter's expression of a strong view of her own.

➤ A daughter's attempt to lessen Mom's authority.

➤ Her determination in trying to change Mom's response to her.

Pearls of Wisdom

"Girls fight against motherly intervention not because they resent her closeness but because they think it shows a lack of faith and appreciation in her own ability to make good decisions."

—Terri Apter, author of *Altered Lives*

Cannon Fodder: A Mother's Constraint

Moms, you inadvertently give your daughter more fire power if you …

➤ Fail to restrain your own temper within reason.

➤ Have to be right.

➤ Want to make your daughter feel guilty.

➤ Don't let her vent when necessary.

➤ Choose your battles unwisely.

➤ Fail to be silent and listen when it's best.

➤ Fail to sympathize with her feelings.

➤ Can't see the positives in a fair fight.

➤ Don't recognize your daughter's rights.

➤ Fail to trust her judgment.

➤ Can't seem to hold your frustration in check.

These lists ought to give both moms and daughters something to talk and think about. It takes two to fight!

Reaping the Spoils: The Positives of a Fair Battle

It may be hard for you or your daughter to believe it in the heat of battle, but fighting is and can be productive. Fair fighting can …

➤ Release tension and clear the air.

➤ Keep important issues from festering, growing, and erupting into major warfare later.

➤ Resolve issues and promote worthwhile change.

➤ Serve as a vehicle to express emotions and problems that need attention and keep mother and daughter close.

➤ Help your daughter build problem-solving skills.

Stay tuned: Which battles are worth fighting will be addressed in Chapter 7, "Dousing the Flames of Adolescent Fires."

Mom, Don't Despair, All Is Not Lost

Do not throw your hands up in despair or give up parental control in the face of these overwhelming forces confronting your daughter. You are still a major influence in her life. There is evidence that the way a child has grown before entering adolescence continues into adolescence. Specifically, children grow and develop their sense of self-esteem in relationship to their parents' views. Children also require validation and confirmation from parents.

Before we get into how you might go about helping your adolescent daughter and dealing with her in the next chapters, there are still a few fundamentals you should have under your belt. You should be aware that …

1. Your daughter may be blaming you for her misery. It is normal.
2. Your daughter thought you would be able to protect her from pain and is angry you cannot.
3. Your daughter is torn between you and her peers.

This is a time moms must be observant and skillful in their mothering. Too many things can go awry.

Explosives

The American Association of University Women Study found significant differences among adolescent girls from a variety of backgrounds. African American girls were twice as happy with themselves during adolescence and retained more of their self-esteem than white or Latino adolescents did. African American girls reported a 7 percent drop is self-esteem, compared to a 38 percent drop among Latino girls and a 33 percent drop among white girls.

Adolescence Gone Awry

It certainly isn't hard to imagine how a girl could make a turn for the worse during adolescence. Some are luckier than others and don't get bogged down in the agony of adolescence or least emerge less scathed. What is alarming is that the onset of eating disorders such as anorexia that can prove to be fatal are practically exclusive to adolescence. Adolescents who fail to resolve the split between their personalities and societal pressures often succumb to other stress-related disorders and illnesses. Some young women simply shut down, withdrawing completely.

The Effects of Early Physical Development

Girls who mature early, developing breasts before the average age of 12$\frac{1}{2}$, have more problems than other adolescents. Jeanne Brooks-Gunn, professor of child development at Columbia University, found that girls who mature prematurely experience three times greater risk of depression, eating disorders, and behavioral problems during adolescence. The problems do not only arise from all of the factors we have already discussed but also from the tendency of the young adolescents with mature bodies to hang out with older girls.

Building Blocks

Vibrancy is a state of mental health that denotes acceptance of self and is not dependent on another person's acceptance.

The Importance of Being on the Lookout

Dr. Brooks-Gunn says that parents must be vigilant in supervising and monitoring their adolescent daughters in order to avoid future problems. Take a look at the following table to see what lies at the end of the adolescent road for further verification that your attention and presence are acutely needed.

Emerging Voice and Persona

Emerging with a Healthy Voice and Persona	Emerging with an Unhealthy Voice and Persona
Increased empathy	Distrust adults
Good balance between caring for others and caring for self	Elusive
Ability to interact successfully	Co-dependent personality
Development of core self	Loss of self in relationships
Strong but pliable identity	A victim mentality
Abundance of family	Builds lop-sided relationships
Extended relationality	Hold onto family feuds
Greater intuition into self and others	Substance abuse or eating disorders
Ability to build authentic relationships	Unhappy
Vibrancy	Lethargic, sullen

Where Do You Go from Here?

Answer: Straight to the next chapter. It is full of answers on how moms can help themselves and their daughters get through adolescence.

The Least You Need to Know

➤ Adolescent girls look for validation and approval from Mom.

➤ There are significant pressures in contemporary society for girls to abandon their true selves.

➤ Adolescent girls are in turmoil and need the support and love of their parents, especially moms.

➤ Behavior that has the appearance of rebellion and confrontation must be understood in the unique light of adolescence.

➤ There are serious, even deadly, consequences of falling through the serious chasms of adolescence.

Dousing the Flames of Adolescent Fires

Author's warning: Before you read this chapter, make sure you finished Chapter 6, "What's Happened to My Sweet Little Girl?" That very important question is answered in that chapter, an answer that is essential to understanding this chapter. You cannot begin to put out the flames of adolescent fires until you know what started burning in your daughter's mind, attitude, and body. Furthermore, to garner the patience, sympathy, stamina, and know-how required to intervene depends entirely on understanding your daughter's travails.

So, now we can begin the difficult, but not impossible, task of improving the quality of life for you and your daughter during this era of growth. Do not dismiss it as a normal phase of your daughter's personal development and necessary turmoil that excludes you. Do not close your eyes or turn your head out of frustration. Do not assume that you can ease all of her pain and make things "all better."

What you must be aware of is that your presence and reactions can play a significant part. Furthermore, her future happiness, well-being, and relationship with you can be greatly affected by the years between ages 11 and 21. Consequently, this chapter provides some prescriptions for action and helps you see where you fit into the scheme of things.

Mothers Going Through Adolescence

In the last chapter we focused on the adolescent daughter. In this discussion moms share the spotlight. The reason being, moms aren't always cognizant of the factors that affect their reactions to their daughter's adolescent behavior, nor are they aware of the consequences.

Some points to consider are ...

➤ Most mothers watch their daughter go through stages of her life and remember past events and emotions they went through during a similar time period. With regard to adolescence, there is likely to be reflection on unresolved issues with their own mothers and fathers as well as personal regrets, glories, and hurts.

➤ Some moms react to a daughter's distress by personalizing it, seeing it through their own eyes and experience, instead of through their child's perspective.

➤ Many moms continue to look at their adolescent daughters with the same mind-set as they did when she was younger. That won't work. You need to adjust your thinking. She's older now.

➤ Some moms have control issues that need to be curbed and desires to always be right that must be eliminated.

➤ Other moms cannot bear to internalize their daughters' pain and, therefore, ignore the real issues presented to them.

Woman to Woman

A mother of an adult daughter made a heavy-hearted confession. "After my daughter had her first child she called daily to apologize for all the things she did wrong in childhood, particularly during her adolescent years. Now that my granddaughter is a teenager, I ravenously read the latest explanations of what happens to adolescent girls, have realized all of the things I did wrong, and call my daughter daily to apologize."

Guidelines for a Mother's Reactions

I have sifted and sorted out the most convincing and sound guidelines for you to consider while living with an adolescent daughter. You may not be able to immediately incorporate each of these into your automatic-response mode, however, practice and repetition will improve this over time.

One very important factor that should drive many of your reactions at this point in time is your daughter's newly developed capacity for suffering humiliation, says author Teri Apter. You may never guess why she is completely humiliated—breaks down in tears, feels totally crushed and overwhelmingly embarrassed, and possibly retreats from you. Unknowingly, experts say, even the tone of sincerely spoken praise or misinterpreted signs of motherly friendship can pierce your daughter like a sharp knife and be resented for a lengthy period of time.

That's how important your validation is!

Eleven Steps of Motherly Reassurance

To help portray the proper message, here is what moms should be working on:

1. Showing and giving all the empathy you can muster.

2. Trying to be more accommodating than your daughter during this time in your relationship.

3. Seeing more clearly when your daughter needs help in problem-solving, dealing with her peers, or feeling the comfort of your sympathy.

4. Achieving a delicate balance of watching but not intruding, and understanding but not misunderstanding.

5. Showing that you trust your daughter's ability to make sound judgments.

6. Making sure that you aren't holding on too tightly.

7. Realizing that you have a big potential to humiliate her in front of friends.

8. Showing your approval to convincingly validate your daughter's new self.

9. Being fully alert to the fact that during this era mothers and daughters are prone to misunderstand one another.

10. Allowing your daughter to have more control over decision making. Stop seeing this as a sign of rejection or being argumentative.

Explosives

A survey of 500 women conducted by Bruskin/Golding Research revealed that daughters apologize first more often than moms after a battle. Forty-seven percent of daughters said, "I'm sorry" before their moms, 29 percent of the moms before their daughters.

11. Accepting that disagreements should sometimes be considered part of a process in which your daughter is trying to change your older, habitual responses to fit who she is now. She may take pride in these battles.

Pearls of Wisdom

"Don't get caught up in trying to make every moment, interaction, or event perfect with your daughter. You will look back and think there are some things you should have done differently. You should offer support by being her friend, listen to her, be there when she falls, spend time together, go to her plays or sporting events, and explain what it means to be a woman at every stage of her life. The mistakes you make along the way don't matter if the relationship and friendship is solid. It is the whole relationship that counts."

—Halley Rosen, 28, Maryland

A Test to See If You Feed the Seeds of Misunderstanding

Are you and your daughter doing all you can to put an end to misunderstandings? Take this little quiz and find out. Fill in the blank with "Never," "Sometimes," or "Always."

1. Do I overreact when my mother or daughter tells me something I don't like?

   Daughter's answer: _____

   Mother's answer: _____

2. Am I overly sensitive to comments from my mother or daughter?

   Daughter's answer: _____

   Mother's answer: _____

3. Do I have an open mind when my mother or daughter disagrees with me?

   Daughter's answer: _____

   Mother's answer: _____

4. Do I ever check to see that what I thought I heard my mother or daughter say was actually what she meant?

   Daughter's answer: _____

   Mother's answer: _____

5. Do I stop to consider my mother's or daughter's point of view?

Daughter's answer: _____

Mother's answer: _____

"Sometimes" is an acceptable and honest answer to these questions. "Never" means you are both much too rigid. If you used "Always" to answer every question, be sure that your mother or daughter verifies this. It is highly unlikely any of us are that empathetic, understanding, or perfect all the time. Still it is something to strive for.

Hints on How to Help Your Daughter Through Adolescence

There are very specific steps that moms can and should take to help their daughters get through adolescence with the least number of bumps and bruises. More importantly, these steps will help them emerge into healthy adulthood. Now that you have been educated and are aware of what your daughter is going through, the benefit of each step should be self-evident.

Give these generalized suggestions some intense and creative thought in order to tailor them to fit your daughter's needs.

Explosives

It is a proven fact that teenagers are good at picking up nuances. That's positive in many situations. However, it can be precarious when it comes to moms who are trying to send a positive message or show approval but signs of their disapproval are peeking through. Once your daughter picks up on the negative, she is likely to surrender this judgment.

Things You Want to Express Often

Remember, we established early on that when it comes to your daughters, actions speak louder than words. That does not, however, alleviate the need for good clear statement of support. Be sure to voice these often:

➤ "I love you."

➤ "I am here to help you."

➤ "Would you like to talk?"

➤ "It's normal to be confused at this time of your life."

➤ "You may feel happy one minute and sad the next. Other girls probably feel that way, too. Maybe if we talk about it I can help you."

➤ "You don't always have to do what your friends want you to do."

➤ "I value your opinions."

➤ "You are talented in many ways."

➤ "I think you are wonderful."

➤ "I am always here if you need me."

➤ "I will try to be open and understanding if you have something you need to say."

➤ "Whatever you do, respect yourself and demand others treat you accordingly."

➤ "It's strange to have a new body all of the sudden, isn't it? But you are the same wonderful person inside of it. Never lose who you are."

➤ "I like being your mom and your friend. We can work through anything together."

Actions You Should Undertake

Here are those important actions. They are not substitutes for words. But doing these seemingly simple things for your daughter goes a long way in helping her through adolescence.

Help her to value herself by making more positive than negative statements about and to your daughter.

➤ Empower your daughter by making her feel capable and confident to manage the world around her.

➤ Demonstrate that you value her opinions and prove that you are willing to consider them.

➤ Encourage your daughter to express her strong feelings and take positive social action in the face of perceived wrongs.

➤ Encourage and help her learn to make good decisions for herself.

➤ Do not turn clothes shopping or an afternoon out into an impromptu battleground.

➤ Demonstrate sincerely that you are a good and willing listener and a trustworthy and flexible mom who is always there for her.

➤ Plan activities and share time doing things together.

➤ Do some serious confidence building by praising her for a job well done.

➤ Don't back down or be afraid to fight necessary battles that can affect her health, well-being, or future happiness.

➤ Allow your daughter space and privacy. She doesn't have to tell you everything.

➤ Never suggest your daughter go on a diet, even though she may have begun to gain weight.

How Your Daughter May Interpret Approval and Disapproval

As we discussed in the last chapter, every daughter wants Mom's approval. The tricky part is whether or not she believes she is getting it. This little true-life tale illustrates how hard that is to come by.

Dressed in Black

Laurie felt confident that she was a model for motherhood after her daughter, then in junior high school, consciously chose to exhibit a lifestyle that was in sharp contrast to the upper-middle class suburb she lived in. Sandra, a bright, liberal free-thinker, dressed in black and rejected the outward standards of her community.

"I thought I was very open-minded and very accepting," Laurie says. "I saw her as a person with an artistic personality. She probably did some things because she didn't fit in. So that no one would tell her she didn't fit, she made a stronger statement that she was different.

"I didn't object to the friends she brought home from schools other than her own. We called one guy 'Flower Pot' though of course not to her face. His hair was green and stood straight up. I always tried to be warm and hospitable when these kids came over.

"I respected that she was an animal rights activist and a vegetarian. I thought it incredibly ambitious of her when she found an alternative way to learn about the frog and not have to dissect one in class.

"I swear I was never critical of what she wore. I am sure my friends were more critical of their children's dress and they weren't wearing ripped things from the thrift shop.

Pearls of Wisdom

"The more time your child spends seeking—and getting—your approval for the right things, the less time she will spend on the wrong things."

—Kyle D. Pruett, M.D., *Me, Myself and I*

Pearls of Wisdom

"The person who praises must be viewed as an ally by the girl being praised, or she will not accept the praise and may consider it manipulation. If she views it as manipulation, she may feel angry."

—Dr. Sylvia Rimm, *See Jane Win*

Sometimes I would fault myself for being too accepting, but the things I thought I was being accepting of were the harmless things that didn't make necessarily make a good appearance."

Despite this mother's actions and words that indicate a genuine acceptance of her daughter, Sandra evidently thought otherwise. Several years later Sandra showed up at the graduation of her preppy-cheerleader sister wearing new clothes she paid for from a recent paycheck. But here's what happened.

"I complimented Sandra on how great she looked. Her response knocked me over," says Laurie. "She said she dressed up to get my approval because I never approved of how she dressed. That was the message I got that indicated she never felt she had my approval. She didn't feel it whether I was giving it or not."

Pearls of Wisdom

"When you listen to your daughter's arguments (not necessarily agreeing with them), you are encouraging her to reason. When you negotiate with her, you are building her problem-solving skills. You are teaching her to use her resources to get what she wants. There is, like any negotiation, give-and-take. You are showing your daughter you are committed to this process."

—Roni Cohen-Sandler, Ph.D., and Michelle Silver, authors of *"I'm not mad, I just hate you!"*

Understanding and Controlling Risky Business

One of the most exasperating aspects of raising a teenage daughter is figuring out why she makes such ridiculous and dangerous mistakes with consequences that have been forewarned loud and clear!

Consider the following:

➤ Among honor students surveyed in 1997 by *Who's Who Among American High School Students,* only half of those who admitted to being sexually active said they actually use condoms. Even fewer were concerned about HIV or AIDS.

➤ The same survey reported that 50 percent of the honor students drank and 10 percent admitted to driving while drunk.

➤ Despite full comprehension of the "reproductive birds and bees," a third of the sexually active teenage girls in Apter's research turned up pregnant.

➤ By age 18, 65 percent of girls will have had intercourse and by age 20, 4 out of 10 will have become pregnant.

➤ Smoking is in again even though kids have been taught about the serious health risks cigarettes pose. Furthermore, nearly 62 percent of teens, according to a 1996 *Time* magazine survey, have friends who smoke marijuana.

Explosives

Religious participation is the most reliable predictor of adolescent sexual attitudes and behavior, according to a study reported in the fall 1998 journal of *Adolescence*. "Regular religious participation might provide adolescents with a value system that encourages responsible sexual behavior in the form of abstinence," wrote the study's author, assistant professor Ronald Jay Werner-Wilson. Other factors that affect decisions to engage in sex include the biological and psychological makeup of the adolescent, her relationships to family members and peers, and sociocultural factors such as race, religion, school, and media exposure.

What Could She Possibly Be Thinking?

The most sound, convincing, and well-developed answer to this question is, I think, given by psychologist Terri Apter. Her thinking goes hand in hand with the biological and brain development we discussed in Part 1, "Growing Up Female," and the emotional maturity we have elaborated on in Part 2, "Raising Daughters."

They look grown-up. Sometimes these daughters of ours even act grown-up. But the fact remains, they are not grown up; nor have they made the transition from irresponsibility to responsibility; nor are they capable of sound thinking during most of adolescence.

The problem is, they really are not capable of thinking the way they did as preadolescents. Back then, you could put terror into their hearts by describing an eminent and certain consequence of their actions. The image of a truck whizzing by and squashing a bug in the road could be translated into what would undoubtedly happen to them if they ran blindsighted out into the street.

Adolescence is not necessarily a time when these girls of ours become suddenly reck-less or act without thinking, nor is it a time when they consciously set out to defy us and ruin our lives and theirs. They know, for instance, that intercourse can lead to pregnancy and that their parents would kill them if they came home and announced that a baby was growing inside of them.

So what happens in between stating this to a girlfriend, hopping into bed with a boyfriend, and then singing the baby blues months later?

Apter says it has to do with the fact that adolescent girls, more so than boys, develop a split between their ability to reason and their ability to predict the outcome of behavior. Therefore, your adolescent daughter may think she is acting safely. The catch is she does not have access to the cognitive skills that enable her to assess the probability of risk or danger. (Note the honor students mentioned earlier.)

One must assume something like that was going on in the head of a teenager one mom told me about. This teen's mom was an emergency room nurse in a hospital where a large number of trauma victims were teenagers involved in car accidents. Her daughter grew up with the constant reminder that death could await any child around the corner. Ignoring the odds, she decided that they didn't pertain to her. Those consequences were for someone else. Unfortunately she ended up in her mother's emergency room and remained in a coma for months after driving with kids who had been drinking.

Pearls of Wisdom

"Conflict is a necessary part of relationships, essential for the changes that must be made so that the relationship and each person in it can change and grow."

—Alexandra G. Kaplan and Rona Klein, *Women's Growth in Connection*

What Are the Important Issues to Confront?

Often it is hard to think clearly and determine whether or not something is worth confronting your daughter with when you are in the middle of a questionable situation. To help you decide, Cohen-Sandler and Silver, authors of *"I'm not mad, I just hate you!"* suggest you consider a checklist of the things that should always be attended to promptly.

Matters you shouldn't let slide by include …

➤ Questions of safety.

➤ Circumstances involving lack of school achievement.

➤ Practices that compromise character.

➤ Situations that take advantage of you and other family members.

➤ Situations involving sexual activity.

Several of these points are discussed in more depth by other experts in later chapters.

What About S-E-X?

Mom, you cannot afford to ignore your role in educating your daughter about sex. Psychologist and author Dr. Nathalie Bartle (*Venus in Blue Jeans: Why Mothers and Daughters Need to Talk About Sex* [Dell, 1999]) found in her study that adolescent girls have more questions than they admit about the subject of sex.

Where adolescents are getting most of their ill-informed answers are from the explicit treatment of sex on TV, in movies, records, and advertisements—as well as peers. They are aware of the risk of AIDS but not of other sexually transmitted diseases. Nor are they cognizant that they might incur surprising emotional consequences from becoming sexually active.

Moms must take a proactive stance when it comes to sex. There are ample studies that show honest and early discussion of sex with Mom:

➤ Does not encourage daughters to become sexually active.

➤ Deters the adolescent girl from early experimentation.

➤ Promotes successful use of birth control.

➤ Lessens high-risk sexual behaviors.

How Do You Handle Sex and Violence Vis à Vis E-Mail, the Internet, and TV?

With the advent of new technology comes new concerns for parents of adolescents. Boys are saying excessively provocative and sexy things in e-mails they would never say to a girl's face, one teenage mom reports after sorting through her daughter's computer mailbox. Furthermore, take Michelle Warren, a mom who told a *New York Times* reporter (September 25, 2000), that she found her 13-year-old daughter "talking" in an Internet chat room and describing herself this way, "I have green eyes, and I'm wearing a towel."

Both examples are why experts suggest three things:

1. Put the computer in a common space where you can be aware of what Web sites your daughters are connecting with.

Explosives

According to a 1999 survey by the Kaiser Foundation, 65 percent of kids between the ages of 8 and 18 have televisions and 21 percent have computers in their bedrooms. Not only is there a loss of important supervision, but professor of developmental psychology at Kansas State University John Murray said the location of these devices also contributes to the "fracturing of family life."

2. Don't hesitate to put some parental controls on computer use. Some providers give kids mailboxes but can restrict which channels they tune into. It is also possible to have web browsers record a history.

3. Professor Murray thinks it is important to discuss with your daughter whether or not a program or video game is "demeaning to women."

Explosives

The joy of motherhood falls to an all time low during adolescence. It is a difficult time for mothers because, "Unlike the earlier stages that are marked by a great deal of reciprocity, during the rebellious years reciprocity is low and rejection is the norm," say the authors of *The Motherhood Report*.

Can More Discipline Solve the Problem?

It is true that children of all ages need some parental control and discipline. The quality just may be more important than the quantity. Learn to use authoritative, not authoritarian, control over your adolescent daughter. The authoritarian parent may be less tired at day's end but the final result won't be nearly as good.

Dr. Jeanne Brooks-Gunn, professor of child development at Columbia University, says that well-adjusted and happy adolescent girls have mothers who avoid using authoritarian behavior. Good parental discipline is authoritative versus authoritarian. Look at the list below to get a good grasp of the differences.

The Authoritative Parent	The Authoritarian Parent
Presents rules based on reason	Assumes absolute power
Maintains control through argument	Coerces through force
Says don't do it, there is a good reason	Says do it, because I say so
Uses logic that can then be used by daughter to further exhaustive discussion	Prevents daughter from learning to use logic
Connects child to sources of discipline and promotes maturity of self-control	Disconnects child from sources of discipline and denies development of mature self-control
Negotiates day-to-day conflicts	

Punishment and Grounding

You probably won't know it by looking at her, but your daughter is afraid of confrontation and punishment. Nonetheless, there are times when her misbehavior must be accounted for and punishment must be meted out with the same good rationale demonstrated by authoritative parental models.

Rules of Punishment

1. Apply reason and rationale behind taking the car away, lowering her curfew time, or issuing those effective grounding orders.

2. Emphasize that the punishment is being given because you are concerned about your child's well-being.

3. Do not give a punishment that humiliates your daughter.

4. Do not punish your daughter to a degree that will alienate her from you and make it impossible for her to love and trust you.

Woman to Woman

Here are a few adolescent survival tips:

➤ Maintain faith in your own intuition and parenting skills.

➤ Stop feeling guilty about your daughter's intermittent lack of complete euphoria and happiness.

➤ Remember to laugh.

➤ Be reassured by the fact that better times are in store.

A Case of Grounding

Grounding appears to be one of the most popular forms of punishment these days. Here's one mom's rationale.

Charlene is 45 years old and the mother of a 15-year-old daughter, Kelly. She doesn't ground her daughter often, but when she does it's for real.

"Grounding is the only thing you can do to make my daughter pay attention," says Charlene. "She is so stubborn, so I take away what she loves most. I think the first time I grounded her she was in sixth grade. I haven't had to ground her that often since."

"My husband and I dropped Kelly off at the movies with a girlfriend. They were supposed to meet another girl there. Early in the evening I got a call from that child's mother. She said that Kelly and her friend left her daughter and went off with two boys to a restaurant.

"I went to the mall and waited until they came back. Boy was I steaming. She had to go and apologize to the other child and was grounded—no TV, no phone, no going out. I really think you have to show kids that they have to be accountable for their actions."

How Far Should a Mother Go?

Kelly got caught in the act. Not all kids do. That's why Sabrina, an upper-middle-class married professional, maintains that she has no choice but to sneak to read her daughter's diary. I am not shaking my finger at this mom in disgust, nor am I condoning her action. However, in light of what she told me, you might find it enlightening to consider her argument.

Sabrina says she is realistic about teenagers. Fooling yourself into believing they aren't having sex, drinking, or doing a number of other things is foolish, she says. Sabrina isn't one to put her head in the sand. "I don't live in a dream world," she said. "I keep track of what Heather and her friends are doing to head off future trouble and prevent her from acting in ways she isn't emotionally ready to handle yet."

"I read her journal to keep me on my toes," Sabrina continued. "And it is absolutely shocking what these girls are up against. Boys send them notes that they want blow jobs. I think she is the only virgin left in her group."

"I did find out about a night she was supposed to be at a friend's house. A few boys showed up, guys that drove, and took them out. The other mom evidently didn't have a problem with this. Heather knew she wouldn't have been allowed to do this. These seniors took them to eat and drink and dropped them off on a street corner. It's frightening what could have happened to them. Fortunately the boys came back and took them home. I didn't know how I was going to get her to tell me about it, but I knew I had to.

"What I finally did was ask her if she had something to tell me about Saturday night. She kept saying no and I kept saying, I think you have something you want to tell me. I asked her if she wanted me to tell her what I knew first. I told her that a friend of mine had seen her out and commented about it to me. She came out with the whole story.

Woman to Woman

Mom, if you wrongfully or excessively punished your daughter, an apology is very healing. According to a study on empathy, forgiveness, and apologizing, apologies lead to empathy and empathy leads to forgiveness. Speak your heart and encourage your daughter to speak hers.

Pearls of Wisdom

"We asked them (mothers and daughters) to tell us the things they were having conflict over. One mother and daughter said they disagreed about nothing. We decided that was pathological."

—Dr. Jeanne Brooks-Gunn and associates at Columbia University

Explosives

Blatantly blaming your daughter for all the tensions and problems between the two of you means you aren't taking any of the responsibility for the situation. If you lay the blame on your daughter by saying, "It's all your fault," that will be the end of the conversation and the beginning of her estrangement. Steer clear of blaming if you want to find yourself among the mutually loved and respected moms after the adolescent dust settles.

"This gave me the opportunity to talk to her about how the boys behave and what they say. I told her that she had to think about where she was going to fit in society and what kind of reputation she wanted. I like to emphasize that as a woman she can set herself apart. She doesn't have to give blow jobs, like so many of the girls at her school do, to fit in.

"Her peers are very important to her, but I do think that she knows we love her and think she is a special person. So if reading her diary is what's going to help me keep her on track, I'm all for it."

The Least You Need to Know

➤ A mother's actions and reactions need to be evaluated and considered in light of her own emotional makeup.

➤ The greatest gifts a mother can give her adolescent daughter are genuine approval and the value of self.

➤ A mother's work may never be done, but it's double-time during raising adolescent girls.

➤ A daughter needs and wants her mother's protection.

➤ It isn't rebellion; it's the inability to apply the odds of risk that puts your daughter in harm's way.

➤ Punishment must meet the crime, not mom's exasperated interpretation of it.

➤ The discussion of sex should be high on mom's agenda.

Chapter 8

Daughters, Out on Their Own

In This Chapter

➤ Saying good-bye to a college-bound daughter

➤ Talking about financial responsibility

➤ Spying on the "unlaunched generation"

➤ Saying "no" to unnecessary demands

➤ Good mothering tips for moms of the 20+ generation

Your daughter is moving out, perhaps into her own apartment or off to a college campus. Whichever, this is a definitive and emotional break with her childhood and an even bigger break for you, Mom. This is when it hits home that your daughter has a path of life that's all hers.

It is also a time when she needs tremendous support, different from the brand you marketed during the throes of adolescence. Remember, if your daughter has just graduated high school she is at the tail end of adolescence and at the doorway of adulthood.

The temptations of prolonging dependency and unintentionally aiding and abetting an unhealthy mother-daughter connection are ever present. However, others provide plenty of guidance on how to set your daughter free. Heed their advice. This is not the time to let emotions overtake reason and good sense.

The Angst of Motherly Separation

Transitional phases or *rites of passage* from youth to adulthood may result in emotional upheaval for both mother and daughter, say Nancy Cocola and Arlene Matthews, authors of *How to Manage Your Mother* (Simon & Schuster, 1992). The results are anxiety, stress, and guilt across the board and an exaggeration of mothering styles. (The style of motherhood will be discussed in Part 3, "Establishing Patterns and Legacies.")

Cocola and Matthews wisely suggest that their readers look at going to college as a rite of passage and accept that while change brings uneasiness to both parent and child, it also brings expansion.

Building Blocks

A **rite of passage** is a formal or customary ceremony or event that marks the transition by an individual into a group, be it adulthood or an organization.

As traumatic and emotional as a departure for college may be, it does not signify a complete break. There are still specified school holidays during which time you know your daughter will be home. Once her career begins, she sets up permanent residence elsewhere, and her room is cleared out, then Mom must truly acknowledge that her daughter has a new address that represents home.

A Tale of Good-Byes

You aren't alone in your emotional ambivalence or misery. Though this is my story, I think it expresses the pain of physical separation for all of us.

As my husband struggled to load the van with a black footlocker, four suitcases, six armloads of hanging clothes, and five boxes, I shook my head. Our college-bound daughter, a freshman at the University of Wisconsin, was convinced she packed only those things essential for her survival. Is this what my friends were referring to the past week when they repeatedly asked me, "How are you doing?"

We squeezed into the car for the nine-hour journey that I used to further instruct my daughter on how to handle the checkbook, to be aware of drunken fraternity boys, and to remember that her primary objective was to get an education.

Explosives

Adult sons live at home with their parents longer than adult daughters do, reported Interep Research in 1997. Eighty-one percent of 18- to 19-year-old men live at home with one parent compared to 67 percent of young women.

We arrived in Madison eager to inspect the campus my oldest daughter would call home for the next four years. Once out on the street I was ordered by her,

"Don't touch me here, please." Slowly I withdrew my overprotective arm from around her shoulder.

Second order, "Don't ask anyone for directions. It's so obvious I'm a freshman."

Just before turning a corner, I remarked what unusually well-groomed college students there seemed to be on campus. Precisely at that moment we came face to face with a group of six performing to loud, dissonant music under a sign, "Our lives are a drama." I couldn't take my eyes off of one of them, a young man dressed in red tights with paper wadded inside around his buttocks and thighs. Instantly I recited a line from my repertoire of lectures, "Don't get mixed up with the wrong people and don't experiment with seemingly innocent, illegal drugs!"

We stumbled upon my daughter's dorm. I tried to stay in the background while she introduced herself in an outgoing, confident manner. In response she was handed a key to her third-floor room.

I blinked my eyes in disbelief. Could this be the same daughter who never put her clothes away or rarely threw a towel in the laundry hamper? Suddenly she was unpacking and arranging her things in such an orderly fashion. I really became suspicious of her identity when she said, "I hope my roommate is neat. I won't be able to live with clutter."

Minutes later she approached me for advice. "I need help. I just don't know where to put everything."

In retrospect I am sure she sensed my angst over her new life that excluded my physical presence and said, "You always know what to do."

During that day as boys and girls wandered in and out of her room issuing invitations to parties, I observed that she teetered between childhood and adulthood. I alternated between wanting to hold her tight and wanting to set her free. How ironic that the magnificent view from our hotel window looked so similar to a view of Lake Washington in Seattle. When I had temporarily moved there 18 years ago, I had been three months pregnant with this young woman who now sat staring at me.

Explosives

Here are some stats that ought to reassure you that absence makes the heart stay fond. According to a poll reported by *USA Today* in 1997, 69 percent of women said "their relationship with mom is very important." Sixty-five percent said they talk with their moms several times a week and 61 percent still call her for advice.

Explosives

According to FinAid, a financial aid Web site for college students (www.finaid.org), the typical coed walks away with an undergrad degree and $16,500 in financial aid debt. This is after scholarships, work-study programs or other gift aid packages.

We decided to say our good-byes late Saturday before the parties began. Is seemed as if it would be easier than putting it off until Sunday morning. This way we could also hide behind the darkness and just guess who had the most tears rolling down their cheeks. I hugged my daughter tightly and said, "Just remember everything I told you in the last 18 years."

Driving home in the early hours on Sunday, I could only guess what time she got in from the parties, what time the boys left her room, what time she got up, and what she would do that day. Reading my thoughts, my husband started to lecture. "Don't write every day. Don't call either. Don't ask her what she is doing. Just let her go."

I knew it would be hard to do. She was on her own and so was I.

Contemporary Send-Offs

Let's be practical. Most send-offs today comprise another major element in addition to the emotional. Plain and simple it's the financial—the dollars and cents of college or setting up a household in another space.

Barbara, a librarian and divorced mom, is a model of good sense and motherly compassion. She worked hard, lived in a one room apartment, and deferred her retirement savings to ensure that her children would enter a debt-free world when they graduated college.

"This was a shared endeavor," Barbara said. "My daughter knew my income. I told her what I was willing to give or not. I always sat down and said, 'What do you need? Here is what I have to contribute. What can you give?'"

When Charlene received her diploma at age 26, Barbara made another deal. She was closing the hometown bank account—after one more withdrawal, that is, for a few months of car insurance and a little transitional money.

Explosives

In 1970 the average woman married at age 20. Today that has risen to age 25, with many women waiting into their 30s.

Looking at the Delayed Generation

Charlene is part of what's known as the delayed, unlatched, or postponed generation. They are five years behind their parents' generation in assuming the trappings of grown-up life. They stay in school longer, marry and begin families later, and find it more difficult to reach financial independence.

Between the ages of 20 to 24, 50 percent of men and 33 percent of women live at home. That falls to 20 percent of men 8 percent of women between the ages of 25 to 29. Sylvia Auerback, author of *How to Be Smart Parents … Now That Your Kids Are Adults*

(Silvercat Publications, 1995), says the lifestyle these young adults want isn't afford-able to them on their entry-level salaries. Expensive housing costs, competition in the job market, and high divorce rates make it harder for many in their 20s, 30s, or 40s to reach and sustain the lifestyle they grew up enjoying. Hence they remain at home where they have access to comforts they are unwilling to give up.

Parental Welfare: When Kids Expect Mom to Support a Yuppie Lifestyle

Just because she has left the nest doesn't mean your daughter won't continue to ask for financial favors either outright or in a less obvious way. Nor will you be rid of the temptation to write out the check. A growing number of young adults have become accustomed to a system of "parental welfare" that encourages a sense of entitlement, says Auerback.

In an era when transfers of wealth from living parents to adult offspring are up three-fold, and 25 percent of home buyers receive down-payment money from parents, the issue of squelching self-reliance through gift-giving is particularly poignant.

Rescues That Send Dangerous Messages

Emotional and financial rescues are not always the best lifeline for your daughter. Sometimes it's better to sink and learn how to swim on one's own.

Financial Rescue

Gil Greene, associate professor in Ohio State University's School of Social Work, says rescuing your kids financially is not in their best interest. It sends a message that life is supposed to be hassle- and pain-free.

The mother that keeps rescuing her daughter keeps her from tackling situations outside the "comfort zone." This prevents your daughter from learning how to handle hurdles that foster growth, matur-ity, and independence.

Emotional Rescue

It's hard to hold back and not book that plane tick-et when Stephanie sounds like she has a case of the new city blues, especially after a bleak week of not finding an apartment and being disappointed in her first job.

However, according to a host of experts, Stephanie's mom made a wise decision to stay at home. Allowing her daughter to solve her own

Explosives

A 1996 *Wall Street Journal* article related how young adults with adequate salaries are asking, even expecting, their moms and dads to fund luxury items that surpass their parents' lifestyle. That in-cludes big screen TVs, vacations, clothes, and cars.

problems was beneficial for her own growth as well as her daughter's. Just as important, showing up on the spot with good intentions sends a message like, "I really didn't think you could get out of this slump on your own."

Woman to Woman

Here's a piece of know-how from a mom with a college-aged daughter. When her coed would return during the summers, come in late and keep Mom up with worry, they devised an ingenious plan. They set an alarm clock at a mutually agreed upon hour that enabled Mom to go to sleep and gave daughter plenty of time for nighttime play. If the alarm clock went off, it meant the coed had not come home and the mom could start worrying. Otherwise her daughter would turn off the alarm when she arrived home and everybody could get a good night's sleep.

A vote of confidence in this instance would be a far better lesson and more beneficial for Stephanie's future happiness than an emotional rescue in the present.

When to Give or Not Give Financial Help

These handy little questions ought to help you decide when giving or not giving is in your daughter's best interest and will or won't curb her growth, maturity, and independence.

The Giving Benchmark

1. Is my daughter moving forward in life?	Yes	No
2. Does she have a direction and a goal?	Yes	No
3. Is she exhibiting responsible behavior?	Yes	No
4. Is she trying to be self-supporting?	Yes	No
5. Is she at least moderately established on her own?	Yes	No

If you racked up five in the yes column, giving large or small gifts probably won't corrupt your daughter or turn her around into a financial dependent. A "No" to any question requires more prudent giving.

The Benchmark for Not Giving

1.	Is my daughter floundering and directionless?	Yes	No
2.	Is my daughter still trying to find herself?	Yes	No
3.	Is my daughter underachieving?	Yes	No
4.	Is my daughter unable to hold a job?	Yes	No
5.	Does my daughter look for handouts?	Yes	No

It ought to be obvious. If your checkmarks are predominantly in the yes category, giving indiscriminately will prolong your daughter's dependency and her habit of financially relying on you. Therefore, not giving might be in her best interest.

Indicators of Adult Behavior

This is an appropriate time to provide you with a reliable list of behaviors that demonstrate your gal is on the road to adulthood. Reviewing these indicators will help gauge your daughter's level of maturity and might make it easier for you to take your financial stand.

An adult …

➤ Is self-supporting.

➤ Can function socially.

➤ Acts responsibly.

➤ Handles *diversity*.

➤ Exhibits mutual respect.

➤ Thinks for his or herself.

➤ Shows concern for others.

➤ Is in charge of one's own life.

➤ Makes decisions.

It is worth your while to ask yourself how your daughter stacks up against these criteria.

The Boomerang Effect

Get this one. You have gone through the angst of physical separation, maybe even the joys of a wedding, and then found your daughter at your doorstep, bags in hand. If this describes you and

Pearls of Wisdom

"The first time you give your adult daughter money, it is an act of faith. If she squanders the money or acts in an irresponsible manner, then you don't have to give again."

—Nick Marzella, psychologist

Building Blocks

Diversity in the formal sense means "variety." As the buzzword of the new millennium, diversity signifies a positive state and acceptance of individual differences.

your daughter, we have a name for it: the boomerang effect. What you may not initially see is that boomerang kids, according to Seattle psychotherapists Jean Okimoto and Phyllis Stegall, feel disillusioned and disappointed by their failure to achieve independence.

Serving Boomerang Style

The best things to serve your daughters when they show up at home as a boomerang kid are portions of encouragement and autonomy. These have the nutrients that will help them retain competence, confidence, and self-esteem. And these are three qualities demonstrated by emotionally mature and responsible young adults able to live on their own.

Woman to Woman

Psychologists tell us moms what we already know but don't want to hear. We are uncomfortable when our daughters are not 100 percent happy. But that's the time they tell us that we have to be particularly careful not to give into their spoken or unspoken pleas for expensive items or money for credit card payments. If you fall into this habit you will prolong their dependency.

How to Avoid Feathering the Nest

Should you find yourself in the same predicament as Julia's mom, follow these four critical steps:

1. Put a limit on time your daughter can nest with you.
2. Expect your daughter to have a well-defined plan of action.
3. Create mutual agreements for living together.
4. Insist on setting up a formal loan and payment schedule.

Good Rules for Adult Mothering

Okay Mom, your daughter is working her way into fiscal, physical, and emotional independence. Don't get in her way. The same rules apply for moms with daughters who are doing well on their own and for those whose gals are stumbling:

1. Do not use dollars and cents to buy attention and devotion.

2. Do not try to fund a lifestyle that fits the vision you had of your daughter's future.

3. Allow your daughter to make her own blueprint for life that incorporates her lifestyle and identity, not yours.

4. Work hard to control your pangs for intervention by achieving a reasonable degree of emotional detachment and physical distance.

5. Develop motherly objectivity.

6. Offer friendly help and advice when solicited.

7. Maintain mother-daughter harmony through discussion, compromise, and problem solving.

8. Insist on and show mutual respect for each other.

9. Respect your daughter's right to privacy.

10. Be cautious about commenting on her love life or making harsh judgments of her lovers.

Woman to Woman

At age 16, Hilari said her relationship with her mother was in the dumpster. Listen to what she has to say at age 22. "Although my mother is a nurturer and will always be that to me, she is also my friend. My mother is someone who I look up to because of her accomplishments and experiences. My mother offers great encouragement and warmth. She is a good-hearted person. I am proud to have some of her traits."

You should commit these rules to memory. There is no doubt you will need each and every one of them when you confront your adult daughter with her adult concerns.

The Least You Need to Know

➤ Your daughter will probably not be completely independent of your support or resources when she moves out on her own.

➤ There is the likelihood your daughter may return home, so don't burn her bed.

➤ The subject of economic independence should be discussed with your daughter because it is so difficult to achieve.

➤ The daughter who returns home should not be smothered with the same motherly acts rendered in childhood.

➤ Don't feel guilty for setting a daughter free to explore and live life on her own; it is an emotional and selfless act.

Chapter 9

Adult Realities, Fodder for Strive and Worries

In This Chapter

➤ Moms' issues and daughters' answers at odds

➤ Mom's unacceptable intrusions

➤ The inside scoop on worrying

➤ The perfect mother of the bride

Daughters who are now in their 20s and early 30s were raised to believe they could have it all and be independent enough not to need husbands. The world was supposed to be at their feet and they would be its mistresses. While that may be the fable of their youth, it is not the reality of their adulthood. Their more immediate landscape is marred by momentous hurdles, substantial pressures, and serious self-doubts.

The backdrop for young adult women's contemporary drama, mothers' responses, and daughters' dilemmas, conclude Part 2, "Raising Daughters." As we progress through this chapter and map the terrain of the new millennium, we will reveal hidden stumbling blocks, gain clarity, and find recommended paths for alert and caring moms.

Peggy Orenstein writes in her book, *Flux: Women on Sex, Work, Kids, Love, and Life in a Half-Changed World*, "In their professional lives, their personal lives, and their dreams of the future, young women face a series of external obstacles and internal contradictions that push them simultaneously toward autonomy and dependence, modernity and tradition—that leaves them in a state of flux."

The Backdrop for Female Adulthood, Here and Now

Women in their 20s and 30s have one foot in the new world of espoused contemporary values and one foot in the traditional world of yesteryear. The result is a state of flux, ambivalence, and confusion that is compounded by the many choices available to them, specifically include: whether to marry, stay single, live together, or divorce; who to marry; and, whether to have children or an abortion. Other contemporary choices include sexual orientation, parenting without a partner, and career paths.

To understand daughters' frustrations and subsequent interactions with their moms, we must spell out how their expectations stack up to reality at hand. (For more information see Chapter 3, "Forces That Shape Women's Lives.")

As they enter adulthood, women have high expectations for their lives. Women believe ...

➤ Once out of college, their opportunities will be equivalent to those of men.

➤ Their femininity shouldn't be a problem in the workplace.

➤ Marriage is a personal choice and an option.

➤ They can have it all—family, career, love, and success.

➤ Their career track will not affect their personal lives.

➤ Childrearing will be an equal partnership.

➤ They will achieve financial independence.

➤ They will have careers.

➤ They will enter the social world on equal ground with men.

➤ They are sexually liberated and entitled to equal sexual satisfaction.

However, as their adult lives get underway, women encounter different realities:

➤ Women report becoming acutely stressed working in male-dominated fields.

Woman to Woman

Nancy Friday, author of *My Mother, Myself* and *My Secret Garden* describes a young woman's dreams and desires. "I want a big life. I want to move on. I want to see the world, I want to do this, I want to be like my mother, yes, I want to get married and have a home, maybe ..."

Explosives

A study by sociologist Anne Machung revealed that men view work in terms of earning money, reaching for the best paying jobs, the highest entry-level positions, and the best titles. They are more future-oriented than women graduating college and seeking employment.

➤ Women find that competing in tough professions, meant wearing a mask and selling their souls to make progress.

➤ Women report encountering more limitations placed on them than they expected. Today, only 13 percent of law partners, 26 percent of tenured professors, and 12 percent of corporate officers are women.

➤ Families and society are still putting tremendous pressure on women to marry and have children.

➤ Women are discovering that there are many more trade-offs than they perceived there would be.

➤ The norm for most men at the top still involves having children and stay-at-home wives.

➤ Work requires more time and energy than assumed, leaving less time for dating, socializing, finding husbands, and having families.

➤ Women are realizing that society still sees and expects the woman to be the primary parent.

➤ Women find themselves *self-supporting,* not *financially independent.* They are choosing flexible, accommodating, and lower-paying jobs that work with raising children.

➤ Work is more akin to a job than a career, providing no real sense of identity, self-fulfillment, and personal satisfaction. In fact, 7 out of 10 women report that they plan to marry, at which time their spouses' jobs will take priority over their careers.

➤ A National Opinion Research Center poll showed that nearly a quarter of women did not want sex the first time they had it. Rather, they succumbed to pressure or the fear of abandonment.

Building Blocks

To be **self-supporting** means to be able to support oneself. To be **financially independent** means to achieve economic self-sufficiency without the financial assistance from a spouse or parent whether single or head of a household.

Powerwoman Meets Man

Problems in the dating world abound and are complicated by the "flux" Orenstein has aptly chronicled in her book.

Sex and the City, the mega TV hit starring Sarah Jessica Parker, accurately reflects the dilemma of today's young woman. One of the principal female characters, a lawyer, couldn't get a date, not even a nibble, at a whirlwind session for singles until she lied and said she was something sexy like a stewardess.

Explosives

A recent nationwide survey by OfficeTeam found that 84 of 100 of the nation's largest companies offer either formal or informal flex hours that accommodate childcare. However, another survey of the 1996 corporate world revealed that bosses view their female underlings with children as women lacking true commitment to their careers.

Woman to Woman

Women who never married include: Jane Austen, author; Elizabeth I, Queen of England; Maria Montessori, physician and educator; and Susan B. Anthony, a pioneer of women's rights. Interestingly, up-to-date research found that as single women age compared to their married peers, they become happier, develop greater independence, are more assertive, and strive toward more personal growth.

Orenstein found plenty of women who said that men are weary of women who earn more than they do. The percent of stay-at-home-dads is still negligible and men who are "backstage" providers (those take secondary financial roles to wives) remain notably in the minority.

A typical 28-year-old young professional woman in Washington, D.C., cites problems of balancing work and meeting eligible men. "There is only so much time I can devote to dating. I work long hours, travel on the job, and have leisure-time activities I don't want to give up. That leaves one night either to go out and meet men or go out on a date."

What follows, research shows, is that the transition into the decade of one's 30s (a reassessment of life and natural part of adult development for both sexes) results in a panic over marriage for women and the fear of being alone. Accompanying those emotions is the fear of falling short and loosing out on their career path.

Conflicted Views on Marriage

If and when your daughter finds a man, her expectations of marriage might be inflated but countered with cynicism. In other words she wants to marry as a way to avoid isolation, find intimacy, and have an anchor in a difficult world. But, she is faced with lots of unhappily married friends, a high divorce rate, and in all probability, a secondary role and a potential loss of identity.

One of my favorite comments that Orenstein reports was made by 36-year-old marketing director Barb Wieneke. "She wanted to marry without turning into a 'wife.'"

This all makes sense in the context of findings by sociologist Kim Ducats, who asserts that the new romantic fantasy of single young women has to do with motherhood, not men. These gals expect motherhood to be wonderful, full of self-nurturance, unconditional love, and permanence. These are all things they doubt they can find long-term in partnerships with men.

Pearls of Wisdom

Dr. Frank Pittman, author of *Grow Up! How Taking Responsibility Can Make You a Happy Adult* (Golden Books Publishing Co., 1999), says marriage is about commitment, self-control, personal responsibility, and reality-based thinking. "When you are married you have a partner in life whose life is affected by everything that affects your life and shares your fate. They can, therefore, be relied upon in times of crises to put your best interest first. There are a lot of logical reasons that you and your spouse should be in love with each other, especially if you have children, share values, are integrated into the family and have finances that are tied together. It make sense for these people to be in love."

Moms and Their Young Adult Daughters, Generations in Conflict

According to research, the primary difference that separates mothers and daughters is the younger generation's "social and psychological freedom to defer motherhood" and develop their own potential.

A secondary difference among factions of younger women, depending on their upbringing, includes a rejection of the supermom format or the adoption of motherhood as their primary identity. The following sections explain this in detail.

Rejecting the Supermom Syndrome

Let's compare supermoms and their daughters.

Daughters' Points of View

Women now in their 20s and 30s who grew up with supermoms who worked hard to reap the rewards of feminist ideology and liberation aren't necessarily buying into their mom's lifestyle. In fact large numbers are rejecting it, much to their mothers' dismay and disapproval. These gals admire the success their moms worked hard to obtain but aren't buying into that model of motherhood and are lowering their career sights.

Here's why:

1. Management psychologist, Harry Levison, told the media that many young women of supermoms today don't feel like they can fill her shoes and be as good at this role as she was.

2. Many of those from the younger generation resented absentee moms who were never at home. Take 26-year-old Marda Herz, daughter of a psychologist. Here's what she told a *Wall Street Journal* reporter. "I grew up without a mom. I don't want to see my children go through what we had to go through."

Supermoms' Points of View

Those who have investigated this phenomenon found that mothers who worked hard to take advantage of new opportunities afforded as a result of the women's movement …

1. Burn when daughters reject their ethics.

2. Interpret their daughter's attitudes as a lack of ambition.

3. Disapprove of their ability to be financially self-sufficient, particularly in light of the high divorce rate.

4. See this rejection as a lack of validation of what supermoms were all about.

Explosives

Not all women have their sights on joining the cadre of liberated females who marched into the workforce during the last several decades. The number of women entering the workforce has leveled off. Two factors reported by the *Wall Street Journal* December 28, 1995, are the primary cause: 1) the extent of job opportunities, and 2) women's desire to spend more of their time with their families.

Understanding Mom's Evaluation of It All

Unless mom and daughter are on the same track, there is room for greater conflict over lifestyles and less empathy. Moms reveal a variety of factors that appear different in their daughters' lives these days that they have difficulty with:

1. Moms cannot envision themselves being able to do what their daughters are doing—traveling, living alone, or chasing after careers.

2. Moms see single life outside the loop and think that marriage is not only natural, but the happiest position for an adult woman. Hence, they expect and want their daughters to marry.

3. Moms admit, "My biggest fear is she won't find a husband."

4. The "sexual thing" grabs other moms' attention and result in shaking heads. "On the one hand I think it is great to be more sexually free. But on the other hand, it bothers me because I come from another world. I listened to a talk radio show about how to bag a woman on the first date and all this macho crap. I find it pathetic."

5. A lot of moms applaud their daughter's super-mom line until their grandchildren go into daycare or their daughters appear overworked and frazzled. Then they advocate staying home.

Pearls of Wisdom

"She believed that decent and caring human relationships are sustained by courtesy. Thus, in talking about sexuality and about the functions of the body, she clearly wanted me to be pleased to be woman and unconstrained by gender."

—Mary Bateson about her mother Margaret Mead, *With a Daughter's Eye* (Harper, 1993)

Discovering How Expression of Generation Differences Affect Your Daughter

Disparity over viewpoints not only produces conflict but it also …

➤ Puts added pressure on your daughter.

➤ Makes her feel guilty.

➤ Increases her desperation.

➤ Intensifies her ambivalence and confusion.

Giving Moms Some Expert Advice

Psychotherapist, Susan Forward, Ph.D., author of *Emotional Blackmail* (HarperCollins, 1997), says moms, beware. In expressing your own lack of assertiveness or fear, you may be making statements that cut down your daughter. Examples Forward cites include telling your daughter …

➤ You won't find the perfect man, he doesn't exist.

➤ You are up against more qualified women for the job.

➤ Why are you working so hard? Relax.

A better strategy for moms and healthier for your relationship with your daughter would be to …

➤ Trust your daughter to make herself happy.

➤ Give her the confidence to do that.

➤ Accept her choices.

➤ Show acceptance of her.

The Dynamics of Worry

Worrying is a natural response to stress, anxiety, and fear that makes you feel vulnerable and powerless. How you worry is a matter of habit and family background. One out of four individuals is an excessive and problematic worrier. Perpetual worriers suffer from more stress, and have a lesser level of comfort, happiness, and peace of mind.

Worry is exacerbated by imagination, anticipation, and emotions. Worries compound worries, says Brad Schmidt, associate professor of psychology at Ohio State University. "You worry more about your kids when you are under more stress yourself."

A Mother's Worried Voice

In the event you don't know a worried mom, which is highly unlikely, or you want someone to empathize with, check out this 60-year-old Midwestern mom with a mid-20s daughter.

> "I worry over Carin maybe every day. I worry about my son, too, but I worry about him differently than my daughter. I worry that Carin will get stressed and hassled or harried and worry that she will break down or do something foolish. I worry that she will falter in some way. I worry her job and her career won't work out for her. She is more positive. I don't like to project that but I do. I think the worst. My biggest worry is that she won't settle down and find satisfaction, productivity, and love. I have to talk to myself a lot not to think about it."

Counterproductive Worries

There are worries that are counterproductive for your daughter and that sap you, Mom, of good energy. So here are some things you had best do:

➤ Stop worrying about situations you have no control over.

➤ Refrain from expressing excessive worries that could cause a rift between you and your daughter. (You may want to take a look at Fix-It Moms in Chapter 13, "Why Mothers and Daughters Drive Each Other Crazy.")

➤ Avoid worrying in a way that tells your daughter you don't think she is capable of handling a situation and thwarts her sense of self.

➤ Do not express worries that make your daughter uncomfortable or encourage her to be inhibited and feel guilty.

➤ Tell your daughters that they can curb your worrying with reassurances and a little more time spent on conversing.

Pearls of Wisdom

"You don't owe each other anything. You just love each other."

—Ruth Bader Ginsburg, Supreme Court Justice, on mothers and daughters

How to Curb Your Worries

In addition to methods that will relax you—like worry beads—Schmidt advises a thoughtful three-step method:

1. Identify the nature of your worry or thought. Determine precisely what it is you are worrying about.

2. Evaluate whether your worry is realistic or unrealistic. Ask yourself whether your worry is helpful, whether any real threat is present, or whether your worrying primarily because of habit.

3. If you can't make a determination, gather more information and seek verification—not sympathy—that will reinforce your worries.

In order to gauge how well this method is working when it comes to your daughter, keep a log of your worries and see if your entries decrease over time.

The Least You Need to Know

➤ Your daughter's expectations of her adult future do not match up with the reality she encounters.

➤ Young women in their 20s and 30s are caught betwixt and between two ideologies that leave them in a state of flux.

➤ Most young women want to marry, but many of them find it difficult to balance their personal and professional lives.

➤ In view of the inequities that your daughter faces, she needs support and comfort not criticism or advice based on personal interests.

➤ Daughters do not necessarily follow their mother's footsteps.

➤ Worrying is bad for your health and hazardous to your mother–daughter relationship.

Chapter 10

Daughters in Love, Time for a New Set of Motherly Instructions

---

In This Chapter

➤ Why Mom may feel happy but disenfranchised by Mr. Right

➤ How to avoid conflict and competition with your daughter's lover

➤ Keeping a footing in your daughter's life

➤ Defining restricted areas for Mother's intervention

➤ Helpful hints for handling Mom

➤ The renewed opportunity for love when daughters become mothers

---

Wishes do come true. First of all, your daughter is all grown-up, self-sufficient, and in love. That guy she is bringing home to dinner just may be the one who walks her down the aisle.

Don't ruin the payoff years that can easily lead to a marvelous mother-daughter friendship by overstepping your bounds Mom. A lot of the rules change once your daughter falls in love.

And daughters, pay close attention! With adulthood comes more responsibility on your shoulders to understand your mom and nurture your relationship.

It is a new era in both of your lives. However, some things never change. Family therapist Nora Isaeli, warns, moms and daughters remain very reactive to each other. They are keenly sensitive to one another's nuances. So watch out!

The following chapter will, therefore, help guide moms and daughters—who find themselves in love—to a happy ending.

Woman to Woman

A real trick for Mom is knowing how far to go when inquiring about her adult daughter's love and sex life. It sounds like Charlene and her mom respect one another's boundaries.

"In college after noticing the wear and tear in my chair, my mother asked, 'Is this from you and Bill?' She was implying that the damage resulted from extracurricular usage by Bill and I. I was surprised by the comment, but we both rolled with it and laughed. I honestly think that she didn't really mean to ask the question, it just blurted out. Nevertheless, it was a turning point in our relationship because it was like opening the door to a sometimes forbidden subject. Still, no details are ever given, nor are they asked for."

What to Expect When Mr. Right Enters the Picture

Both mother and daughter will be overcome with joy if Mr. Right seems perfect to both of you. In addition to the euphoria, you may be surprised at some of the other emotions that surface. Getting prepared in advance for their entering the scene will promote mutual understanding and smooth over misunderstandings.

Here's what to expect and how to handle it:

➤ Mom, you may feel tossed out of the picture. A wise woman cut right to the core. "It takes time for your daughter to learn that she can love more than one person."

But be patient. She will come around, although it could take a while.

➤ Chances are, once your daughter falls in love you may lose the primary position as her confidante. A 1993 "New Woman" survey found that a majority of single women view their moms as the person who supports, appreciates, and loves them the most—before marriage that is. With matrimony on the horizon all that changes. Her primary confidante, supporter, and advice-giver becomes her soon-to-be spouse.

Do not compete for intimacy with her new partner in life. In fact, you should encourage their teamwork. Learning to share a daughter is traumatic for some women. But if you fight it, put pressure on her and create unnecessary tensions by demanding her child-like loyalty, you will embark on a contest you cannot and should not win. Such actions will only result in alienating you from her in the long run.

Mom's have to adjust to what is no longer their business. However, if you play your cards right, a new era of mother-daughter love is just around the corner.

➤ The need for your approval also seems to diminish once your daughter commits to a lifetime partner.

While these facts may throw moms into a fit of despair, there is a brighter more reassuring side of the coin. Life changes often become a time of mother-daughter reconciliation.

Getting Over These New Humps

Okay Mom, here is your first list of new instructions once your daughter falls in love:

1. Don't sulk or punish your daughter because of your ambivalent emotions.

2. Gently express your feelings and ask for your daughter's understanding.

3. Provide your daughter and her new partner with the space they need and want at this juncture.

4. Whatever you do, don't make your daughter feel guilty about her new and critical alliance with the man she loves.

Moms don't have to do all the work alone. The longer list of instructions is for mother and daughter together.

Pearls of Wisdom

"When your darling daughter wants to marry a man of whom you disapprove, smile, be gracious, and help out with the wedding. When the marriage is over, you are the supportive mom and the man is the jerk! It's hard, but it's usually worth it in the end."

—Jeni, Phoenix, Arizona

Reviewing a Mother-Daughter Laundry List of New Instructions

Don't blow it, either one of you. If you survived the war years of adolescence, this ought to be easy. Here is what mom and daughter need to do to preserve the peace when love walks into the picture:

1. Talk it out. Respond tactfully to one another, but allow the other to be candid and honest about their new feelings.

2. Lessen expectations of one another during this transitional period. Now is not the time to be nitpicking.

3. Maintain a willingness to bend for each other.

4. Develop keener powers of empathy and keep each other's perspective in mind.

5. Make it easier, not harder for each other.

6. Work on developing realistic expectations of each other.

7. Respect each other's privacy. (Mom, that means she doesn't have to give you a key to her love nest.)

These seven points ought to get you started. Planning the wedding calls for more wisdom.

Pearls of Wisdom

Your mother has been planning your wedding since the day you were born. It's part of 'the good life' she wants for you. She doesn't just want a wedding—she wants the perfect wedding for you and nothing less than 'storybook' will do."

—Denise McGregor, author *Mama Drama* (St. Martin's Press, 1998)

Marriage May Not Be the Next Step

Chances are that even after your daughter falls in love, marriage may not be her next step. Living together without the benefit of formal matrimony may be your daughter's first-union relationship. It is considered part of the normative dating pattern these days.

Some mothers heartily agree with the decision while others strongly disapprove. Try to understand her decision and do not alienate her with ultimatums or demands. You do have the right to express your concerns. Depending on the age of your daughter, it may be helpful for both of you to engage in a conversation that includes her lover.

You may feel better after evaluating their goals and motives with those that proved the most beneficial or least productive in my book *The Complete Idiot's Guide to Living Together* (Alpha Books, 1999).

Your Daughter's Love Problems, Do's and Don'ts

There is one more lesson to be learned in this chapter. By now it should be apparent that your adult daughter may be worrying about hooking up with a love partner. It should also be obvious that your worrying isn't doing her any good.

For some role modeling, take a look at Ann Roth and her daughter Kerry. The way in which Ann has handled, and continues to handle, her daughter's love problems is exemplary. The amazing thing is, her daughter agrees. Now that should definitely grab your attention!

What I suggest is to put this type of respectful exchange into play before a crisis in your daughter's love life erupts. This way she will feel comfortable to seek out your help, if only as a sympathetic listener or sounding board.

Kerry and Ann

Mom: Ann

> "I didn't think Kerry would be married at 25 and I didn't want her to get married until her late 20s, after she found she could live on her own free of domestic responsibilities. But I don't talk to her about things like that unless she brings it up. I don't want her to marry just because it is time. That isn't a good reason, and I don't want her to be pressured into marriage."

Ann admits she isn't the "perfect" mom. "If I open up and get the brunt of it, I get a little hurt and then I keep quiet, take 50,000 breaths and don't touch that again. Or at least if I do, I try in a better way. In my mind I hold back, but I probably give Kerry looks that show disapproval or worry. It's hard because I can tell by her tone of voice if she is stressed or frustrated or down."

Nonetheless, her daughter Kerry is getting Ann's message—she cares and is ready and willing to listen.

Daughter: Kerry

> "I am open with my thoughts because I think Mom and I have a lot of the same thoughts and feelings about life and we can relate like that. I am comfortable with myself so that I can accept advice. I am not trying to get approval from her, just trying to figure things out myself.
>
> "Mom is definitely unobtrusive in my love life. She will wait for me to come to her and I appreciate that. She will bring things up to me that enable me to bring it up on my own time. She trusts the person I am. A few of my friends don't have that with their moms, which is very frustrating. That is huge!!!!! So I don't feel the need to lie to her.
>
> "Recently I told her I feel I need to discuss some issues with her. I wanted to prepare her because I was going to tell her how I was feeling about this man I have been with for five years."

Kerry admitted she had been grappling with whether after all this time, he was Mr. Right or Mr. Wrong. At the moment she had serious, perplexing, and troublesome doubts he could make her happy for a lifetime.

Woman to Woman

Moms, a recommendation for your confused, lovesick daughters is get them a book that realistically looks at modern marriage. One of the best I have found is *The Seven Principles for Making Marriage Work* (Crown Publishers, 1999) by relationship professor and guru, John M. Gottman, Ph.D.

"I know she feels sad this relationship may not be working out. She feels the same emotion I do. In fact she feels it so much she won't interfere. She is very respectful and that is very good. Maybe I do need a kick in the ass but she won't give it to me. She says I am here for you. It is good that you are thinking this over carefully. I hope you sleep well tonight. It's amazing!

"The best thing my mother could be doing for me right now is exactly what she is doing. Being there. I know I can go to her without her jumping to conclusions or being judgmental, which she has never been with any situation. I don't want her to give me the answer or wring me out like a sponge of all my thoughts and feelings. I want her to be the wall. She's doing everything good.

"I know she wants to talk about the situation, but I control when to talk or not. I have to figure it out on my own first."

Extracting the Lesson

What we can discern from our role models:

➤ Ann was respectful of Kerry's privacy.

➤ Ann admitted to herself that she wasn't perfect, but she was willing to try harder.

➤ Ann trusted her daughter's ability to solve the problem and was willing to give guidance instead of a lecture.

➤ Kerry was receptive to her mother's opinions because she had no self-confidence or autonomy issues.

➤ Kerry was careful to maintain boundaries with her mother.

➤ Kerry was specific in telling her mother what she wanted and needed from her.

What's important here is how both mother and daughter acted. This isn't a one-sided lesson.

A Quick Lesson to Learn for the Mother of the Bride

Rachel Menke and Ryan Borland got engaged on Friday night. On Monday morning, Rachel's mom began showing signs of wedding madness. She was sitting in the rain drinking coffee with a friend at 7 A.M. waiting for the office of the cathedral to open. She was determined to reserve it for her daughter on the wedding date they had chosen.

Although this may sound obsessive, there is a hidden purpose behind the mad wedding planning: It helps keep mom's emotions in tow. However, before promising your daughter the moon, get a game plan:

➤ Do not jump the gun.

➤ Do not promise your daughter anything until you check out the price (if you are footing the bill).

➤ Do establish a budget if you are footing the bill.

➤ Do determine from the get-go which decisions each of you has a right to make.

➤ Do not give the groom's parents or your daughter carte blanche for a guest list unless you mean to honor it.

➤ Do not forget for one second who the bride and groom are, nor that it is their wedding.

Pearls of Wisdom

I cannot attribute this pearl to just one mom or one daughter. Too many have and will say it about the period of engagement and wedding planning. "This will be the best and the worst year of your life."

How to Keep Your Nose Out of Your Daughter's House

Dr. Charney Herst, author of *For Mothers of Difficult Daughters* (Villard, 1998) believes, "If you want to share a marital coping strategy with your daughter every now and then, that's fine. But 99 percent of the time, acting as her marriage counselor will backfire—*even if she asks for your help.*" Your daughter will patch things up and be embarrassed or resentful that you know so much about her relationship and her husband.

Furthermore, you cannot be objective. We all know that. Perhaps a good rule of thumb is not to offer advice with one exception—if she is being abused. That calls for immediate intervention. Otherwise, try to be satisfied being her mother.

Add to that the wisdom a young married woman imparted to her mother. "My marriage is different than yours. We work things out to suit us, our personalities, and our needs. I don't expect the same things you do from Dad."

Topics Off-Limits for Moms

Other areas besides marital counseling to steer clear of include …

➤ How your daughter and her husband spend their money.

➤ How they raise their kids.

➤ How clean they keep their house.

➤ How they manage their household.

➤ How they celebrate their anniversary.

➤ How they spend their leisure time—whether together or separately.

➤ What you deem to be appropriate or acceptable gift-giving.

Without respecting these as zones of "no admittance" you could seriously jeopardize the good feelings your daughter and her husband have toward you.

Pearls of Wisdom

"I am so very lucky to have a wonderful mom who loves me so much and wants the best for me. I have moved over and over, farther and farther away from her, and now that I have a child I wish I hadn't done that. I wasn't moving away from her. I was just trying to find my way and my place and she let me do that. So now, here I am—too far from her."

—Toby Sugarman, Kapahu, Hawaii, age 40, mother of a daughter

Guidelines for Daughters in Love

There are ways daughters in love can perpetuate the peace and enhance their relationship, appreciation for, and friendship with their mothers. As a daughter, the steps required on your behalf aren't all that difficult.

Here are a few tips to keep in mind:

1. Avoid the temptation to discuss marital fights. Chances are, your mom will suffer through them more intensely than you. Besides, you will get over them more quickly than your mother, who will want to know all the details of the aftermath.

You could just get an e-mail like the one this mom sent. "Okay, so what happened when you got home? Share with me what you will. But ... you should know that your fight with Joe caused me to nervously trim two inches off my hair with a toenail scissors and indulge in a 1,000-calorie cookie binge."

2. Every now and then it might be prudent to allow your mom to think she is right.

3. Listen to what Mom has to say without getting defensive. She may just have a worthwhile point to offer that could be lost if you close your mind to her.

4. Try to gently disagree when she provides you with advice you think is totally wrong. There isn't any need to snap at her unless she persists.

5. Be sure to let her know that you still love her.

6. Don't exclude her from your life nor fail to share small or large plans with her.

When Daughters Turn into Mothers

Perhaps the biggest change in many mother-daughter relationships comes when the daughter has her first child. Assistant professor of human development at Penn State University Karen Fingerman said age strengthens mother-daughter relationship, partially because of shared experiences like having children.

The reasons for moving into a more positive territory and renewed affection are varied.

1. The status of the daughter changes when she becomes a mother. She is emancipated, and it should signal the definitive end to treating her like a child.

2. Roles change to some extent when a daughter becomes a mother. As one daughter aptly put it, they became mother and mother.

3. There is added understanding and clarity when daughters encounter the intensity of the shared experience of motherhood.

4. Daughters tend to seek new guidance from their mothers when they become moms for the first time.

5. It is not uncommon for daughters to feel a new and intense period of bonding with their mothers after having a child.

6. Toronto family therapists and authors of *Goodbye Mother, Hello Woman* (New Harbinger Publications, 1995), Marilyn Irwin Boynton

Pearls of Wisdom

Jane Ginsburg, a Harvard law grad like her mother, Supreme Court Justice Ruth Bader Ginsburg, expressed that motherhood brought the two women closer. "It's easier to understand things that seemed arbitrary in the past."

and Mary Dell, reveal that often having children provides a wonderful opportunity and impetus for children to reevaluate their mother-daughter relationship. A 28-year-old woman called her mother for months after having her first child to praise her endurance, thank her for her love, and apologize for her own adolescent outrages.

7. Daughters appreciate what their own mothers sacrificed to be moms once they, too become a mom.

8. Daughters respond positively to the adoration their mothers hold for their grandchildren.

Do's and Don'ts for the New Mother's Mother

No doubt you will be feeling pleased and confident, if like so many other young women, your daughter's new role as Mom prompts a show of love and appreciation. Nonetheless, this doesn't give your license to drop all other guidelines. In fact, you best read through the following lists of do's and don'ts to steer clear of potential conflict.

Do's

➤ Do continue to see your daughter as a whole person, not just the mother of your grandchildren.

➤ Do compliment her on her mothering. Be sincere and look for the positives.

➤ Do give your daughter a little mothering at this stage. New moms tend to need it.

➤ Do make time to do adult things with her, not just the baby.

➤ Do give her support. New mothering can be overwhelming.

➤ Do listen to her patiently even though she sounds like no one else has ever dealt with an infant and her complaints about no sleep seem trivial. Discussing baby care creates a deeper psychic connection between you and your daughter.

➤ Do show enthusiasm for all the new things she is encountering in her life.

➤ Do make constructive suggestions, but only with a great deal of tact and wisdom.

Woman to Woman

Many young moms say they are surprised even startled when they sound like their moms. However, many experts say that we cannot deny that part of our mothering style comes from our own mothers.

Don'ts

➤ Don't be surprised when your daughter doesn't do things in the nursery or with her baby the way you did.

➤ Don't criticize her mothering.

➤ Don't tell her how to raise her children.

➤ Don't go against her wishes and do things behind her back that she doesn't want you to do.

➤ Don't let her baby or her entire brood of kids replace the special person she is or the place she holds in your life.

➤ Don't put pressure on your daughter to be a stay-at-home mom or a supermom. The choice is hers.

➤ Do not ever say, "I told you so."

➤ Don't pour guilt into wounds.

➤ Do not go to the extremes and either dote on your grandchild relentlessly or neglect him or her either.

Explosives

According to what Naomi Lowinsky, Ph.D., told *Parents Magazine* (May 1998), there are reluctant grandmas. Their reaction to a daughter's motherhood may confound, puzzle, hurt, and anger their offspring. The problem is they have a hard time facing aging, don't want to think of themselves as old enough to be grandmas, are tired after raising kids and working all their lives, may be fearful of the responsibility, are not interested because they have already been there and done that, or may be more consumed by their own lives.

Tips on How to Be a Great Grandma

Don't be a play-it-again mom. It's your daughter's turn. Besides, grandparenting is delicious! Like the 50 million other grandparents in the United States, you will want to spend time and money on these love bundles. And, like many grandparents, you won't live in the same city as your daughter. When you visit, heed these suggestions:

➤ Try not to stay more than a few days.

➤ Do not interrupt the household routine.

➤ Do not take command of the house or the children.

➤ Make yourself helpful.

➤ Don't expect to be waited on.

➤ Baby-sit and give your daughter an afternoon or evening out.

➤ Always clear dates in advance of your visit.

This list should get you started. It does, however, take time to fit into this new mode. Let it evolve slowly.

The Least You Need to Know

➤ Chances are, Mom, you will feel ambivalent and left out when your daughter falls in love.

➤ Mothers and daughters need to increase empathy and understanding when Mr. Right enters the picture.

➤ Your daughter will come to the understanding that she can love her husband and still love you.

➤ You can look forward to increased closeness and bonding when your daughter becomes a mother.

Part 3

Establishing Patterns and Legacies

Patterns and legacies influence how mothers and daughters interact, evolve over time, and continue to exert influence on the relationship later in life. Interpreting this information should help shed light on your mother's actions, your reactions, and your relationship from a vantage point on both sides of the fence.

Part 3 is divided into four critical chapters. The discussion in each chapter builds on the entire process of growth that began on page one of this book.

Chapter 11, "Fingerprinting Mother Types," identifies a number of prevalent mothering types. These handy categories succinctly explain how moms approach their daughters and how each method either positively or negatively contributes to an adult relationship.

The remaining three chapters in Part 3 elaborate upon patterns that create mother-daughter tensions, cycles of blame, spinning wheels of guilt, and impossible expectations. However, not everything can be blamed on Mom—not even those moms adept at using emotional hooks to control their daughters. The family itself and the place each person assumes within its structure plays a meaningful role in determining future patterns and long-term legacies for mothers and daughters.

Fingerprinting Mother Types

In This Chapter

➤ Discovering where mom picked up her mothering style

➤ Pointing a finger at Mom's M.O.

➤ Mothering styles that carry warning labels

➤ Moderating the mother agenda

➤ Daughter's pick—defiant or compliant

It is time to get specific. The basic style or combination of styles that comprise one's mothering modus operandi (M.O.) is the first step in understanding the patterns and legacies established over the course of mother-daughter relationships. The styles of mothering set forth in this chapter should offer valuable insights for both mother and daughter. Without such information, delving sensibly and logically into mother-daughter conflicts and compatibility would be impossible.

However, as you read this chapter don't jump the gun and say, "Ah ha! That's my mom—the monster mother or the smothering motherer." And Mom, don't cower with fright if you identify too closely with those mothers that come with a warning label. Chances are much more likely that without such an emotional knee-jerk response, you will concede that your true mothering style is less exaggerated and more moderated.

Understanding How Mom Developed Her Mothering Style

There are several factors that contribute to the development of a woman's mothering style. Chances are the mom in question arrived at a style that was affected by all of the following circumstances:

➤ Childhood and adult interactions with her mom

➤ Her cultural and religious background

➤ The number of children she has delivered

➤ Her financial well-being or pressures

➤ Her responsibility to older family members

➤ The quality of relationship she has with her husband or the father of her children

➤ Her level of education

➤ Her personality characteristics and self-concept

➤ The condition of her health

➤ Her mother's style of mothering

➤ Her childhood experiences and upbringing

Assessing Mother's Style

Whoever is doing the picking—deciding if Mom is wonderful or horrible, the best or the worst—remember a lot of it has to do with a matter of perception. After all, two daughters in one family could match Mom up with different titles and even paint entirely different pictures of their childhood under her care.

Secondly, it is difficult to pigeonhole anyone into one pattern. It is for the sake of discussion that we define and use handy but often-exaggerated categories prepared from a variety of sources. The reality is many a mom is a mixture of salt, pepper, and a number of spices—not a solid rock of salt like the authors of these categories suggest.

Profiling the Ideal Mother

Why not start with the best first! If one were the absolute ideal mom this is how they would operate 100 percent of the time. This selfless mom would ...

➤ Separate her needs from her daughter's and never inflict her own needs onto her offspring.

➤ Accept and never be threatened by her daughter's aggressive behavior or independence.

➤ Be realistic enough to know that no matter what, her daughter would have both good and bad feelings toward her.

➤ Respect a daughter's differences and not treat this as a personal betrayal.

➤ Be loving and caring.

The reality is that while the ideal mom is worth emulating, most women cannot be all of these things all of the time. Every now and then they display characteristics that belong to those moms who come with warning labels.

Woman to Woman

Research shows that moms who acknowledge their own imperfections enable daughters to assume the healthy posture that it all right for them to be imperfect as well.

Identifying Mothers with Warning Labels

In their book *How to Manage Your Mother* (Simon & Schuster, 1992), psychotherapists Nancy Wasserman Cocola and Arlene Modica Matthews discuss six extreme mother types that are troubling for daughters and frustrating for mothers. I think of these as "fingerprints" that can illuminate the cause and effect of various behaviors by moms, perceptions of daughters, and their ensuing relationships. Not only do these fingerprints reveal an identity, but they also leave behind what can be a "sticky residue" that affects the mother-daughter relationship.

Most women and their daughters will recognize a little of their mothering self in each of these fingerprints. It's the mom who sees herself clearly and completely in one of the categories that may be in for the most trouble.

When One Plus One Equals One

This is the fingerprint of a mother who cannot distinguish herself from her daughter. Mother and daughter are as inseparable as they were when daughter resided in her womb, in Mom's perspective. Cocola and Matthews call this the "merged mothering style."

This mom exhibits …

➤ An inability to separate her daughter's identity from hers.

➤ An inability to separate what is hers or her daughters.

➤ A deep concern about all aspects of her daughter's life.

➤ The need to know everything about her daughter.

➤ A failure to have a full and enjoyable life apart from her daughter.

➤ The desire to hang onto a feeling of oneness with her daughter.

➤ The need to have a life that revolves around her daughter.

➤ A conscious or unconscious behavior that allows for little fatherly participation.

The Residue of Sticky Fingerprints

According to authors Cocola and Matthews, the merged mother places a tremendous burden on her daughter. It is difficult for the younger woman to feel like a good daughter because of her mom's need never to want her to grow up. This mom also produces excessive guilt and other feelings in daughters, despite appropriate time spent with and for Mom. It is never adequate. (A more in-depth look at how guilt plays a part in driving a wedge between mothers and daughters is presented in Chapter 13, "Why Mothers and Daughters Drive Each Other Crazy.")

When Worry Is the All-Consuming Face of Motherhood

The mom whose world revolves around worry is what Cocola and Matthews call the "chronically worried mothering style." This mom …

➤ Uses words like don't, can't, and watch out, be careful, don't fall, are you crazy, you'll kill yourself.

➤ Is disaster-oriented.

➤ Continually warns of impending dangers.

Pearls of Wisdom

"… mothers and daughters relate best when they have a sense of independence from each other." This is particularly true when mothers are not defined entirely through their relationships with their daughters.

—Alexis J. Walker, author and human development expert

Pearls of Wisdom

"… mothers in this day and age, even more so, I think, try to control their daughters. There is a line here. And daughters, I feel, desperately need their fathers. I'm very big on this business of getting men into the nursery."

—Nancy Friday, author of *My Mother, Myself: The Daughter's Search for Identity* (Delacorte Press, 1977; available Doubleday 1997)

➤ Has difficulty with separation because she is fearful for their daughter's future.

➤ Is overly cautious and concerned with preventative health measures.

➤ Is overly protective and tries to fix anything she thinks may be problematic for her daughter, (which is also a characteristic of the smothering or overly protective mom; more on this a little later in this chapter.

The Residue of Sticky Fingerprints

The daughter of the genuine chronic worrier is at a distinct disadvantage. She focuses on Mom's fears, avoids things she disapproves of, and formulates an identity based on Mom's version of the world around her. If and when she recognizes the ill effects of her mom's behavior, chances are she will become antagonistic and angry toward this dominant female figure.

When the Critical Hand Keeps Shaking a Finger

Nothing makes this mother happy. She finds fault in everything her daughter does. Cocola and Matthews call her the "hypercritical mother." This mom has a strong tendency to …

➤ Want her daughter to do well and make her proud.

➤ Use negative tactics and control through demands to inspire her daughter.

➤ Express everything in a negative way.

➤ Find fault in everything, be opinionated, be critical of other moms, and have all the correct answers.

➤ Question the validity and right of her daughter's independent emotions.

➤ Be ready to criticize and to condemn others.

➤ Have high energy, be married to a passive male, and always need to be the winner.

➤ Pit one child against another.

Explosives

Denise McGregor, author of *Mama Drama: Making Peace with the Woman Who Can Push Your Buttons, Make You Cry, and Drive You Crazy*, thinks that the hypercritical mom may also be motivated by competition, overprotectiveness, emotional neediness, and the desire to control.

The Residue of Sticky Fingerprints

The daughter of the hypercritical mom, Cocola and Matthews say, lives in a state of tension over getting her mother's approval. Her primary concern in interacting with her mom is whether or not she is doing something right or wrong. Further consequences for the daughter of a finger-pointing mother is the constant questioning of her own feelings and opinions, the tendency to formulate addictive self-punishing habits, and development of a low self-esteem.

When Mom Is Right in Her Daughter's Face

Some moms have to not only know everything but also control everything in their daughters' lives (and often in the lives of others). Cocola and Matthews call this mothering type the "controlling mom." This mom …

➤ Knows everything about her daughter.

➤ Anticipates her daughter's thoughts and needs, is manipulative, and is always telling her daughter what to do.

➤ Takes charge of everything—her daughter, home, friends, and community.

➤ Is intrusive to the extent that she would rearrange her daughter's dresser drawers or bedroom, purchase her clothes, or sign her up for classes without consulting her.

➤ Plans ahead in order to remove obstacles she thinks are in her daughter's way.

The Residue of Sticky Fingerprints

The daughter raised in the clutches of the controlling mom will find herself with an opponent who is difficult to argue against. Her mom has more stamina and sticking power to her point of view than her daughter, and does not respond to the word no. Her daughter is likely to fail to develop her own life skills, and remain reliant on her mom.

Pearls of Wisdom

Jessica from Miami, Florida, said that her pediatrician gave her the best motherly advice when her daughter was young that alleviated a lot of stress, friction and arguments. She used it consistently all through the years. "Give your daughter choices, but don't give her a choice if you truly aren't going to give her the freedom to make that choice."

When Mom Vies for Equal Billing

Some moms compete with their daughters, which Cocola and Matthews call the "competitive style mom." The mom who must be on equal footing with her daughter turns a mother-daughter relationship into a contest. She …

➤ Does everything her daughter does and tries to do it better.

➤ Wears her daughter's clothes to show she looks better.

➤ Must be the center of the family, the first to get attention for anything.

➤ Doesn't allow Daddy to pay a lot of attention to his little girl.

➤ Strives to be the focus of everyone's attention, including her daughter and her daughter's friends.

➤ Competes physically and beauty-wise with her daughter, to try and outshine her offspring.

➤ Resents getting older.

The Residue of Sticky Fingerprints

Living with this kind of mom can't help but make a daughter feel unimportant. To survive, she aggressively competes or quietly languishes in resentment.

Explosives

Experts may put your mind at ease and tell you that it is absolutely normal for moms to envy their daughters' youthfulness. However, when moms start to act out that envy and begin to compete with their daughters, someone is going to suffer serious consequences. Actions of this nature not only adversely affect the relationship between mothers and daughters, but also the self-image of the younger party.

When Mom Is Simply Too Good to Be True

This mom has Miss Manners and Emily Post beat! Cocola and Matthews call her the "pseudo-perfect style mom." Because she is overly concerned about social appropriateness and has a limited sense of self-worth, her public and private behavior is …

➤ Never without perfect manners.

➤ Marked by saying the right words and expressing the right sentiments.

➤ Never relaxed enough to let family or friends know how she is really feeling.

➤ Calculated in a way that will win affection by giving things or gifts she herself wants or needs.

➤ Marred by the difficulty of understanding her daughter's needs or point of view.

➤ Marked by generosity that is motivated out of selfishness.

➤ Developed around the hope to gain the admiration of those around her.

➤ Motivated by a sense of obligation; full of pretense to the point that she behaves toward her daughter the way she is supposed to, not necessarily how she feels.

➤ Meant to convince her daughter to feel as if she still needs her mother's care.

➤ Lacking in sincerity or feels false.

➤ Centered around doing things she thinks will make her worthy of someone's love.

The Residue of Sticky Fingerprints

These moms, say Cocola and Matthews, have a M.O. that is subtle and elusive. They attach conditions to loving them and normally form little more than superficial relationships with their daughters because of their inability to achieve real intimacy.

Explosives

Roni Cohen-Sandler, Ph.D., uses the term "Monster Mothers." These are women who are abusive, neglectful, and intolerable of a daughter's individuality. They fail to be empathetic during teen years and are uncommunicative because they cannot express themselves. Fortunately, they are the exception to most mothers rather than the rule.

Understanding the Smothering Mother

Everyone has a name for these moms. However, the one that is universally understood is "overprotective." She will hide behind bushes to make sure her children walk safely into the school building and double-check their homework to ensure passing grades.

The name, overprotective mom, conjures up a character. The comical, exaggerated image is one of a mother who will follow her kids anywhere, from the bathroom to college, and wipe their teenage noses as if they were toddlers.

The point is, you won't find a mom in the world who doesn't possess some degree of zealous enthusiasm for protecting her children. But that doesn't constitute smothering. The concept of motherly protection is so important that it merits a separate discussion.

Legitimizing the Need to Protect

Most women view protection of their daughters as a form of nurturing, not controlling! Keeping children safe—and we all know that your daughter is your child for life—is a major concern for moms. The anxiety over protecting daughters from school violence, abductions, and gun-toting youngsters merely changes focus in adulthood to college acceptances, broken hearts, fertility, career disappointments, and marital or singlehood happiness.

"It is hard for parents to do less and still feel they are doing a good job," said Janis Keyers, M.A., faculty member in human development at Carillo College and author (*Becoming the Parent You Want to Be,* Broadway Books, 1997).

Woman to Woman

Dr. Hiasako M. Koizumi, associate professor of child and adolescent psychiatry at Ohio State University, explains that a true overprotective mom interferes with normal child development. She manages their environment to the extent that she prevents them from learning how to handle stress, inhibits healthy exploration, denies the growth of autonomy, limits self-confidence, and nurtures socially isolated and inadequate teenagers.

The tricky part for well-meaning moms at any stage is to promote a balance between exploration and a safe environment without putting obstacles in the way for an autonomous, self-directed life.

Controlling the Urge to Protect

It is wise for each parent to consider her own actions and determine their motivation for decisions says Dr. Hiasako M. Koizumi. The number one question moms need to ask themselves is, "Am I doing this because of my own anxiety or is there a real and justified concern for my daughter's safety, happiness and well-being?"

A rule of thumb Koizumi suggests is arriving at a balance that promotes safety but allows growth in younger years. The same is true in adulthood with some conceptual adjustments. The following diagram visually depicts the concern that must be balanced between a protective mother and her daughter during adulthood.

Pearls of Wisdom

Overprotective parenting may be in the eye of the beholder. "To the watcher it might look like overprotecting, but for the child it might just be right."

—Kyle D. Pruett, clinical psychiatrist at Yale University's Child Study Center and author of *Me, Myself and I: How Children Build Their Sense of Self* (Goddard, 1999)

Determining If You Are an Overprotective Mother

Various stages prompt different motherly responses to daughters that could be suffocating and construed as overprotective. Have your responses crossed the line? Here's a short quiz that can help you find out.

1. Do you have excessive fears about your daughter?
   Mostly Yes   Sometimes   Mostly No

2. Do you worry unnecessarily about her?
   Mostly Yes   Sometimes   Mostly No

3. Do you feel she is unsafe in the world?
   Mostly Yes   Sometimes   Mostly No

4. Do you have the need to control your daughter's destiny?
   Mostly Yes   Sometimes   Mostly No

5. Do you have difficulty separating from your daughter?
   Mostly Yes   Sometimes   Mostly No

6. Do you discourage joint parental decision-making and participation?
   Mostly Yes   Sometimes   Mostly No

7. Do you try to keep your daughter from experiencing disappointment, pain, or hurt?
   Mostly Yes   Sometimes   Mostly No

8. Do you try not to allow your daughter to feel failure?
   Mostly Yes   Sometimes   Mostly No

9. Do you try to inflict your opinions onto her decision-making process?
   Mostly Yes   Sometimes   Mostly No

10. Do you check on her to make sure she is back from business trips, home from dates, or up-to-date on her rent?
    Mostly Yes   Sometimes   Mostly No

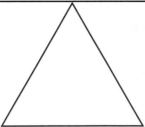

| Mother's actions that reflect her fears, worries, and concerns for her daughter's well-being and happiness | Daughter's right to privacy and ability to remain independent and autonomous |

Balancing a mother's need to protect and an adult child's need for independent growth and decision-making.

If you answered "Mostly Yes" to all 10 questions, you are without a doubt an overprotective mother. In fact, unanimous answers in this category may suggest a need for professional counseling. A perfect set of "Sometimes" represents the most honest and healthy responses. Ten "Mostly No" answers may send a message to your daughter that you are wrapped up in your own life and aren't concerned about her.

Mothers Meshing with Daughters

The entire exercise of discussing mother types will enable us to explore in the next few chapters why some mothers and daughters are predestined for a troubled relationship. Inherent in each of the types presented were qualities that could conceivably grate against the nerves of daughters. How these younger women respond or how their mothers learn to temper these characteristics account in part for how each mother and daughter type mesh.

The options for meshing are defiance or rebellion, or compliance or passivity. As we will see in the remaining parts of the book, both mothers and daughters with the best relationships fall somewhere in the middle—not at either end of the continuum.

Pearls of Wisdom

No matter how accurately any of these prototypes fit mothers and daughters, there is hope for a better future. "It's not where you start in life, it's how you end up that counts."

—Susan Merinoff, New York, mother of five adults (two boys and three girls)

The Least You Need to Know

➤ Mothering styles develop in response to numerous factors in addition to personality.

➤ The ideal mother is something to strive for although it is an impossible ideal to achieve and maintain all the time.

➤ The best mother is likely to exhibit a combination of good and bad qualities, recognizes that she is fallible, and demonstrates a willingness to change.

➤ Chances are your daughter sees you often in exaggerated terms that either focus entirely on your good or bad points.

➤ Most mothers are a blend of styles that vary according to life stages and internal and external factors.

Chapter 12

The Mother-Daughter Dilemma in a Nutshell

> **In This Chapter**
>
> ➤ Understanding the inherent tensions in the mother-daughter relationship
>
> ➤ Realizing you cannot leave the voice of mother behind
>
> ➤ Understanding why mom always gets the blame
>
> ➤ Defining the "blame cycle"
>
> ➤ Identifying factors that keep blame on the front burner

Mothers and daughters are notorious for forming close relationships, but their battles are even more notorious! Sometimes these differences produce a rift that endures and over-shadows the bond of younger years. What does all this animosity evolve from and why the staying power?

These are questions that will be answered in this chapter. We have already hinted at some roots of the problems. The period of adolescence, exaggerated mothering personalities, and differences in generational goals all spark conflict. However, many of the problems that ensue, particularly in later years, are much more deep seated and rooted in one's own unique bias filters. Those are the ones we will unearth now.

Describing the Core of the Dilemma

There are three basic theories that I want to offer up for your consideration. Each researcher assumes the answer to finding the core of the mother-daughter dilemma.

Victoria Secunda, author of *When You and Your Mother Can't Be Friends* and feminist theorist S. Ruddick each talk about an inherent conflict in the mother-daughter relationship. Dr. Charney Hearst focuses more on a theme she found pervasive throughout most mother-daughter relationships. All three theories, in my estimation, offer valuable points that warrant our attention and merit the fame to blame!

Behind Theory Number 1

Ruddick points out two primary factors that in her opinion form the basis of the conflict:

1. The simple fact that a mother and her daughter are and should be two separate persons.

2. What fosters growth or happiness in one does not always do the same for the other.

Behind Theory Number 2

Secunda thinks the problem lies more in the fact that mothers and daughters have an inherent position of being allies and enemies. Here is what she means:

1. Mothers and daughters share some aspects of their identities. However, there is just as much of a need to be different as there is to be similar.

2. There is "a built-in and unavoidable tension that goes with being someone's child."

3. There is a competition that mothers and daughters feel that encourages daughters to do things as well as or better than their moms.

4. Daughters frequently feel that survival without their mothers would be impossible, despite the feelings that put moms and daughters at odds.

Behind Theory Number 3

Psychotherapist and author of *For Mothers of Difficult Daughters* (Villard, 1998), Dr. Charney Hearts claims that all mother-daughter relationships are set up for misunderstanding due to each participant's expectations. Mothers expect a reincarnation of self and an imitation of their behaviors. Daughters expect encouragement for individuality, approval of everything and all decisions, and lifetime nurturing. Both mothers and daughters feel disappointment in each other for

Pearls of Wisdom

"... you don't have to love your mother totally."

—Nancy Friday, author of *My Mother, Myself*

Woman to Woman

How sad! When mothers and daughters get wrapped up in blaming each other for ill feelings or a conflict between them—wrong decisions, unhappiness, or any other possible conceivable problem—hostility arises that blocks the release of love. And love is the bond that puts everything else into its proper perspective.

not living up to these impossible expectations, Hearst concludes. (More discussion on these unmet expectations will follow in Part 4, "The Age of Discovery.")

Getting Away from Your Mother Is Impossible!

Wherever you go, you take your mother with you. It is as if you swallowed a miniature version of her that somehow lodged itself in your brain. Her little voice inside your head is called a *maternal introject*. Most often this introject includes Mom's values, traits, attitudes, habits, and outlook. There is a negative and a positive side to the maternal introject. You may either accept and find comfort in the maternal introject or experience a *reaction formation*.

The Positive Side of "Mother's Words"

The big plus for the maternal introject is when aspects of the voice build egos and confidence. The introject is working in a positive manner if the voice you hear is saying something like …

➤ You can do it.

➤ You are special.

➤ Your good judgment will carry you through.

➤ You should follow your own instincts.

➤ You look great.

➤ You are worthy of love and respect.

Two Concrete Examples of the Positive Introject

A Voice of Love and Comfort

The maternal introject is a universally applicable concept. On a ship in the Aegean Sea, I met Ivona and was introduced to the voice of her grandmother. Twenty-nine-year-old Ivona Golubic was born in Croatia and raised by her grandmother. "She was my real mother," Ivona said.

Building Blocks

Bias filters are factors that affect your perception of the world around you, including how you see or hear other people—that means your mom, too! These filters include life experiences, preferences, expectations, and individual personality differences.

Building Blocks

Maternal introject is a psychological term referring to that part of your mother that lives within the psyche. It is a voice both men and women hear and feel, but is more powerful for daughters. When the motive for a daughter's reaction is to thwart or reject the mother introject, the action is called a **reaction formation**.

"I could never cheat or hurt anyone now because of my grandmother. If there is a small part of me that is different, I try to get rid of this part just by thinking about my grandmother. She told me what goes around comes around. My grandmother taught me to respect what is good and not to harm anyone."

A Voice of Memory and Connection

Halley, a 28-year-old woman who has lived thousands of miles from her mother, expressed, "Sometimes I go places—like to an art museum—or see things that I know my mom would like and I have a reaction or feeling that I know she would have. When I do that it makes me smile or laugh, because I feel close to her."

Explosives

If you have a low rapport with your mom, you aren't alone. In a study titled "Lifeprints: New Patterns of Love and Work for Today's Women," 25 percent of the women reported feeling like you do.

The Negative Voice Within

On the other hand, Mom's voice can take a turn for the negative. The maternal introject can pose a rift between mother and daughter if the later is unable to control, ignore, or block this voice at appropriate times.

The mother-daughter relationship is in trouble if …

➤ Daughters reject opportunities and make life decisions that are counter to their own desires and preferences, but in accordance with the internalized mother.

➤ The voice makes a woman self-conscious or unsure of herself and unable to act independently.

➤ The voice is debilitating (in extreme cases).

➤ The maternal introject creates blame directed inward and results in self-punishment.

In the next chapter, you will see how the maternal introject has the power and the probability to drive daughters crazy! For now we will accept that it contributes to the cycle of "mother blame."

Understanding "Mother Blame"

Everyone talks about it. Mother blaming is in all of the books, it simply isn't fair to place all the blame on Mom for a poor relationship with her daughter. By

Explosives

A 1998–1999 U.S. Department of Labor report revealed that individuals who care for animals and aren't even employed in a supervisory capacity make 19 to 27 percent more money than child-care workers or home health aides, who exhibit many of the same skills ascribed to mothers.

definition, a relationship must include more than one party. The mother-daughter relationship, good or bad, is a reflection on two generations not just one.

Determining Who Is to Blame

Society is partly to blame for Mom's dilemma here. Motherhood is undervalued in the media and the butt of jokes. Professions that use skills akin to those of mothers are paid less and mother's work garners a low fee when it comes to divorce cases. Caplan, author of *The New Don't Blame Mother,* says, "the less a group is valued or respected, the easier it is to target them for ills." In this case the ills include some more of those impossible expectations first introduced in the last chapter.

Setting Mom Up for Blame

When Mom cannot fill the mandate of the following four myths, Caplan says she is poised for blame. The four myths that Caplan refers to are …

Myth #1: The measure of a good mother is a "perfect" daughter.

Myth #2: Mothers are endless founts of nurturance.

Myth #3: Mothers naturally know how to raise children.

Myth #4: Mothers don't get angry.

Pearls of Wisdom

"Even as we grew up, my mother could not help imposing herself between her children and whatever it was they might take it in mind to reach for in the world …. A way had to be found around her love sometimes … I think she was relieved when I chose to be a writer of stories, for she thought writing was safe."

—Pulitzer Prize winner and Southern novelist Eudora Welty, in her memoir *One Writer's Beginning*

Accepting the Blame, Moms Who Feel Guilty

We all know moms that are racked with guilt and without sufficient logic or investigation accept blame for their mother-daughter dilemma. No doubt, some are playing the role of martyr. Others genuinely wear the cloak of responsibility and ponder what it is they didn't say that could have made a difference, what they could have possibly done wrong or how they could have done things differently.

What they should do and what we will do is address how to climb out of the murky present in Part 5, "Sharing Revelations, Making Adjustments." Accepting blame without doing anything to alleviate or rectify the problem is not sufficient restitution for any wrongdoing!

Sprouting a Blame Cycle

"It is important to recognize that motherhood is a two-way street. It is almost never an issue of just a mother and a daughter but rather an evolving relationship between the two," write Roni Cohen-Sandler, Ph.D., and Michelle Silver in their book *"I'm not mad, I just hate you!"* When that relationship evolves sprouting a cycle of blame, here's what it looks like:

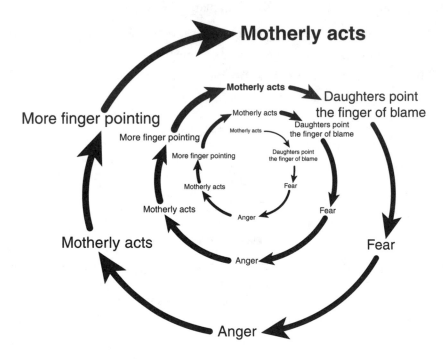

The self-perpetuating growth of a blame cycle.

Whether or not the cycle of blame is justified depends on each unique pair of mother and daughter. In Parts 4 and 5 of this book, ways to evaluate the validity of a cycle of blame as well as how to break it will be presented. In the meantime, it is important to further identify factors that get the cycle spinning.

Generating Energy for the Blame Cycle

You can visualize the cycle of blame in the diagram and how it keeps turning and growing with more anger, fear, blame, and actions. However, what produces the real energy for this cycle to spin out of control is what we need to uncover.

Mothers Who Evoke a Special Brand of Anger

In Chapter 11, "Fingerprinting Mother Types," we identified a number of mother types or mothering fingerprints. In the extreme, these have the potential to evoke anger and fear: fear if one does not comply with an overbearing mother's wishes, and anger if a different direction is sought. However, remember that mothers and daughters form a reactive relationship. Just imagine the sparks when …

➤ A defiant daughter of a chronically worried mother type takes a potentially dangerous or diverse road in life.

➤ A daughter of a merged mother type marries and refuses to share the details of her life or include her mother 100 percent in her new life.

➤ Any daughter of an extreme mother style drives to establish a sense of self and wage a fight to throw off the yoke of her mother and become free.

Explosives

Authors Nancy Cocola and Arlene Matthews say that the mother types that are most likely to create tensions and produce self-doubt and low self-esteem in daughter's are controlling, competitive, and hypercritical moms. Daughters of pseudo-perfect moms may be more compliant and do the right things in order to preserve the perfect image their mothers' project.

When Daughters Point the Finger of Blame

Daughters point the finger of blame at their mothers for creating the problems in mother-daughter relationships. Their accusations include …

➤ Distorted memories or perceptions of events that carry bad feelings.

➤ Failure of Mom to meet all of her needs.

➤ Lack of shared values.

➤ Inadequate support.

➤ Rivalry.

➤ Disappointment in Mom's shortcomings.

➤ Inability to protect Mom from pain, hurt, or unhappiness.

➤ Inability to completely understand Mom.

➤ Failure of Mom to provide adequate empathy.

➤ Their own failure.

➤ Mom's feelings toward siblings.

➤ The maternal introject.

Woman to Woman

What daughters may be missing in understanding their moms in later years is that much of mom's behavior can be attributed to the natural way in which one ages, according to Dr. Joseph Russell, retired professor of geriatrics and consultant in adult care. For instance her presumed lack of interest in your work may actually be more a function of her forgetting to ask you questions. Loss of memory is one of those factors Russell says daughters must be sensitive to.

Explosives

An uncontrollable eruption of anger may feel like a good release of emotions for the moment. However, it is rarely constructive, merely masks the problem, and normally creates latent feelings of guilt.

Anger Keeps the Blame Cycle in Motion

There are several common causes of anger that are likely to arise on a daughter's behalf. The more personal ones, deep-seated within each reader, will be unearthed in explorations conducted in Part 4. The ones we discuss here are more general and universal.

Paula J. Caplan, author of *The New Don't Blame Mother*, says that we are angry and hate our mothers because they have the "power to make us feel infantile, ridiculous, and inadequate." Anger also seethes when …

➤ We assume different realities, or the one we have that is different from our mothers makes mother or daughter uncomfortable.

➤ Mothers deliberately or inadvertently hurt their daughters.

➤ Daughters have to find a way to feel empowered or express themselves.

➤ It is the emotional response chosen as a means of protection.

➤ Daughters are unable to garner their mothers' approval.

➤ Moms criticize too much, making their daughters feel inadequate and insecure.

Fear Adds to the Emotional Uproar

Three forms of fear prevent real mother-daughter communication and perpetuate a poor relationship that culminates in a cycle of blame. Caplan identifies these three:

1. Daughters fear risking the loss of their mother's love when they displease her or don't meet her standards.

2. Daughters fear emulating the negative extremes they see in their mother. Recognizing these characteristics in themselves deprecates who they are as well.

3. Daughters fear their mothers' shortcomings negatively reflecting on themselves.

The Least You Need to Know

➤ A mother and daughter may share similarities in aspects of their personalities but must always regard themselves as two very distinct women.

➤ Expectations and misperceptions on both the part of the mother and the daughter can sabotage hopes of a harmonious relationship.

➤ A mother's voice echoes in a daughter's head forever in the form of a maternal introject.

➤ There is no reason to believe that a satisfying, loving relationship cannot be achieved, despite the inherent tension between mother and daughter.

➤ Understanding the "blame cycle" is the only way to overcome its ill effects.

Chapter 13

Why Mothers and Daughters Drive Each Other Crazy

In This Chapter

➤ Battling opposite temperaments

➤ Pleasing and unpleasing personality types

➤ Controlling mothers and defiant daughters

➤ Exorcising mom's ever-present voice

➤ Not letting guilt get the best of both of you

➤ Handling mom's subversive emotional hooks

➤ Those annoying, well-meaning fix-it moms

The description of the mother-daughter dilemma in the previous chapter does not tell the entire story. Mother-types, expectations, personal perceptions, and blame are not sufficient to express why some mothers and daughters drive each other absolutely bonkers. There are a number of other factors that may catapult a normal or moderate level of friction into the realm that drives mom and daughter crazy.

The purpose of our discussion in this chapter is to reveal and describe those factors that perpetuate, widen, or create rifts that may arise between pairs of mothers and daughters and affect their adult relationships. The intensity of these circumstances and the damage they cause to that relationship varies.

Without addressing differences in temperaments, a resounding maternal introject voice, reasonable levels of closeness or a potpourri of critical emotions, it would be impossible to isolate the roots of many problems. Furthermore, without going through this exercise it is highly improbable that any mother-daughter repair work would amount to more than putting a finger in the hole of a dike.

Building Blocks

According to *The Motherhood Report*, **temperament** is "an innate blueprint that determines how a baby, and later a child, will react to his or her environment."

Temperament's Role in the Mother–Daughter Relationship

A child's *temperament* affects how a mother reacts to him or her! Experts used to believe that the mother acted and the child reacted to her. But that belief has been changed. The new mode of thought decrees that mother and child, from infancy on, are interactive. That's a big difference.

Temperament is a significant factor that sets up reactions that can affect the future of the mother-daughter relationship, so remember this important point. In other words, facets of temperament—such as whether a baby is easily frightened, gets excited by noise, is generally happy, distressed, or quickly soothed—affect how Mom reacts.

Temperamental Influences on a Mother's Attitude Toward Her Daughter

This all starts in infancy. Here are some observations that *The Motherhood Report* made:

1. A more pleasing baby evokes a more positive view from the mother.

2. The baby with a negatively perceived temperament elicits a more overall negative response from the mother that can put a lasting strain on the relationship.

3. The early connection between mother and daughter can potentially set the tone of a lifelong relationship. In other words, a relationship that starts out well, ends well. However, a relationship that starts out poorly may also end up poorly.

4. The researchers studied relationships that started out on the wrong foot and never set a more positive course.

5. Children whose temperament compliments (but is not identical) to that of his or her mother, brings out the best in their nurturer.

6. However, this doesn't mean that opposites have the best track record. On the contrary, the personality must be different and complimentary.

The secret in all of this is how Mom perceives her child's temperamental traits. Does she perceive them as positive or negative? The answer is strictly in the eye of the beholder!

Woman to Woman

One's temperament may not be able to be completely changed, but it can be altered and channeled into more positive or negative behavior. For instance, *The Motherhood Report* said that "an easy-going child who does not have limits set by a parent may begin to exhibit disobedient behavior. In the reverse, a disobedient child who does not initially have an easy going temperament can become more adaptive and less problematic to handle through parental persistence, love, and patience."

The Most Pleasing Personality Types

Despite personal preferences or the uniqueness of each mom's personality, *The Motherhood Report* identifies core traits of temperament and personality that are deemed "easy" or "difficult" by the majority of maternal caretakers.

Easy kids tend to easily establish routines, have good sleep patterns, easily adapt, readily meet new situations, be easy going, and generally have a positive, cheerful, and affectionate outlook. Difficult kids, by contrast, tend to be high intensity, resist new things, establish few routines, be poor eaters and sleepers, frequently have negative or cranky moods, be stubborn, and scream and throw tantrums.

Go back and take a look at the characteristics for easy kids. These are the kids' moms who find it more natural to view them as positive and pleasing. Now glance at the difficult characteristics. Kids who claim a preponderance of these traits are viewed as less positive and pleasing.

Mixes and Matches

It isn't pervasive by any means, but therapists have reported finding mothers and daughters whose temperaments are mismatched in a way that the pair is unable to arrive at anything but a poor relationship. When this happens, the daughter's temperament is unable to fulfill the temperamental moods of the mother—and vice versa.

Here are examples of positive and negative matches that researchers have reported finding.

Bad Mixes

Little monsters + a mom with little patience

Very active daughter + low-key mom

Good Matches

Active child + active mom

Nonpersistent child + persistent mom

These examples of positive and negative matches are prevalent, but the combinations are endless. Many good matches are dependent on individual factors. For instance, this example might seem to go against the grain except for the fact that the women mentioned in this case are single. Some experts have found independent women who have been well matched with a clinging baby.

Compliant or Defiant? That Is the Question!

Compliant daughters are well-behaved and easy to discipline in their youth. They follow Mom's lead, and don't make waves in their adult years. They make Mom feel good! But, that could be at a price to themselves. They may be ignoring their inner selves to please Mom, keep the peace, and comply with her personality type of wishes.

Explosives

The problem with bad mixes of temperament is that Mom may begin to question her own parenting abilities. For instance, when Mom's little monster or active princess doesn't behave like she does, Mom may begin to question her own mothering abilities, and this could lead to negative feelings about herself.

Defiant daughters are more difficult all the way around. They shake up the household, go against Mom's natural instincts, and put obstacles in Mom's way to effectively mother her other children. In essence they may be struggling to express their own identity that clashes with that of their mothers'. Nonetheless, their defiance may cause Mom embarrassment, and the expression of hostility makes Mom feel hurt. Either significant expression of defiance can take a big toll on the mother-daughter relationship.

Fortunately, most of us daughters and mothers exhibit a mixture of compliant and defiant behaviors toward each other that allows for free expression of self.

Defiant Behaviors That Drive Mom Crazy

The most significant behaviors that send moms who have adult daughters over the top have to do with values and lifestyle. Particularly potent factors have to do with morality, substance abuse, or lack of direction and achievement. Half of the mothers in the landmark study reported by Louis Genevie, Ph.D., and Eva Margolies in *The Motherhood Report* said they had one child with an emotional or behavioral problem.

Sometimes mothers find the difficulty of dealing with different lifestyles so intense that the only way they can handle this is to distance themselves from their children. It should be noted that adult daughters have been known to react in the same way. Their specific cases will be addressed later.

Origins of Defiant Daughters Whose Moms Make Them Nuts!

Temperament is one origin we can point to at the root of defiant daughters. Mother types are another. In Chapter 11, "Fingerprinting Mother Types," we explained the mother types. Let's examine why some of their daughters are aggressively defiant. You will need these descriptions in order to complete the self-analysis in Part 4, "The Age of Discovery," and determine the state of your own mother-daughter relationship.

➤ Daughters of merged mothers express rage over being controlled and have at times created physical and psychological distance to free themselves of Mom's constant pressure.

➤ Once daughters of hypercritical moms get their own wings and manage to develop a good sense of self, they express anger toward their mothers. In order to avoid her criticism or outwardly display their defiance, they forego sharing information with their moms.

➤ On the other hand, daughters who remain compliant—and do not become somewhat defiant when faced with any of the exaggerated mother-types discussed earlier—may suffer from poor images of self, feelings of inadequacy, or fears ingrained by Mom.

What to Do When Daughters Cannot Turn Down the Heat from the Maternal Introject

The maternal introject can be likened to the gas burner under a pot of water. An intense flame or introject can cause water—and a daughter—to boil. The following examples demonstrate how the maternal introject may work on daughters.

Example #1

"Sometimes when I used to hear my mother's voice it pissed me off and I got defensive. To some extent I still do. I am 28 years old and at this point I know what is best for me.

"In my very early 20s, every time I would be physically close to a man I could hear my mother telling me not to have sex and I didn't. By around 22, I still heard the voice and was angry with my mother. I wanted to feel more sexually free, but I couldn't. Finally I translated the words from her voice into something that was meaningful for me—only have sex if I am in love. Now I don't hear that voice anymore at all. It isn't for Mom to tell me what to do with my body. I outgrew her statements."

Woman to Woman

Here's some good advice Marcia Douglass and Lisa Douglass give in their book *Are We Having Fun Yet? The Intelligent Woman's Guide to Sex* (Hyperion, 1997).

These researchers say it is understandable that Mom is worried about your sex life considering date rape, the potential for pregnancy, and HIV. So, they suggest, "While it makes you mad that she's butting in, let her know she raised you to have good judgment."

Example #2

"It took me a while to get rid of my mother's fears that I carried around in my head every time I was confronted with a situation I knew she would find frightening for me. It was ruining the way I like to travel and approach life in general. It was preventing me from enjoying myself and instilling fears I didn't want to have.

"At first I just didn't tell her about things I was doing so that she couldn't put more thoughts into my head. I felt like I was doing a lot of lying and sealing myself off from her. Finally I had to turn off her voice myself and come right out and tell her not to make anymore statements that related to my safety. I just told her she would have to learn to value my judgment and keep her worries to herself.

"I think that was a turning point in our adult relationship. It was something I had to do for myself."

The Moral of These Stories

Daughters, take charge and use your own good sense to adjust the heat of your mom's internal voice. Without doing so in adulthood, that whisper in your head is bound to drive you crazy.

Emotional Hooks

Moms have a way of getting under their daughters' skin. There are a variety of home-grown moms that do it intentionally and others who do not. Emotional hooks come in a wide variety. However, four major categories include …

1. Spoken phrases.

2. Guilt-induced stabs.

3. Overriding fear.

4. The "mama drama" syndrome described by author Denise McGregor.

Moms use these emotional hooks to …

1. Get their daughters' attention and affection.

2. Maintain control.

3. Punish.

4. Inflict guilt.

Woman to Woman

Research has revealed that physical likeness between mother and daughter is a positive or complimentary vantage point for moms. It feeds their egos, makes them identify more readily with their daughters, and adds a dimension of connectedness.

Each of these four categories deserves your undying attention. Rarely are any of them considered positive behaviors or responses. Daughters, you best wise up as to how mothers use these techniques. Moms, once they are pointed out to you in black and white, you have no excuse not to abandon these annoying, subversive, and divisive behaviors.

Verbal Hooks

Here are some popular verbal hooks used far and wide by moms. Moms and daughters may want to try the following exercise. Each of you put a check next to the ones you think are present in your relationship. Then add some of your own.

Moms	Daughters	Hooks
1. ___	___	"Do you want me to leave the house and never come back?"
2. ___	___	"You should never know what it is like to be alone."

	Moms	Daughters	Hooks
3.	___	___	"I'm only one person."
4.	___	___	"I hope you have a daughter just like you!"
5.	___	___	"That's what you get for not listening to me."
6.	___	___	"That dress is pretty but I've seen you look better."
7.	___	___	(add your own)
8.	___	___	(add your own)
9.	___	___	(add your own)
10.	___	___	(add your own)

Woman to Woman

A few of the unique verbal hooks admitted to me by moms sound like these. "I'm going to change my name and I'm not going to tell you what it is," said one mother about being "mommied" to death.

One politically conscientious mom—who checks labels of items to make sure they aren't produced in countries where human rights violations abound—admits she finds herself inserting information to maneuver her daughter onto the side of political correctness. Signs of her daughter's exasperation were apparent recently after a recent grocery store excursion together.

"Do you always have to tell me everything?" her daughter announced upon hearing the woeful tale of animals turned into the veal steak she wanted for dinner.

Feeling Guilty, One of the Most Potent Emotional Hooks

Dishing out *guilt* is hard to stop doing and so is feeling guilty! It is an emotion used by both mother and daughter to control responses or impose feelings of hopelessness or powerless. A few of the phrases above evoke a message of guilt. But guilt can also be imposed upon one another through a tone, gesture, and lack of words.

Guilt works on daughters who feel ...

➤ They have done something wrong and let their mothers down.

➤ They should do things to make their mothers happy.

➤ They owe their mothers something because they feel beholden to them.

➤ They are unable to fulfill unrealistic expectations, and are feeling the effects of that failure.

Building Blocks

Guilt, according to *Webster's New Twentieth Century Dictionary Unabridged Second Edition,* is "the act or state of having done a wrong or committed an offense, culpability, legal or ethical." When applied specifically to mother-daughter relationships, mothers feel guilty if they become aware that they have done something wrong. Frequently, they are unable to rationalize the guilt away and find comfort in a more healthy state.

Fearing Guilt

Fear of feeling guilty poses a special burden on daughters. It can prevent daughters who are fearful of losing Mom's love and approval from confronting their mothers. It can make them obsess about how their mothers will think about their life decisions. It can keep a mother and daughter roaming the landscape of conflicts and remorse. It can result in self-punishment.

An Initial Test of Your Mother-Daughter Relationship

Denise McGregor uses her book, *Mama Drama: Making Peace with the One Woman Who Can Push Your Buttons, Make Your Cry, and Drive You Crazy,* as the platform to launch her description of a specific syndrome. Mama drama, she writes, is

Pearls of Wisdom

"We are often mad at our mothers because we think we don't live up to their standards, when in fact, they don't live up to ours."

—Denise McGregor, *Mama Drama*

"the ongoing conflict with your mother that never seems to go away and is often perpetuated from generation to generation."

McGregor, therefore, asserts that you can be unaware that you may be afflicted by this syndrome. To test whether your relationship is affected, take the following quiz. Answer "Yes" or "No" to each question.

1. My mother has the ability to quickly and frequently make me feel guilty.
   Yes   No

2. I frequently feel that what I say or do may not be perceived as good enough by my mother.
   Yes   No

3. I find myself acting like an adult except when I am around my mother.
   Yes   No

4. I do not stop my mother from interfering in my marriage or private life.
   Yes   No

5. Sometimes I either indulge myself with food or withhold it from myself to cope with the feelings I have toward my mother.
   Yes   No

6. I live with the hope that one day my mom will change, suddenly appreciate me, and be receptive to what I have to say.
   Yes   No

A string of "Yes" answers undoubtedly demonstrates that you have the affliction. None of the above are happy, healthy, or satisfying conditions under which daughters should live. This is admittedly an initial, not the final, definitive test of your relationship.

If you have been a particularly compliant daughter, this may be an overwhelming revelation. For others, it may have merely confirmed your suspicion that it is Mom who is driving you crazy and that your relationship needs some serious work!

Woman to Woman

Just in case you skipped or forgot about the discussion in Chapter 8, "Daughters, Out on Their Own," this is a good time to go back for a review. It might just heighten your awareness, cause you to let lose of the reins, and enter a new era of mother-daughter harmony.

Does Mom Have an Inalienable Right to Come to the Rescue?

Moms have a tendency to need to rescue their daughters from perceived danger. As daughters get older, they have less of a need to be rescued. However, that doesn't stop moms from feeling the need to be in control, alleviate guilt for past mistakes, or act out of pure altruism.

Not only can this drive daughters right to the brink of insanity, but it also turns them into dependent women. And dependent women, according to Dr. Charney Herst, are sullen, angry, and hostile individuals toward their mother. Independent daughters are more gracious, helpful, and cooperative.

Mothers must learn that 1) they cannot solve their daughters' problems, nor do they have the right to, and 2) assuming the role of rescuer is a no-win situation and can turn their daughters into angry victims of their good intentions.

The No-Win Triangle of Rescuers

A succinct way to view the no-win dynamics of rescuers and victims is by applying the Karpman Drama Triangle. The rescuer mom in the end can do no right and is persecuted by the daughter for not doing enough or doing it wrong.

Woman to Woman

Learning how to deal with stress or suffering the consequences of mistakes, romantic disasters, or workday problems will make your daughter stronger. It is best to allow children to begin accepting responsibility for their actions when they are young, says Dr. Thomas R. Linscheid. Doing so will better prepare them better for their adult years.

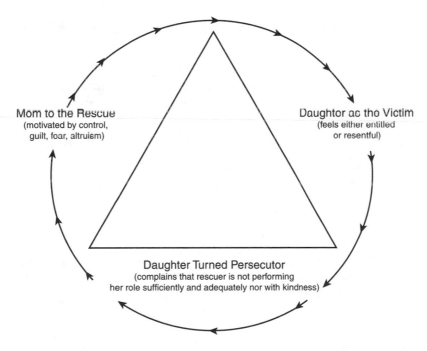

Rescuer moms caught by angry daughters on the pointed edges of sharp triangles.

The Fix-It Fixation

A lot of moms have this fixation. The fix-it fixation is the uncontrollable urge to eradicate your child's pain, whether it is real or created by your imagination. The need to fix something is brought on by that queasy feeling in the parental stomach when you sense your child's sadness, regardless of your child's age.

It drives moms to extremes that annoy the living daylights out of their kids. A mom may plan a party for a daughter who appears to be left out of a social group only to find out later that she declined an invitation to become part of the clique. Or, she may scour the city for a sweater she thinks will cheer up her daughter who had a fight with her boyfriend only to find that she already made up with him, hates the sweater, and is annoyed she told her mom about the disagreement in the first place.

One young woman who was the subject of one too many impromptu interrogations by her mom to determine if any distress lurked deep within her daughter's mind, screamed in self-defense: "Mother, I swear I am happy! Okay? Now leave me alone. Please."

Woman to Woman

Margaret Mead, noted anthropologist, wrote about her mother in a way that any fix-it mom could relate to. "I know that if I had written to her (mother) to say, 'Please go and wait for me on the corner of Thirteenth and Chestnut streets,' she would have stayed there until I came or she dropped from sheer fatigue."

Beyond the Realm of Normalcy

Most behavior associated with the fix-it fixation is within the range of normal, even if it does have the capacity to drive your daughter crazy. However, a mother may be reaching beyond the realm of normal if she …

➤ Stays up nights plotting ways to make her daughter's life easier.

➤ Feels compelled to solve her daughter's problems.

➤ Makes it her goal to make sure that her daughter is always happy.

➤ Continues to do things that her daughter can and wants to do for herself.

➤ Needlessly worries about her daughter's welfare.

Exhibiting all five signs places a mom beyond the realm of a normal fix-it fixation. Anyone who recognizes she exhibits all of these identifying marks should consider seeking expert counseling.

The Least You Need to Know

➤ The temperament of both mother and daughter plays a significant role in how Mom views and relates to her daughter.

➤ Defiant daughters may drive their mothers crazy, but sometimes defiance is the only choice they have to make and preserve their individual identities.

➤ A daughter must take the initiative and put her mom's maternal introject into perspective.

➤ Mothers use potent emotional hooks, intentionally and unintentionally, that are read by daughters and drive them off the wall.

Chapter 14

Mothers and Daughters Within the Family Circle

In This Chapter

➤ Can family influences override Mom's impact on a daughter?

➤ Mom, the mighty micromanager

➤ How family alliances affect a daughter's relationship with different family members

➤ The "Big Four" family factors

➤ The extent to which birth order determines family roles

➤ Circumstances beyond Mom's control

Who we are as women can't entirely be blamed on or claimed by one member of the family—Mom. Therefore, we will examine the major factors within the family unit that play a role in shaping the destiny of a daughter. Much of the relationship between mothers and daughters is determined by the dynamics of the entire family. Granted, that family may be very different and more loosely defined today. Nonetheless, the point is: Whoever comprises a family unit and how those individuals interact impacts the relationship between mother and daughter.

It is impossible to fully understand dynamics—good or bad—between a mother and daughter without looking into how each fit into the family unit. Not only will this discussion assist in repairing mother-daughter relationships, but it also helps a new generation of moms develop greater insight into the workings of their own immediate family circle.

The Family Circle

In Chapter 3, "Forces That Shape Women's Lives," the new definition of a family that is accepted by most professionals was presented—that a family is two or more people who not only share a common residence and economy, but also affection. The family unit we are interested in must obviously, at the very least, be comprised of a mother and a daughter. However, whether a father or siblings are all living within one residence, our discussion in this chapter primarily refers to family units that involve more than the mother and one or more daughters.

Woman to Woman

Ladies, instead of complaining that your partner doesn't do enough when it comes to helping in the house or caring for the children, ask yourself if you are discouraging your partner's assistance. Many women do because they will only accept help on their terms.

Building Blocks

A **dysfunctional family** is a family unit that functions abnormally or inadequately and is, therefore, considered impaired.

The family represents a structure with various parts. These parts function in a way that affects all of the parts, hence all of family members. The family affects an individual's physical and emotional growth, emotional well-being, self-image, behavior, and intellectual, physical, and personal skills. It should be apparent that one's family unit can have a tremendous impact on an individual.

Healthy vs. Unhealthy Family Structures

When the family structure functions effectively and positively nurtures individual members it is called a functional family. When parts do not work well or are not in equilibrium, it is called a *dysfunctional family*. Members of dysfunctional families more readily have problems forming other relationships. Part of the reason is that individuals learn how to interact by watching members of their family and imitate behavior that is not conducive to forming healthy, equal, or functional relationships.

Two Sides of Family Interaction

Family members interact in two fashions, outward and inward. Both sides of family interaction affect the dynamics of the family and the self-image of the individual member.

The outward interaction is how members respond and overtly interact with one another. The inner interaction has more to do with each member's perception of interacting. Perceptions, as we have mentioned throughout earlier chapters, can carry more influence than the reality of the act or interaction. And, perceptions as we know are influenced by individual personality differences, previous experience, and self-image.

The fact that there are two sides to family interaction make family dynamics much more complex and account for family members harboring different feelings and perceptions of the same event.

Mom, the Micromanager

Mom is the member of the family who tries to *micromanage* her domain and her subjects. Hence she is more …

➤ Aware of shaping the destinies of family members.

➤ Sensitive to mediating the interaction between other family members.

➤ Cognizant of the family dynamics.

➤ Hesitant to allow others to take a role in the family more active than her own—that includes making family decisions, caring for the children, or managing the household.

➤ Determined, according to research at the University of Washington, to be "first among equals" when it comes to home and hearth, and, to cling to control.

Sometimes a mom likes micromanaging her family because it enables her to feel in control, it makes her feel like a good mother, and it may be the only source of real power to which she has access.

Building Blocks

Micromanager is an individual who oversees and takes responsibility for the tiniest details in a plan family, business, or organization.

Pearls of Wisdom

"Responsible mothering, by definition, means support of the father-child bond."

—Kyle D. Pruett, M.D.

Mom Tends to Play the Role of Gatekeeper

Moms don't need to, nor should they, bear the brunt of parenthood. But frequently they deliberately or unconsciously do just that, says Dr. Kyle D. Pruett of Yale University and author of *Fatherneed: Why Father Care Is as Essential as Mother Care for Your Child* (Free Press, 2000). The phenomenon is called "gatekeeping." In her role as gatekeeper, a mom tends to …

➤ Act as sentry, regulating access to children.

➤ Resist surrendering authority to Dad.

➤ Limit Dad's access to decision making or participation in parenting.

Mother's Role as Micromanager and Sentry May Change

Research by John Snarey found that with a wife's increased role as breadwinner, fathers assumed greater childrearing responsibilities and had more time with their kids. One might assume that necessity is the motherhood of invention. In light of the very newest statistics, moms may in the future be forced to limit their roles as micromanagers and sentries.

A report by the U.S. Census Bureau made public in October 2000, revealed some important new trends:

1. The number of moms with infants who return to work is up 31 percent from 1976. In 1998 59 percent of these women went back to work. Thirty-seven percent of these work full time, and the remainder work part time.

Pearls of Wisdom

"Mothers, be forewarned: there are grave consequences to ignoring your husband's input. The immediate result is that he'll feel impotent in his own house and unimportant in your eyes. The feeling of being left out can, and very often does, wreak havoc in a marriage."

—Dr. Charney Herst, author of *For Moms of Difficult Daughters*

2. For the first time, families with married moms and dads who both work moves into the majority. Only 24 percent of families in which married moms and dads live together represent households where the father is the only breadwinner.

3. Eighty percent of moms with associate degrees who have older children and a combined family of $50,000 to $75,000 are now returning to work.

4. Mothers with higher family income and education are returning to work in greater numbers during the first year of their child's life.

Nonetheless, as revolutionary as these statistics may appear, none indicate that Mom is currently the primary breadwinner. We can, therefore, assume that while the future places her role as micromanager and sentry in jeopardy, currently she bears title to these positions.

Moms Shouldn't Dismiss Dad's Importance

The truth of the matter is moms and dads have different effects on a child's development. An overzealous, gate-keeping mom could rob her daughter of fatherly benefits. Pruett, a champion of dads' active fathering, reminds moms that ...

1. Well-fathered infants are more secure in exploring their world, more curious, and less hesitant or fearful with unfamiliar stimuli.

2. Children who have ample contact with dads are more tolerant when faced with stress.

3. Girls deprived of paternal contact have more difficulty with self-control.

Family Alliances

Family alliances are formed between family members who affect the structure and functioning of the entire unit. The combinations are plentiful. In this section we will deal with the most common alliances that influence a daughter's position in the family and the overall relationship with her mother and other family members. The order in which these are presented is random and does not suggest a hierarchy of importance.

Alliance #1: Dads + Daughters

Daughters who align themselves with Dad may get a good go-between for themselves and Mom, but the conspiratorial closeness they exhibit with Dad may make Mom resentful and jealous.

Alliance #2: Mom + Daughter

The alliance between mother and daughter is a natural one despite their conflicts, particularly during adolescence. Sharing the same gender and identifying with one's mom is a strong reason to become allies. On the other side of the coin, situations when Moms align themselves with their daughters can get sticky for several reasons:

➤ An alliance can pit one sibling against another when there is more than one child, particularly another daughter.

➤ Usually Mom aligns herself with the child she can manipulate the most.

➤ Sometimes the mother-daughter alliance is formed in order to present a united, confrontational, and protective front where Dad is concerned.

➤ In some cases, a mother forms too close of an alliance with a daughter, and turning her into a friend at too early of a age and confiding in her inappropriately.

Building Blocks

A **family alliance** is a connection or union of individual family members that demonstrate an affinity for one another and are joined by a mutual interest.

Pearls of Wisdom

"Mothers have a special bond with all of their children, but I think the mother-daughter relationship is extra special. Even when we aren't getting along, my mother is the first person I want to call when I have a problem."

—Lisa Gomes-Casseres, 22, Washington, D.C.

Alliance #3: Sibling + Sibling

The coalition formed by cooperative siblings is called "sibling axis." This type of alliance inside the family gives siblings leverage with the older generation, namely Mom and Dad. It's the old story of strength in numbers.

Alliance #4: Mother + Son

A mother may form an alliance with a son for some of the same reasons she created one with her daughter. However, as we shall see shortly, a son is viewed and treated differently by his mom. This may particularly affect the quality and intimacy of the alliance as well as the determination whether or not to select a son because expectations of him are less when compared with daughters.

The next step it to watch these alliances in action and see how they affect the family dynamics.

Pearls of Wisdom

"Advice primarily directed towards her daughters, 'Be true to yourself and trust in yourself.'"

—Charlotte Mussafer, Montgomery, Alabama attorney and mother of three adult children

Two Real–Life Dramas of Mother + Daughter Alliances

Each alliance has a unique affect on the dynamics of the family and the mother-daughter relationship. In order to see how an alliance functions within a family setting and how it influences the mother-daughter relationship, I have selected two very different stories that were entrusted to me.

No doubt each alliance has its own little nuances, purpose, and modus operandi. The more obvious, positive alliances are readily visible to the observer; it is for that reason I am presenting cases that are a bit more complicated.

Alliances That Place Mom in Peril

Estella's mom can't seem to win when she aligns herself with her daughter. Nonetheless, she feels compelled to do just that. Estella, Mom thinks, is too much like her dad—gregarious, stubborn, set in her ways, and determined. Consequently, clashes between the two have become notorious in the household. That's when Mom jumps in.

For instance Estella's mom sided with her recently and told her husband that their daughter didn't need to answer all of his questions regarding why she broke up with her most recent boyfriend. Estella is after all in her early 20s and as Mom put it, "She doesn't like to have to explain herself, and he asked her 300 questions."

Nonetheless, Dad was hell bent on finding out what Estella could possibly have found objectionable in yet another young man. Mom's persistence to create an alliance that would put Dad in his place backfired yet another time. "My husband got mad at me because I was siding with Estella and said I should stay out of it. He blamed me for the conflict."

Alliances Too Heavy for a Daughter's Delicate Shoulders

A young woman from Connecticut has an entirely different story. Her mother formed an alliance with her when she was less than six years of age. Now that she has a daughter that age herself, she realizes she was just a baby when her mother tried to make her an inappropriate ally.

"Literally I was my mother's crutch. I was the oldest of two other girls and one boy. My brother developed leukemia and died at age five. He was sick the first five years of my life. I was my mother's emotional link and her emotional sounding board. My father wasn't around mentally. That's how he dealt with it. Mother told me things I didn't need to hear as a six-year-old, even issues between her and my father. I don't blame her but it was too heavy for me. I was too aware at that age of all that was going on."

We will follow this young woman's story and see how the drama played out in the next few pages.

Explosives

Mothers beware! There are a number of tempting circumstances that make daughters an appealing but inappropriate ally. Think before acting and consider whether what you are asking of your daughter is good or bad for her, not just you.

The "Big Four" That Affect a Daughter's Growth, Image, and Family Relationships

There are at least four more factors that play an important role in a daughter's position within the family structure. Each influences who she becomes as an adult and how she relates to Mom as a child and in the future:

The "Big Four" include:

1. The number and sex of other children in the household
2. One's birth order

Building Blocks

Sibling rivalry isn't a competition for the largest steak on the family platter. The rivalry is between siblings and the prize that is sought after is the affection and attention of Mom and Dad.

3. How an individual child fits within the family structure

4. Timing and circumstances during youth

Understanding Sibling Rivalry

Siblings affect each other in both positive and negatives way within the family.

For Better	For Worse
More than one child in the family helps a daughter form a healthier relationship with Mother because it is more balanced	*Sibling rivalry*
	Favoring the super-achiever or perfect angel
Less intrusive, concentration on just one child that might inhibit growth and independence	Loving the most pliable

It is a wise woman who made the point about raising five children. "They all have to think of themselves as perfect children. You can't let one feel more special than any of the other four."

Understanding the Importance of Birth Order

Some experts place more value on it than others. The misconception of birth order arises, in my opinion, when it is given single billing. Birth order, like any other personal influence, must be viewed as one among many interplaying factors within the family framework.

Pearls of Wisdom

"A mother caters to the child who needs her the most." However, she must do it in a discreet way.

—Sarah Kanter (1869–1962), highly self-educated immigrant who came to the United States around 1910 and the mother of two sons who became physicians and a daughter who practiced law

Having said that, here are the generalizations applied to birth order:

1. Birth order affects jobs and roles one takes on in family such as helper or confident. The most responsibility is given to the oldest and then chronologically dispersed after that. If that oldest child is a daughter, she is often viewed prematurely by her mother as a little grown-up.

2. The first child is theorized to develop natural leadership qualities.

3. The oldest daughter is frequently her mother's angel, a loving position full of glory, devotion, and attention. She also, however, gets the brunt of strong parental supervision. Generally firstborns are reprimanded or punished earlier and more severely than their younger siblings.

4. The second child is supposed to benefit from older sibling's mistakes, and, therefore, be more adept in handling family dynamics and parents.

5. The middle child some say is lost in the shuffle. Others identify the middle child as the peacemaker and nonconfrontational member of the tribe.

6. The youngest child is usually babied longer and may maintain a position of dependency.

The problem with these generalizations is that we all know tons of exceptions to these supposed rules!

Finding a Place in the Family Structure

Keep these two rules of thumb in mind:

1. Most experts agree, "How a child is treated is more important than birth order."

2. A daughter's treatment garnered within the family framework affects how she views her mother and the opinion she forms of her mother.

Significant factors in determining her place in the family structure are whether or not the daughter is the prize child, the one that gets blamed, the one who is in trouble all the time, the favorite, the ally, the friend, the confident, the enemy, the competitor, or "Daddy's girl."

What it means to be a daddy's girl is to have an attachment to that parent and model oneself after him. Normally young girls who do this form not only a strong emotional connection with their father but accept his ethic of achievement without abandoning their femininity. The affects of father-daughter relationships are peppered throughout this guide.

Explosives

Some parents feel that raising the oldest child is trial and error from which subsequent offspring benefit. That's why one Nebraska mother tells her friends that with the first child, "you ought to be able to chew them up, spit them out, and then start all over again."

Woman to Woman

Being a daddy's girl has been an accepted position for a daughter more so than a mamma's boy, reported Perry Buffington, Ph.D. Still, Buffington identifies some very famous mamma's boys who did alright for themselves and obviously were not hampered by the attachment to their mothers. These notables include Douglas MacArthur, Franklin Delano Roosevelt, and Harry Truman.

Competing for the Place of Honor in Mom's Heart

The answer to this question is not gender related. Researchers discovered that sons and daughters have equally positive relationships with moms. However, the qualitative content of that relationship is different:

➤ Mothers feel closer to daughters because they are more open and less distant than boys, envision a greater "sense of permanency" with daughters, and see them in their own likeness.

➤ Boys receive more lenient treatment than daughters, a cause of resentment among their sisters. Mothers do not place as many demands or expectations on sons in terms of their responsibilities within the family and to others. Furthermore, they are also given more leeway to deviate from acceptable behavior. A lot of moms are known to go so far as to adopt the attitude that their sons can do no wrong.

➤ Daughters can also prove to be more tiring than boys and evoke more agitated motherly responses that result in friction between the two. The reason being girls are more difficult and more demanding emotionally than their brothers. Additionally, moms sometimes put added pressure on daughters if they see their own image in her and feel the need to redo themselves.

What is of particular importance here is how a daughter perceives the treatment her brother is getting in contrast and comparison to herself. If a rivalry for Mom's attention is ignited or if a daughter feels like she is second fiddle, the mother-daughter relationship could easily be negatively impacted.

Pearls of Wisdom

A 27-year-old man from Athens, Greece, said that his mother always tells him, "You be happy. I will be happy." Evidently the sentiments and wishes of mothers are the same the world over!

Timing Is Everything

Victoria Secunda, author of *When You and Your Mother Can't Be Friends,* stresses the importance of timing—meaning the time period and circumstances that influence the quality of a daughter's childhood.

These extraneous circumstances that can affect how Mom goes about mothering include:

➤ Menopause

➤ Stress

➤ Family problems

➤ Sick grandparents

➤ Husband-wife relationships

➤ Financial insecurity

➤ Employment problems

➤ Marital status

Any of the above can detour Mom's attention, love, affection, approval, and protection.

Act 2, the Daughter from Connecticut

The young woman from Connecticut who became her mom's early ally and confident because of a brother's death was also handed a megadose of mother-like responsibility by age four. Her story is a perfect example of how out-of-the-ordinary circumstances impact a mother's ability to fulfill her role and how that in turn affects the mother-daughter relationship.

> "Today there is a lot of competition between my mother and me for the attention of my sisters and how we manage our households. I think it all stems back to the period of my little brother's illness. Even though I was young I felt like the mom. Many days I had to get breakfast for my sisters even though I could hardly peel a banana myself and do all that baby stuff like changing diapers. My youngest sister was only a year old.
>
> "I am still vying to be the leader in the family. I feel I need to be the matriarch while I know my mother should be. It is evident I still worry about my sisters today and keep in touch with them all."

Woman to Woman

The death of a child turns even the best marriage upside down. The combination of misplaced blame, personality differences, and the vicissitudes of the healing process all contribute to the decline of the marital relationship. In fact, a large majority of couples never get over the impasse and end up in a divorce.

An Era of New-Found Wisdom

We have spent a great deal of time outlining the development of mother-daughter relationships, how they flourish, and where they go wrong. The information is interesting and juicy. For some it may serve as ammunition to confront a mother; for the wiser ones, it is food for thought and understanding.

At the very least, it serves as a foundation from which we will jointly make discoveries about ourselves, our mothers, our mothering style, and our position as daughters.

The Least You Need to Know

➤ The entire family circle plays a significant part in formulating the mother-daughter relationship.

➤ Mothers micromanage the family unit and assume more responsibility than is absolutely necessary because it is often the only place they exert genuine power.

➤ Moms who dismiss the influence and helpfulness of dads are wrong, and are cutting off their own noses to spite their own faces.

➤ Mothers should be cognizant of family alliances and consider what's best for all their children when making them.

➤ Inadvertently, special treatment of one child negatively impacts another, and may create long-lasting friction or resentment between mother and daughter.

➤ How a child is treated within the family unit is more important than gender and birth order.

Part 4

The Age of Discovery

Daughters, you are all grown up. You have a past to reflect upon, a present to understand, and a future you can affect. In order to accomplish all of this, you may need to take a close look at yourself and your mom. To give everyone equal opportunities to make pertinent discoveries, moms included, the following chapters are filled with the usual, the unusual, the norm, and the non-traditional.

The revelations you come to in the following pages will help serve your leap into Part 5, "Sharing Revelations, Making Adjustments," when you take an in-depth look at your own mother-daughter relationship. For the moment, shed your preconceived notions and peel back the protective coverings. Both mothers and daughters have reached the "Age of Discovery."

Daughters, Inside and Out

Stop, look, and listen before your proceed! This is the first of the chapters that takes you on your very own road to self-discovery. It is an intimate journey that requires bravery, open-mindedness, and honesty. You may or may not want to accept the feelings you uncover. That applies to both mother and daughter as they travel these pages.

For daughters, this chapter encourages you to look deep inside and come face to face with personal attitudes, actions, and reactions that relate to your mom. For moms looking in, this chapter encourages you to consider your daughter's position in a way that you may not have before.

The tables will be turned in Chapter 16, "Who Is This Woman I Call Mother?" Moms will do the self-discovering and daughters will do the listening. Concluding both chapters should lead to new understanding and insights that are critical for mothers and daughters who wish to objectively evaluate their relationships and ensure a loving future.

How Reliable Is Your Memory?

Daughters, how you feel about your mothers is based on memories that may or may not be reliable, claims Alyce Faye Cleese, psychotherapist and author of *How to Manage Your Mother* (Regan Books, 1999). Here are some thoughts to keep in mind the next time you adamantly defend your version of an event recalled from the past.

Memories are jumbled mixtures of emotions and individual perceptions that cloud the facts. This is why siblings express completely different recollections of the same shared past. There are some events from the past that we don't wish to recall, so we repress them instead. Leaving out these *repressed memories* affects the accurate accounting of other past events.

Memories are constantly changing and being updated by the new person we are continually becoming. Cleese makes a good point when she says that memories "fit the person we are today." Events that occurred in the past, which evoked strong negative feelings at the time, assume a more prominent place in our memories. When it comes to our moms, Cleese says for daughters, these negative memories have greater impact on how we view or treat our mothers than do the positive memories.

Explosives

Daughters, did you ever consider the disadvantage your mother may play in your relationship? Most likely she has to deal with, interpret, please, and maintain harmony with more than one child—you and your siblings. That can be wearing. On the other hand, daughters only have one mother to combat.

How Your Mom Remembers It

Chances are that you and your mother have different perceptions of the past, stated a study reported in a 1997 summer issue of *Current Psychology*. When it comes to your childhood memories …

➤ Your mother remembers the facts of your mutual conflicts rather clearly. What she seems to be tainted by her biases are the memories of her attitudes associated with these conflicts.

Building Blocks

Repressed memories are those events from the past that an individual buries or hides in her unconscious mind in order not to have to deal with them.

➤ Your mother remembers that if your childhood relationship with her was full of problems, so, too, were your teenage years.

➤ Your mother over-rates the positive and undervalues the negative aspects of your relationships.

Mothers and Daughters Remember the Past Differently

Take a look at ways in which your mother's recollections of the past differ from yours. Your mother is likely overall to evaluate all periods of your growing up with less degree of conflict than will you.

According to the current research of Karen J. Fingerman, professor of human development and family studies, when asked to define which periods of their relationships with their daughters were more conflicted, moms said that time period before age 25. However, daughters rate the period after age 25 with more conflict than do their moms.

There seems to be a general consensus among moms and daughters that most past conflict dealt with daily matters. However, daughters, more than their mothers, believed many conflicts dealt with questions of their need for independence. Mothers tended to report more conflicts that had to do with their daughter's sexuality. Moms who viewed their past relationships with their daughters as very positive failed to agree with their daughters on the times in the past that were most problematic.

Explosives

According to detailed studies among those daughters who describe their current relationship with their moms as being relatively conflicted, their mothers tended to rate their past relationship more conflicted.

What Happened to Mother's Little Angel?

According to Victoria Secunda, author of *Why You and Your Mother Can't Be Friends*, daughters start out as their mothers' angels. It is a position of honor that may place an undue burden of responsibility on a daughter. A persistent attitude can materialize that causes daughters—particularly the oldest—to be preoccupied with winning Mom over, having their goodness appreciated but fearing it won't be, and needing to serve Mom to ensure her happiness.

That isn't to say, however, that all of this is abnormal or bad. According to most experts, a daughter is demonstrating a normal, appropriate level of empathy when she is concerned about her mother, wants her mother to be happy, and feels the distress Mom may be experiencing. However, the angelic daughter is off track and tainted with abnormality if she gives up her own life in the pursuit to make her mother happy!

If You're Not an Angel, What Are You?

Most daughters don't maintain their angelic wings. Nor do they burn them in defiant disgust of their mothers. Like mother-types discussed in Chapter 11, "Fingerprinting Mother Types," the vast majority of daughters similarly fall somewhere in the middle of extremes. They don't tend to develop into all-loving, doting, and compliant angels, nor do they become defiant, lifelong *defectors*.

This quick little quiz should shed some light on whether your immediate reactions to Mom are exaggerated by excessive needs to demonstrate compliance or defiance.

You have three choices with which to answer the following questions. Fill in "Always," "Sometimes," or "Never" as it best describes your reactions to the following questions:

1. When my mother asks me to run an errand for her during the middle of my workday, I _____ do it.

2. When my mother buys me a new sweater she thinks I might like, I _____ keep it.

3. I would _____ opt for a college, vacation spot, or movie my mom suggests.

4. If my mother likes someone I am dating, I _____ do.

5. I _____ use the recipes my mother gives me.

6. I _____ consider following in my mother's career footsteps.

7. I _____ join professional or volunteer organizations that my mother belongs to.

8. I _____ respect my mother's opinions.

9. I am _____ on the same wavelength as my mom.

A majority of "Sometimes" answers with a few "Never" or "Always" answers thrown in represents the most healthy combination of answers. One could surmise that a daughter who scored similarly does not feel internally or emotionally compelled to rebuff or accept all of her mother's opinions, actions, or attitudes.

Building Blocks

According to author Victoria Secunda, **defectors** are daughters, psychologically or physically battered by their mothers, who literally left their childhood abode and severed all further contact with their moms.

Explosives

Daughters who are superachievers may have reached this pinnacle in order to disprove a mother's negative messages, win her approval, gain her favor, or to feel loved. It seems that experts have discovered mothers put pressure on their daughters to achieve because it adds to their happiness, not just their daughters', and confirms that they have done a good job mothering.

However, 10 straight "never" answers leaves no room for doubt. You, my dear, are deliberately and obstinately defiant. Ten straight "always" answers would lead one to believe you are ridiculously compliant, trying too hard to please your mother, or trying to maintain her approval at the expense of your personal opinions and choices. Either extreme—being too compliant or being too defiant—suggests ...

➤ A preponderance of unresolved issues with Mom.

➤ A lack of full-fledged independence and no self-motivated identity.

➤ An unwillingness to assume responsibility for your own actions, thereby blaming your foibles or successes completely on Mom.

Should you fall into one of the latter two categories, you better pay close attention to the chapters in Part 5, "Sharing Revelations, Making Adjustments," which deal specifically with repairing the mother-daughter relationship.

Explosives

Daughters, have you ever considered that approval is a two-way street? Your mom may want and need your approval, too. More discussion on this point of view will be offered up to you in Chapter 16.

Are You Hung Up on Approval?

Throughout this book we have referred to a daughter's need to win her mother's approval. It stems back to those early childhood years. Dr. Charney Herst says, "craving Mother's approval is almost a primal urge. Her opinion carriers more weight than anyone else's because it was Mom who first introduced us to life showed us our world when we were infants, and as we grew she taught us right from wrong ..."

Chances are you will always like getting your mother's approval. However, if your mother's approval is an absolute requirement for your general, adult happiness, you may very well have developed a real hang-up over it.

Sorting Out Whose Got the Approval Problem

The tricky thing is that you may not even recognize that you are still battling for Mom's nod of approval. At least Jane said she didn't. Once she had this epiphany, however, her entire outlook changed.

> "It took me a long time to realize what my problem was with my mother," 30-year-old Jane admitted. "I always needed to feel like I was doing the right thing. By 'right thing' I mean what my mother's idea of doing the right thing was. I didn't think there was any other way or possibility to see things. I knew what she considered to be the right way to treat other people, your marriage, your spouse, and other family members."

"I felt that if I emulated her I would be okay, and that if I didn't I wouldn't get her approval. Then she said two things to me in the course of different conversations that really shocked me. My sister, my mom, and I were airing out some grievances, I think about coming to visit her and my dad. Whatever it was I remember she said that she would hope we did something because we wanted to, not because we had to. The way she said it made me realize I had choices that I hadn't been making. It also gave me a lot more confidence in myself and in our relationship. I realized that she wouldn't reject me if I rejected what I thought were her absolute right ways of doing things. It took a lot of pressure off the relationship and me when I realized I didn't have to have her approval, that I needed to trust in myself and find my own rights or wrongs. It took time for me to realize that I was the one that needed to cut the cord and sift through all of the stuff Mom raised us with before I could find out what felt right for me. Whatever was left in the sieve belonged to me.

"I can't say that this one episode changed my entire outlook. It wasn't long ago Mom and I were having a pretty intense conversation. My mother said she didn't expect me to like or approve of everything about her and that I shouldn't want or need her to like or approve of everything about me. She said that was unfair for both of us.

"Now I have a lot more trust in our relationship. I don't feel compelled to do all those things that never felt right to me. I can do them my way."

Pearls of Wisdom

"Respect and acceptance go hand in hand. If you respect a daughter or a mother, then you accept who they are."

—Anonymous

Realizing Your Mom Could Have the Approval Problem

No matter how much we intellectualize or departmentalize approval, Jane's story in the previous section demonstrated that some need for approval continues to pop up. As you get older, a daughter doesn't require her mother's approval in the conventional sense. However, another form of approval that feels good is praise. And, it is a smart mother who knows when to give it.

However, if you are still suffering from approval or praise deprivation your mother may simply …

➤ Not know how to give praise.

➤ Lack empathy.

➤ Be a poor listener.

➤ Be self-absorbed or withhold praise as a way to control you.

➤ Fear you won't continue to work hard to achieve if she gives you praise.

➤ Not realize you need it.

If Mom is the one with the approval or praise problem, it may be time for a heart-to-heart talk. "A good relationship boils down to being able to communicate without tearing at each other's throat," Jane advises.

How to have a productive heart to heart is fully outlined in Chapter 20, "It's Time to Learn How to Talk."

Woman to Woman

Experts tell us that anger is a reaction to something or someone that hurts, disappoints, rejects, or ignores us. Becoming angry at someone doesn't solve the problem. It does, however, combat feelings of powerlessness that arise when faced with these things. The next time you explode in anger at your mom, stop and consider how true this bit of information is and examine what transpired that caused your reaction.

Are These Negative Daughterly Emotions Normal?

There is a whole series of emotions that daughters can expect to have when it comes to their moms. They won't seem nearly as overwhelming when daughters and moms accept that they are part of the normal course of things. You can expect to …

➤ Feel ambivalent toward your mom—there are moments she is your best friend and other moments when you don't want to pick up the phone to talk to her.

➤ Feel despair when you don't think you are able to please your mom.

➤ Feel angry, even betrayed, if your mom fails to nurture you when you feel you need it.

Explosives

Daughters, make sure that you have your maternal introject under control. This isn't something your mom can do for you. You have reached an age of maturity that demands you turn on and off that voice of hers that rings in your head when you feel it is appropriate!

➤ Experience anger because your mom isn't perfect, and won't always understand you and give you what you need.

➤ Feel sad if your relationship with your mother doesn't make you happy.

However, these emotions do come with a warning label. For instance, if you are so angry or sad that you emotionally distance yourself from your mother and are unable to show her love, you have gone beyond the limits of normal emotions.

Are Your Expectations Getting in the Way?

Although there is an old saying that infers your mother knows everything about you—what you are thinking and feeling—and don't have to be told, that isn't necessarily a good adage to buy into. You could be expecting too much from Mom if you expect her to …

➤ Read your mind.

➤ Know what you think is important at all times.

➤ Be ready to drop everything the moment you want her to listen.

➤ Know exactly when or when not to ask questions pertaining to your private life.

➤ Be fully attuned to your moods.

➤ Know what is and isn't important to you.

➤ Not put any demands on you.

➤ Be your friend, supporter, and confidante, but do not allow her to expect the same from you.

If this list sounds all too familiar, your expectations are way out of line, and you will surely meet with disappointment. Some readjusting on your part is in order.

So What Are Reasonable Expectations?

In case you are left in a quandary after going over the previous list of excessive expectations, examine the ideas that follow. They reveal expectations many adult daughters have of their mothers that are more fair and reasonable.

Well-founded, reasonable expectations for a daughter to have of her mom include …

➤ Showing a real interest in your life—career, loves, well-being, hobbies, problems, and children, for starters.

➤ Asking questions about your work and your children.

➤ Demonstrating equal interest in all of her children.

➤ Being able to empathize.

➤ Valuing what is important to you.

➤ Making your relationship a two-way adult street.

➤ Being your friend and supporter.

➤ Demonstrating enthusiasm for your accomplishments.

➤ Respecting your way of doing things.

➤ Appreciating the unique adult you have become.

➤ Discussing with you, not lecturing you, about concerns she has about aspects of your life that may lead you into trouble.

If your mom doesn't meet these expectations, you can be relatively certain the fault is hers, not yours!

Pearls of Wisdom

"A daughter cannot blame her mother for her own faults. She has to start blaming herself eventually."

—Jane, 30-year-old stay-at-home mom of a son says this is a new revelation for her

Woman to Woman

Amy Tan, author of *The Joy Luck Club* (Putnam, 1989), told interviewers Mickey Pearlman and Katherine Usher Henderson, authors of *A Voice of One's Own: Conversations with America's Writing Women* (Houghton Mifflin, 1990) that her mother had expected her to become a brain surgeon since she was six years old. She tried to fulfill this expectation early in her college career at a university selected by her mother. However, after changing colleges, becoming an English and linguistics major, and marrying, she and her mother were estranged from one another for six months because of their differing points of view. Part of this was created by a lack of understanding one another and the worlds each grew up in. Tan said she used her writing to help discover new things about her mother's past and present identity.

Are You an Adult "Mother-Blamer"?

There is one way to quickly find out. Answer the following questions with a "Never," "Sometimes," or "Always."

1. When you are disappointed in your ability to confront a new situation, do you blame this on your mother?
   Never   Sometimes   Always

2. If your marriage is in trouble, do you blame your problems on your mother?
   Never   Sometimes   Always

3. If you fail to win a promotion or get the job you wanted, do you blame it on your mom for not pushing you more in school?
   Never   Sometimes   Always

4. If you have a weight problem, do you blame it on your mom for being too concerned with your body when you were younger?
   Never   Sometimes   Always

5. Do you frequently wish your mother had raised you differently?
   Never   Sometimes   Always

6. When you are unhappy with life in general, do you blame it on your mother?
   Never   Sometimes   Always

7. Do you blame your lack of success, motivation, or development on your mother?
   Never   Sometimes   Always

8. If you are having financial problems, do you blame your mother?
   Never   Sometimes   Always

9. Do you think your mother could have made your life better?
   Never   Sometimes   Always

10. Do you think you would like yourself better if you had a different mother?
    Never   Sometimes   Always

There comes a time when we must accept responsibility for the adults we have become, recognize that free choice allows us to change those things we are unhappy with in our lives, and stop blaming our mothers. You are still stuck in the muck of mother-blaming if you have more than one or two "Always" answers. You have one foot in the muck and one foot out if you have more than three or four "Sometimes" answers. If you have answered the 10 questions all with "Never," you need to take this quiz over and apply a little more honesty.

The Least You Need to Know

➤ Relying on individual memories is not always the most accurate guide to the past.

➤ Accepting that you are overly compliant or childishly defiant is a big step toward improving mother-daughter understanding and relationships.

➤ Needing and wanting Mom's approval are two different issues. As an adult, continually needing her approval signals a serious problem in your level of self-acceptance and confidence.

➤ Your mother may be deliberately withholding approval as a means of maintaining her seniority and control.

➤ You may be harboring unfair grudges toward your mom because of her failure to meet your unrealistic expectations.

➤ Recognizing that as adults, it is our responsibility to change that with which we are unhappy and to stop mother-blaming.

Who Is This Woman I Call Mother?

It is the appointed time to focus on the mother in your life. Who she is, what makes her tick, how she views you, and how she came through motherhood are all part of the "Age of Discovery" for both of you. The exploration should produce some startling revelations, thought provoking considerations, and critical insights. Much of this book has been dedicated to understanding and nurturing daughters. Little of it has had to do with Mom's personal side.

In order to reach the goal of this book—achieving a mutually respectful and loving mother-daughter team—this investigation is an absolute must.

Pearls of Wisdom

"My mother is sending me her journals now ... as she finishes them. I'm seeing her as a person with her own center of gravity and I see in her more than ever, the little lost only child who felt that she never fit in."

—Gail Godwin, novelist (author of *A Mother and Two Daughters*, a National Book Award winner) from *A Voice of One's Own*

Motherly Wisdom Is Found over the Atlantic

On a long flight from Istanbul, Turkey to the United States, I had the opportunity to interview several women. Before takeoff I approached Susan Merrinoff, a New York mother of five adult children—two sons and three daughters. Part way into the flight she handed me a few thoughts she had written out on the bottom of a magazine page. I hope she made another copy and read it to her three daughters after she arrived home. Here is what she wrote:

Woman to Woman

There are significant distinctions between types of motherly need. You may not need your daughters to need you as they did when they were young. You may, however, need to have them want you to share in and be a part of their adult lives for you to be happy.

"Linda, Cathy, Barbara: The best thing about having a daughter is that even though you may be very different we are really best friends forever and ever. I can only talk for me because I appreciate them and feel so very blessed. I can call my daughters at any hour, for me very early in the A.M. They are always there to talk. When they were little, they need me more, now I am older I need them more. In a different way, with so much love, they are there for me always."

What is particularly significant is that Susan came back a little while later to tell me that what she wrote really didn't matter when you consider the mother-daughter relationship. "It's what my daughters' think!" she said.

Moms Must Work Harder at Relationships Than Daughters

This may just be a generational thing, but if you talk to middle-age moms of adult daughters, you will see what I mean. They are singing a different tune than their own mothers, who expected unconditional respect and didn't worry so much about making sure their daughters liked them. The new middle-aged moms confronting adult daughters, many of whom live hundred if not thousands of miles from home, exhibit a new mind set. A good many of them ...

➤ Feel they have to earn and maintain their daughter's love, affection, attention, and respect.

➤ Measure their words more carefully than their mothers to maintain peace, harmony, and closeness.

➤ Are more aware of giving praise, patting their daughters on the back, demonstrating interest, and overlooking what their mothers would have deemed disrespectful behavior.

➤ Are willing to forego the formalities of unconditional respect to promote honest, open communication.

➤ Recognize that their daughters can do without them with fewer emotional difficulties than they can do without their daughters.

➤ Concern themselves more with being on the same wavelength as their daughters.

➤ Go out of their way to do things that will endear their daughters to them and bring them closer.

➤ Repeatedly travel far and wide to have ongoing and meaningful contact with grandchildren.

➤ Are concerned about what their daughters think of them, how they are viewed by these young women, and being loved by them.

Pearls of Wisdom

"The greatest thing in my life has been being their mom. The three of us are so intensely bonded."

—Singer Naomi Judd, *Life* magazine, May 1, 1999

What Most Daughters Think About Mom

For those who want to know what their young adult daughters think of them, the result of this sampling informally conducted in random interviews will be enlightening. Daughters reported appreciating and valuing moms who ...

➤ Are able to be caring, loving, and social people.

➤ Show a willingness to devote time to a daughter's happiness.

➤ Have a sense of humor, individual strength, personal motivation, intelligence, and courage.

➤ Demonstrate a desire for honest and open discussion.

➤ Have the capability to give sound, timely guidance.

These same daughters had no trouble voicing what they disliked or admired least. What they found least appealing in a mom include a lack of activities outside the house, moodiness, the tendency to overanalyze them, and the attempt to manipulate them.

What Mothers Need and Want

This list may look strikingly similar to what their daughters need and want from them: love, praise, approval, kindness, empathy, forgiveness, respect, friendship, time and companionship, understanding, support, and validation. This is probably a good time to pause and consider when, how, and if these needs have been met in your mother-daughter relationship.

A Mother's Wish Come True

This open letter to my daughter was published in a woman's magazine in 1991. Judging by the responses I got, I think it expressed heartfelt sentiments of a large number of us moms. Therefore, I think it will help further your understanding of your mother, or of yourself if you are a mother. Sometimes it takes others to give words to our feelings in order to clarify them. This was written when my oldest daughter Sara Jane was 21. I have sent it to both of my girls when I think we might be getting off track or that I was being misunderstood. This was particularly true during the first few years of Sara Jane's married life when we all had a great deal of adjusting to do.

Dear Sara Jane,

Unknowingly you made me ponder this year's Mother Day with a bit more reverence. Previously, I gave the holiday only token consideration. However, the time we spent alone together last month at the beach prompted me to think a great deal about being both a mother and a daughter.

Do you recall that three days were just long enough for us to concentrate on one another, yet short enough to avoid the eruption of one of our inevitable mother-daughter conflicts? I remember thinking how ironic it was that during our morning walks we exchanged such intimate confidences, revealed our inner-most concerns, spoke of disappointments, and outlined future dreams. After all, it did not seem that long ago that I made endless futile attempts to involve myself in your life or discover your private thoughts. I even dared to wish you might ask me what I was thinking and feeling. I guess the time has now ripened with your emerging equality. You seemed so independent and mature, and I easily accepted you as the adult you had grown into.

Pearls of Wisdom

"I wish my mom would open up to me more about her feelings, anxieties, menopause, stuff like that. Because let's face it, if she's going through it, it's highly likely I will go through it, too. We are peas of the same pod."

—Charlene Garland, New Hampshire, an unmarried environmental professional in her late 20s

I often think of that last night of our getaway when you climbed into my bed and asked, "Do you mind if we cuddle like we used to?" It felt so good when you fit yourself into the niche between my arm and my chest that you could barely fill years ago. The insights of our morning talks lingered over us. As I rubbed your arm and smothered your long dark hair, I knew that this was a special moment.

In fact, the three days were full of special moments. There was no way to package the love and attention you gave me and save it in my top dresser drawer among your childhood offerings of wooden pendants on wool strings or hand decorated cards. I knew these were fleeting moments that would not typify our daily interaction encumbered with work, responsibilities, and friends—all of which draw us into our separate, frenzied lives. I just hoped there would be more times like these.

I wonder if you understood what I felt that evening or if you would have to wait until you had your own child. Climbing into my arms signaled you would always be my little girl, and I your mommy. But in addition, during those days when you were willing to share yourself with me, you were more. You were a wonderful combination of daughter and friend who enjoyed my company as a person and not just your mother. There was a respect for who each of us was—separate and apart from our mother-daughter relationship. You told me you needed my approval. Did I tell you I wanted yours?

It is hard for me to explain after years of nurturing what one expects out of motherhood, out of daughters. Relationships are so fragile. I fear falling into a trap by expecting too much, wanting to be too much a part of your life, and causing you to retreat and move away from me.

Before I fell asleep that night, I tried to retrieve memories of my own mother and myself, examining them for signs of similar moments. I could not pinpoint any, although I was sure they must be there. Perhaps in my self-centered world they had occurred, and I was the one who had missed them. I worried that I had not given Grandma a chance by using the pretense of being too busy for such intimacy when, in reality, I was fearful of motherly criticisms and interferences—relics of childhood misunderstandings. I should have realized that an honest dialogue might rid me of these feelings we grudgingly carry over into adulthood. I should have tried to see my mother as the individual she was and is. I should have grasped what I meant to her. I should have been willing to be a friend. All this is clear, now that I am the mother of a 21-year-old daughter.

So you see Sara why I plan to steal Grandma away for a few days, long enough for the seeds of these moments to germinate, long enough to give her a taste of what you gave me. I think the time is now ripe for me to tell her who I have become and to ask her what she is thinking and feeling.

I love you,
Mom

Pearls of Wisdom

"Disappointments from a daughter can hurt the mother even greater than a boy because the relationship is closer."

—Lasenua Madanguda, Kenya, educator and Masai daughter, mother of two college-age girls and a son

Building Blocks

Parental anxiety is concern by parents over their future needs and whether or not their daughters will be willing to care for them as they age.

The Years Bring Positive Results

If you haven't already experienced it, a study by Karen L. Fingerman published in the *Journals of Gerontology*, March 2000, notes that the mother-daughter relationships shift as the latter moves into adulthood. The diagram below clearly depicts the progression of most relationships. As adult daughters, relationships with our mothers should take on a new hue of mutual concern, maturity, and equality. In addition both experience a new-found parental and filial anxiety.

Broader focus on family ties and
enjoyment for both mother and daughter
**Aging mom appreciates and enjoys
things more that daughter does for her**
Middle-aged daughter feels competition for time
and increased demands by mother and other family members
Mother moves focus to next generation that will be left behind
Mother experiences parental anxiety and concern about
daughter who will turn into caretaker
Daughter expresses positive feelings about future care of mother

Adult to adult relationship
**Daughter feels more connected to mother, recognizes
mom as individual, and enjoys doing things for mother**
Mother still doing many things for daughter
**Both view their relationship more favorably,
accept one another's faults, and enjoy interacting
and spending time with one another, focusing on
each other, not broader family relationship**

Mother experiences satisfaction of daughter's
entry into adult life, proof of her good mothering
**Daughter establishing autonomy and trying
to gain help, guidance, and assistance from mom**

Motherly interest in younger
daughter's psychological development
**Daughter does not yet
recognize mother as individual**

Start here
Focus on daughter's life by mother
Daughter self-absorbed

The advancing years bring along changes to the mother-daughter relationship.

How Well Do You Know Your Mother?

You will be able to achieve the happier levels of mother-daughter relationship presented in the diagram if you look deep inside your mom. See if you have answers for the following questions:

1. Is your mother basically a happy or unhappy person? Why or why not?

2. Does she have a satisfying and fulfilling relationship with a love partner? Why or why not?

3. What are your mother's lifetime regrets, unfulfilled dreams, and future goals?

Building Blocks

Filial anxiety is the worry expressed by middle-aged daughters about their mother's future need for assistance during the time in which she still maintains good health.

4. What are her gravest disappointments and her most rewarding accomplishments?

5. What are her biggest fears?

6. What does she like the most and least about herself?

7. Is she happy with your relationship?

8. What are her strengths and weaknesses?

9. What does she wish she could do that she doesn't?

10. Is she envious of others? Why?

11. Is your mother overly sensitive and vulnerable?

12. Does your mother have special needs? If so, what are they?

If you can't answer these questions, either your relationship with your mother could still be strongly influenced by your childhood status or your mom is uncommunicative. How to begin a dialogue and get to know each other more intimately will be outlined for you in Part 5, "Sharing Revelations, Making Adjustments."

Woman to Woman

The martyr mothers do not want their daughters to forget the life-time sacrifices made for them, says Alyce Faye Cleese, from *How to Manage Your Mother*. Rather, these moms want eternal gratitude and guilt for all they have done. They are not above making constant reminders of all they gave up for their daughters.

Woman to Woman

Experts acknowledge that all mothers think from time to time about what they gave up to become mothers. That's normal and natural. It isn't until she sounds like a broken record, reminding everyone around her of her sacrifices, that she qualifies as a martyr mom.

Mom, the Martyr

Moms of all types sometimes show signs of martyrdom. To get a firm handle on what your mom is all about, take note of the symptoms, causes, and motivations of martyrdom.

The Sounds of Martyrdom

➤ "I was never able to fulfill my dreams or reach self-actualization because I stayed at home with you."

➤ "I gave my life to mothering you and your brothers and sisters."

➤ "I did without many things I would liked to have had to be able to give more to you."

➤ "I did not travel like I would have like to because there were always so many places to take you and your siblings. How could I have possibly left you in someone else's care?"

Personal Contributors to Mother Martyrdom

1. Allows one to avoid taking responsibility for one's choices or disappointments by blaming it on something else.

2. Provides an excuse for one's shortcomings.

3. Masks one's insecurities and lack of courage.

Martyr Mothers and Daughters

Martyr moms are forever reminding you what they gave up to nurture you. Their conscious or unconscious motivation in doing so is to provoke a daughter's guilt, get her approval, enlist her support and sympathy, obtain recognition, garner her attention, secure her love and gratitude, and control and manipulate her.

Explosives

Therapist Alyce Cleese explains that guilt put on daughters by martyr moms is an outgrowth of a mother's regret and a lack of responsibility for her own choices and actions. It is meant to make daughters feel eternally responsible for Mom and her life opportunities or lack thereof.

The Least You Need to Know

➤ The mother-daughter relationship shifts from earlier years when the focus is on the daughter to a more equal and interactive relationship in adulthood.

➤ Mothers in their middle-years express great concern over their relationship with their daughters, including the need to gain their respect and maintain their love.

➤ Daughters value the productive, outgoing, and sensitive qualities exhibited in their mothers.

➤ Mothers need many of the same things that their daughters need from them.

➤ Most mothers will tell you that raising a daughter is worth any or all of the struggles.

➤ Martyr moms are victims of their own problems and create strife between themselves and their daughters.

Mom's Getting Older

Stop and read! Don't neglect this chapter, even if you are a younger mother-daughter duo. This comprehensive mini-course on aging moms, their daughters, and positive responses to common problems applies to everyone. The chapter is filled to the brim with pertinent, factual, and emotional information about the aging process and how mothers and daughters relate during this part of their lives.

One can look at this stage in either a positive or negative light, although a dark, depressing take won't do anyone a bit of good. I think you will see, and agree, that one's mindset has a lot to do with successful aging and a satisfying mother-daughter relationship in the later years.

Acknowledging the Positives of Age

Joan Borysenko, Ph.D., author of *A Woman's Book of Life*, espouses a view of aging that is positive and invigorating. It is congruent with the fact that the majority of women in their 70s have good health and are capable of intellectual and psychological growth. The myth surrounding women's later years that projects an image of inactive, sickly, and passive individuals should not prevail, she says. In fact, Borysenko advises women to set their goals on becoming one of the *young-old*.

The young-old women she refers to …

1. Have most generally used time in their earlier adult life productively, heightened their ability to empathize, and have been compassionate. Normally these women, Borysenko claims, do not become bitter, inhibited, inactive, or destructive later in life.

2. Prevent a loss of function in older age by maintaining an active life that is both physically and intellectually challenging.

3. Do not allow themselves to fall into a state of depression, especially after the loss of a spouse or companion. Instead they flourish in a state of activity and new discovery.

4. Are vessels of wisdom and vision.

What is of added value to the young-old is that they fit the description of what daughters find admirable and likable about their mothers (see Chapter 16, "Who Is This Woman I Call Mother?").

Building Blocks

The **young-old** are individuals over 65 who maintain active, vital lives and an up-to-date interest in larger world around them.

Pearls of Wisdom

"We imagine that she (an aging mom) is always going to be there, and so there will always be time to deal with things. But if we can grasp that our time with her is limited, we can value her presence now more fully."

—Alyce Faye Cleese, *How to Manage Your Mother*

Age with Wisdom

Women who encompass wisdom that comes with age have this to say:

➤ Betty Friedan, feminist and author of *The Feminine Mystique* and *The Fountain of Age:* "I have discovered that there is a crucial difference between society's image of old people and 'us' as we know and feel ourselves to be."

➤ Betty Laverdure, Tribal judge and legislator: "Grandmother, that wonderful name, has always meant teacher in all of our society. That's a good distinction and I'm proud of it."

➤ Katherine Hepburn, actress: "I have no romantic feelings about age. Either you are interesting at any age or you are not."

My Heroine

When I read the novel *Stones of Ibarra* several years ago, I fell in love with the book and the author, Harriet Doerr. Doerr returned to college at age 65, after the death of her husband and raising a daughter and a son. She published her first novel in 1984 at the age of 74. It is obvious age did not limit her in any way. Doerr's example makes all things seem possible to me.

As to the longevity she has enjoyed, she remarked, "If you live a long time you have a long view, you look back a long way. I had a gal in mind and a deadline, so I didn't fool around. Now I feel the same way about the book I'm writing. You cannot just waste time. Otherwise you'll die to regret it."

Woman to Woman

We have said it before but it bears repeating: Women's natural tendency to seek out social connections, discuss their feelings, and look for comfort is a value to their physical and mental health, especially during a period of loss.

Exhibiting the Opposite of the Young-Old

Those women who are not of the young-old mindset exhibit qualities that often tend to make their older years more difficult, their days less productive, and their daughters more frustrated. Take these points, for example:

1. Women who do not handle loss or grief well may retreat from an active life, become bitter and resentful, and allow their feelings of depression and loneliness to cast a shadow over the remainder of their days. This is particularly pertinent because women outlive men by nearly eight years and of the total female population, 12 percent are widows.

2. Women who do not handle their advanced age successfully and tend to become increasingly bitter are those who lived their younger years forming a habit of helplessness and revenge.

3. Elderly women who fail to be or see themselves as active, participatory people, or maintain independent control over their life suffer from ill health earlier than the young-old.

4. Some experts believe the surfacing of negative events and feelings suppressed during younger and busier periods of life is a natural function of aging; however, not all women exhibit this behavior. Those who do may

Building Blocks

Resiliency is the ability to rebound or recover and regain strength, both emotionally and physically, after confronting a situation that compromised one's normal state of being.

complain to their daughters about things they missed out of in life, perhaps even their anger or unhappiness with a spouse.

Thinking About Relocating Home and Hearth

You are about to meet Betty, a 67-year-old widow living alone in a mid-western city where she has become an integral part of her community over the past 44 years. Her one surviving daughter—the only close relative she has—lives in Hawaii. The purpose of Betty's story is twofold:

1. It represents a dilemma many women will increasingly be facing.
2. The methodology she uses to resolve this dilemma is instructive and sound.

Experts tell us that how one copes with a crises—moving out of a home, facing financial reversals, the losing a spouse, or fighting illness—depends upon the meaning we give the circumstances. *Resilient* people look for and find a positive meaning then go on with their lives. Despairing people feel victimized and suffer from hopelessness and depression in the face of a crisis.

The Dilemma

Betty, an independent, resourceful, productive, and interesting woman, retired two years ago from a career in social services. She continues to use her skills to run a weekly support group for pregnant women confined to bed rest and participate in a school reading program. Recently, she began to contemplate moving to Hawaii to begin a new life near her married daughter and primary-school-age granddaughter. "The whole idea scares the hell out of me," Betty admits.

Still there are plenty of reasons for Betty to seriously consider the move: Her daughter, Toby, wants her to be closer; many of her friends (who have been an integral part of her life) now live six months of the year elsewhere, are deceased, or have moved to be closer to their children; she can no longer use work as an excuse; she misses her family; she wants to be a larger part of Cheryl's (her granddaughter) life; and, the idea of moving with a well-thought-out plan is more appealing to Betty than being forced into a sudden move prompted by a health emergency.

Pearls of Wisdom

"You regret the things that you don't do much more than the things you do."

—Betty Sugarman, retired social worker, raised two daughters

The Plan

"Finally I told Toby I would think about how I could do what she was asking of me," Betty said. "I decided to try it for one month in my own apartment. Of course I chose the shortest month, February. It is also the coldest and nastiest month in the Midwest."

During the course of that month Betty has a specific agenda. She wants to see if she could learn the community, find her way around, and meet people with whom she had the potential to become friends. To accomplish this she planned to make contact with local professional social work organizations, attend religious events, and see where she fit in.

Betty has also found that by being open and discussing her feelings with friends about the prospect of a move, she has been able to gain insight, perspective, and support.

The Outcome

"There is only one person who can make this move a success," Betty says. "That's me. I will only make this move if I have a good feel for my own independence. There is an element of challenge and adventure to it."

Although Betty puts the responsibility for a successful move on herself, the quality of her mother-daughter relationship surely will help. "Toby and I are getting closer and closer and closer all the time," Betty said. "Our relationship is changing all the time and we are both changing all the time. It is easier to talk to her now than when she was 15, 17, or 19. She is diplomatic, understanding, and upfront. I don't know if there is anything she wouldn't ask me. I would ask her anything—not about her husband and their relationship—about her feelings."

Pearls of Wisdom

Thirty-nine-year-old Cheryl Oyaski of Phoenix, Arizona, says, "My mother feels that I am mothering her and she resents it. It is the primary factor that causes tension between the two women."

Understanding the Aging Woman

Aging should be met with better understanding, believes Dr. Joseph Russell, retired professor of gerontology at Ohio State University and a consultant on care for the aged. "Don't hold it against Mom. She is making the best adjustment she can out of the circumstances," Russell said.

Therefore, it is important to pinpoint prevalent changes that take place among the aging population. The following list of characteristics isn't unique or peculiar to your mom. These characteristics are part of the aging process, Russell notes. Nonetheless, further reading will prove that mother-daughter relationships can flourish during this time period, and that many, many moms maintain respect, compassion, and appreciation for their children's assistance.

1. Older folks complain about their health in order to obtain love and attention.
2. Older people become more self-absorbed as their world shrinks.

3. Mothers lose appreciation for the tasks children perform and become more demanding.

4. Those affected by the normal aging process become less sensitive to others, regress, and lose interest in the world around them.

5. Cognitive skills become impaired and attention span is limited during the aging process.

6. Expectations and demands continue to build as all of these other changes take place.

Mom's Personal Frustrations

Mom's newfound limits and lessening of capacity can be profoundly frustrating to her. They alter the way in which she reacts with others, put personal constrains on her, and change her role in the family.

Building Blocks

A **reverse mortgage** is a home equity loan that converts equity in a home for cash and is paid in allotments by the lender. The loan is due upon sale of the home, death, or total payout of loaned monies. Upon death, either heirs or one's estate must pay off the loan, normally by sale of the house. In essence, a reverse loan allows you to live in your home and use the equity as readily available cash.

Daughters Reactions and Concerns

Daughters, too, get frustrated and angry with the changes that take place in Mom and about factors that affect their own lives. Russell mentions several to be aware of:

1. The cost of care for the elderly is expensive. Children may become angry and resentful when they see their inheritance being spent and *reverse mortgages* being put on the family home.

2. One daughter most often becomes the primary caretaker of Mom. When there are other siblings, both brothers and sisters, anger and frustration from the over-burdening of responsibility may be directed at them.

3. Chances are that a daughter who takes responsibility for a mother's care may suffer a serious time-crunch when faced with raising children, working, spousal needs, and personal desires.

Mother and Daughter, Creating a Plan Together

The best way to approach the prospect of eventual caretaking is to discuss it with family members before Mom suffers limited capacity. Suggestions on how to go about this have been adopted from the wisdom of experts in gerontology. Plan for the future with a parent so that you can avoid a hasty decision that does not meet with Mom's and your wishes or the realities at hand. Consider, if Mom suffers limited mobility, where she would want to be to receive the necessary care, what her finances are, and what legal steps need to be taken.

In order to make the planning stage work effectively for everyone, both parties must listen carefully to each other and accept the other's viewpoint. Daughters should not shortchange their mother's ability to make decisions. Nor should they make concessions in their plan based on guilt or out of stress.

Getting Along with an Aging Mom

Researcher Alexis J. Walker asserts that caregiving for a parent does not develop suddenly after an era of intergenerational independence and the onset of need. Rather there are many examples of assistance given prior to that time in simple acts of sending left over food to a mother's home, purchasing items for them in the store, running errands, accompanying them to the doctor, and many more. For some mothers and daughters, interaction after loss of independence can be similar to healthier time periods in their relationship.

The Mother-Daughter Relationships That Fair Best in Later Years

According to Walker, how mother and daughter feel about giving and receiving care is dependent upon the quality of their earlier intergenerational relationship when each lived independent lives. Here is what Walker found:

1. Daughters who felt close to their mother during the period of *intergenerational independence* experience less frustration and anxiety when it comes time to giving care.

Building Blocks

Intergenerational independence refers to individuals who belong to different generations and live as independent, autonomous persons during a specific period of time.

201

2. Mothers who feel close to their daughters do not exhibit as much anger as those moms who are not as close to their daughters when the time comes for them to need their [daughters] help.

3. Daughters who were part of pairs of mothers and daughters who thought of themselves as good friends found the caregiving relationship to be rewarding. They had fewer conflicts, expressed concern for each other, respected one another's autonomy, viewed each other as adults, and tried to maintain the mother's independence.

4. Ambivalent pairs of mothers and daughters who expressed both positive and negatives in the intergenerational relationship did not find the period of caregiving as rewarding. They experienced more conflict. Daughters felt that their mothers did not demonstrate a concern for them, respect their autonomy, or appreciate their efforts.

5. Moms and daughters whose younger relationship was full of conflict and individual focus had the least satisfying interaction during the caregiving era. Daughters did not find caregiving rewarding but felt it was a heavy burden.

When Duty Calls and Caretaking Is Not a Labor of Love

It is safe to say that a very big difference in how one feels about the time, effort, and emotion that goes into caring for a mother has a lot to do with the love and pride a mom sends in the direction of her daughter!

Take Jess for example. When I first approached her about sharing thoughts about her adult mother-daughter relationship with me, she said, "I have no relationship with my mother."

Explosives

Therapists have found that those men and women who do not experience a mother's love—either due to death, mistreatment, or abandonment—are often deeply wounded and extremely vulnerable.

That statement made her story all the more important to understand. What I came to learn was that her aging, sick mother had been a self-centered, alcoholic actress and model who had left much of the emotional childrearing responsibilities to her husband. "She didn't do anything for us (Jess and her sister and brother) that she didn't have to."

In later years, this mom has become resentful of everyone and everything. She never gives Jess a compliment about her children or her professional success, and fails to thank her for all the things she does for her since Jess moved her parents to Florida to be closer to her so she could be a more accessible caretaker.

"I do what I have to do. I stop over all the time for a few minutes, take her to the doctor, and do the grocery shopping with my father," Jess said. "My mother and I never go to lunch or anything like that."

"This episode will explain to you what I mean about my mom," Jess continued. "An old friend of hers came to visit. I went to the airport to pick her up and took her to my parent's home. The moment I turned my back and walked out of the room to make them tea my mother gestured with her hands how much weight I had gained. She didn't think I would see her. She hadn't seen this woman in 20 years and that was what was of the utmost in her mind. I was furious and hurt. I left even though I had been looking forward to sitting and talking with this woman and my mother."

Now compare and contrast Jess's feelings toward her infirm mom to those of Nanette's in the following chapter. Then you will see what really matters to daughters and exacerbates a genuine desire to be a sincere, loving caretaker.

Moving into the Caretaking Stage

The facts and figures of the aging population become particularly important to women when one considers that …

➤ Women make up 72 percent of those unpaid family members who serve as caregivers; and, 64 percent of these women also work full or part time.

➤ Daughters make up the largest proportion of these caretakers.

➤ A growing number of caregivers are women over age 65 who face their own "graying" problems.

➤ In the American culture, according to the vast majority of research, it is still regarded as a daughter's responsibility to care for an elderly parent.

➤ Twenty percent of a woman's life span will involve a parent over the age of 65.

Pearls of Wisdom

"A mother can raise five daughters, but five daughters can't even take care of one mother," Tillie tells her adult daughters ranging in age from 40 to 60. Other mothers have stated similar versions of this oft-repeated message.

Shifting from Nursing Homes to a Daughter's Home

In light of the pertinent facts outlined above, consider the impact of a statement made in *Nursing Economics:* The emphasis on caretaking of the elderly is shifting from hospital or skilled nursing facilities to home and family care. The effect this will have on caretakers (primarily daughters) and those who need care (elderly moms) is enormous when you look at the following statistics:

➤ The fastest growing portion of the American population is individuals over age 85. Most of those are women who are widowed or alone due to other circumstances.

➤ Nearly 31 million Americans are over the age of 65. By the year 2025 that number should climb to 62 million. In 1992 there were 19 million women over the age of 65. By the year 2035, it is projected that one in four Americans will be over the age of 65.

➤ Of those over age 65, approximately 1.6 million live in the community (compared to 1.5 million in nursing homes), either alone or with family members, and require assistance in daily activities from dressing to eating. Sixty-two percent of them are women.

Caring for a Parent in Your Own Home

Dr. Joseph Russell said it's important not to overtake tasks older people can still perform. To refrain from doing so requires patience understanding, energy, and love. From his article in *MidLife Woman,* "Caring for Aging Parents," June 1, 1994, is a list of questions and concerns to discuss with Mom:

Building Blocks

Filial responsibility means the perceived level of suitable responsibility by a son or daughter.

1. Would she be able to live in a home where she would not be the reigning lady of the house but a participant and not the primary manager?

2. Would she understand that her needs might not be put first above all other family members, and could she accept that?

3. Would she be able to fit herself into the household style of daily life and activities?

4. Would she be able to maintain her own friendships and social life in this setting?

5. Would living in her daughter's home provide enough privacy for her?

Understanding Expectations: Moms Expect Less and Daughters Expect More

A study of 100 Jewish women discussed in the March 1998 issue of *Contemporary Women's Issues Database* revealed what elderly mothers and their daughters thought about entering a period of necessary caregiving:

1. Daughters expect more *filial responsibility* from themselves with regard to caretaking than their elderly mothers expect from them.

2. Mothers want to spare their children from having to take care of them and becoming a burden.

3. Mothers do not want to live with their children, but do want to maintain close ties.

4. Mothers and daughters value their social and financial independence. Therefore, they each try to prolong those qualities for their elders.

5. Mothers do not give up the role or image of themselves as nurturers and therefore try to protect their daughters.

6. Mothers fear relying too heavily on their children, worrying they may be become resentful.

7. Mothers and daughters in this group try to make their relationship reciprocal and do things for each other.

8. Some mothers voluntarily put themselves into nursing facilities in order not to burden children.

9. Daughters of mothers in residential nursing home settings express less "filial expectations" than daughters whose mothers are still living in the general community.

Pearls of Wisdom

"Recollections of happy times can ameliorate the tedious work of caring for a sick person and the anguish of watching a loved one suffer."

—Anne F. Caron, Ed.D., from *Mothers and Daughters: Searching for New Connections* (Henry Holt, 1998)

The Least You Need to Know

➤ The later years can be productive, meaningful, and happy if one practices the secrets of being a "young-old" woman.

➤ Mothers who do not approach old age optimistically project a negative image that is difficult for daughters to deal with positively.

➤ Daughters need to be sensitive to and accepting of their mothers' concerns as they approach the "graying" years.

➤ The best mother–daughter relationship in later years is hallmarked by mutual love, respect, pride, concern, and appreciation. There are no substitutes for these critical expressions.

➤ The tone of past mother–daughter relationships leads one into the future.

➤ Caretaking may be difficult and demanding, but for many daughters it can also be rewarding.

Mom, I'd like you to meet someone very special to me...

Chapter 18

Mothers and Daughters Living Outside the White Picket Fence

In This Chapter

➤ Coping with mom's mental illness

➤ Understanding the relationship between adoptive mothers and adopted daughters

➤ Coming out: daughters telling moms, "I'm gay"

➤ Choosing to have a child when you're single

➤ Understanding the bottom line: love, support, and caring

There are circumstances between mothers and daughters that go beyond those we have discussed. In this chapter we will take a look at specific situations that add another complex layer on top of the mother-daughter relationships that have been carefully outlined for you. Although the situations here may not apply to the average reader, nor address the unique circumstances of another, there is plenty to be learned.

In each of the cases discussed, you might gain a glimmer of understanding that you may incorporate into your own relationships or offer to a friend or family member. There are so many combinations of mothers and daughters with a wide range of distinct circumstances that it would be impossible to present them all. However, empathizing with these mothers and daughters should provide tips for all others on how to meet situations that are outside the tight little box we conceive as the norm.

When the Table Prematurely Turns, Dependent Moms

I am now introducing you to 30-year-old Nanette because her story demonstrates that expressing and giving love to children is what matters most to daughters—even under the most stressful and unusual set of circumstances.

Nanette's mom had always suffered psychological problems, before and after her divorce. Due to her mother's increasing problems and inability to provide a secure environment, when Nanette was nine she and her sister moved out of their mother's house and in with her dad and his second wife. Her life thereafter was more than tumultuous.

Nanette remembers feeling confused and knowing that it was difficult for her mother to come and see her at her father's home. "She couldn't hop in a car to see us. She was always financially strapped and her mental state held her back from being a part of our lives. She realized we were better off. She would correspond with us through letters and still does today," Nanette said.

It wasn't until the last three or four years that Nanette finally went into therapy and achieved a perspective on her mother she could accept and live with. "I finally gave up the expectations one normally has for a mother. My mom is not able to fulfill those because of her limitations. I needed to be at a point where I could accept who she was. This didn't happen until I graduated college and I got married. It took me moving into my own life as an adult."

Explosives

A report in *Contemporary Women's Issues Database* notes that the homeless population has increased substantially since 1980. Women who become homeless are most often victims of domestic violence, sufferers of a medical or mental health crises, drug-users, or employed in low-paying jobs that provide insufficient economic resources. Due to a shortage of low-income housing, many of these women are unable to get off the streets.

"I have accepted who she is. It took a long time feeling comfortable having her around my friends. She dyes her hair real dark, is unable to appropriately handle her emotions in public, and may wear tattered shoes, but her nails are always perfect. She can't hold a job because of her mental disabilities. I have to remember this is all she can manage. Right now she is living with friends, but she is pretty much homeless. Sometimes in the winter she lives in shelters.

"I know it sounds crazy because I could have a lot of anger and sometimes I do, but I can look at others and say I have it better than they do. I know my mom loves me and will always be there for me. I know I can always depend on her for a hug or to say something positive without having to ask. She is so proud of the women her daughters have become and doesn't hold back telling us. She is genuinely happy for us."

Pearls of Wisdom

Celebrity adoptive mom of three Rosie O'Donnell said, "It's interesting being an adoptive mother. I wonder if you are more open to however they turn out and don't try to mold them because there's not a genetic component to it. I don't know."

The Climate of Adoption

If you look at what experts in the field of adoption have to say, they don't think the climate is optimal for adoptive mothers and daughters. Society still sees adoption as something that is not quite normal and should be hushed up, contend researchers, Mary Watkins, Ph.D., Janet Surrey, Ph.D., and Betsy Smith, Ph.D. They further assert that the sympathetic focal point of the adoption relationship is on the feelings of the birth mother, not the adoptive mom. These prevailing attitudes, they say, affect the "mental health and psychological development" of adoptive moms.

Laura Benkov, Ph.D., a clinical psychologist in Massachusetts, finds evidence that society still reveres genetic similarities in parents and children. The effect of this on one adopted daughter will be clear when you read about Elizabeth's saga further on in this chapter.

Despite these prevailing social winds, non-traditional adoptions are on the rise. Nine percent of the 127,000 legal adoptions in the United States in 1997 involved international pairings. Furthermore, it isn't only unmarried celebrities who are adopting children. A wide variety of women are opting to do so.

Adoptions: The Relationship Side

If you want the real scoop on adoption, consider the findings reported in *The Motherhood Report* by Louis Genevie, Ph.D., and Eva Margolies. The study found:

1. There is no difference in the quality of relationships among adoptive and biological mothers to their children.

2. Moms with both adopted and biological children do not feel any closer to the biological child.

3. Some moms favor their adopted child over their biological child.

4. The relationships between biological moms and their kids, and adoptive moms and their kids are no better or worse.

5. The critical factor in determining the quality of a mother-child relationship depends largely on "who that child is as a person."

6. Mothers who have both biological and adopted children have what authors of study call a *psychological edge* over adoptive moms and are able to combat feelings of insecurity and confidence because they could experience that they are just as real a mother to all of their children.

Building Blocks

A **psychological edge** means to have a greater ability to think logically and systematically than another individual or individuals.

Other research that adds to a fuller picture of adoption tells us that:

1. Adoptive moms worry about whether attachment and love for them could be as strong as that which daughters have for their biological mothers, and whether they will be less attached to a child to which they have not given birth.

2. Adopted daughters may have feelings of loss or abandonment, not having been raised by a biological mother.

3. Many adopted daughters voice the need to search out their biological moms and discover their hereditary background.

Perceptions and Hindsight: An Adopted Daughter Speaks

Read between the lines. It should be clear that Elizabeth's youthful perceptions, the normal feelings of mother-daughter conflict, and a conservative mom who was unable to express adequate empathy added up to a troubled adoption.

Elizabeth said, "I always knew I was adopted. We talked about it. My older brother was adopted. My younger brother was my parents' biological child. I never really felt I belonged. I always felt out of place. It wasn't a question of love and respect. I didn't feel loved, although I don't doubt my mother loved me. I just never really connected with her. I think we both knew it. I think that's the saddest part."

"We were totally different. I have blue eyes, blonde hair, and am 5'9". My adopted mom is 4'11" and has dark eyes and hair. I am very passionate and emotional. My mother seemed to be very factual and not very emotional. I never saw her cry. She was very strict and religious. She didn't like it if I wore makeup and she told me that I dressed like a floozy. As far as I am concerned it was a total mismatch.

"There was an incident in kindergarten when all the kids were supposed to bring eggs to paint. My mom didn't make one for me and couldn't understand why I was so angry that I destroyed everyone else's. It never got resolved. My mom considered it going off the deep end and said I made a mountain out of a molehill. I always felt like I was doing something wrong. There was a lot of tension in the family that centered around me. She would get mad and say mean things and I would get angry and withdraw. We blamed each other.

"I always thought about my birth mother and felt she must love me. I carried her love around with me. At 17 I ran away. I saw my mother when I was 23, but I haven't seen her in years. I am 30 now.

"I never looked at the adoption from her side and the loss she must have felt not being able to have kids. I would like to have a relationship with my adopted mom now. I need to have courage to do that. I want my adopted mom to approve of me, but I'm afraid she won't."

Building Blocks

Diversity, in the loosest sense, is a variety. It is the buzzword of the new millennium and signifies a positive state and an acceptance of individual, cultural, and ethnic differences.

Sounds like the dilemma many young women encounter. In Elizabeth's case, it is compounded by the adoption factor—her perceptions and her mom's.

Adoption: An Adoptive Mother Shares Her Story

Caroline—a successful administrator in an educational setting who was raised at country clubs and boarding schools in an exclusive, conservative environment that allowed for little diversity—broke the mold of her family's tradition. Unmarried and childless with several disappointing love affairs under her belt, she suddenly found herself approaching age 40 and asked herself, "When I am 80 years old and looking back, what will I regret the most?"

Explosives

According to an *ABC World News Sunday Report* in 1997, more children are adopted from China by American parents than any other country. Part of the reason is that Americans who have difficulty adopting in the United States, for example single women, will not encounter the same problems in China.

"Not being somebody's mom," she answered and seriously began to think about adopting. Not long thereafter she adopted a six-month old baby girl from China. "It was a big leap of faith. I jumped off and hoped there would be water in the pool."

Woman to Woman

Caroline, an advocate and activist for the adoption of abandoned Chinese and Russian children, is eager to encourage anyone thinking about adopting. A favorite resource of hers is *Adoptive Families* magazine and can be found online at www.adoptivefam.org.

Caroline explains that she was motivated to specifically adopt a little girl from China by her concern about birth mothers in the United States reclaiming children as well as her love of the Asian culture and her empathy for kids who have truly been abandoned.

"I felt I would have more in common with a girl if I should remain single, and it would be better to have that bond with the same sex child. I was one of four girls and adore my sisters. I didn't select the idea of in vitro fertilization because I thought the issues with adoption would be easier, discussing abandonment rather than an unknown father. I also felt with my parents' conservative traditional and social background, adoption would be more easily accepted by them. I am not driven biologically to have my own child or one that shares my gene pool. I love seeing the way my daughter is different than me."

Woman to Woman

According to a U.S. Census Bureau report entitled "Fertility of American Women," the number of women between ages 40 and 44 who do not have children have doubled since 1976 and now comprise approximately 19 percent of the female population. However, in response to a question addressed to women between the ages of 18 and 34, only 10 percent said they did not want to raise children. One can surmise, therefore, that the other 90 percent are seeking ways to experience the joy of children in their lives.

Caroline has carefully crafted a life that will ensure that her daughter feels as comfortable and accepted as possible. She attends a school with a diverse student body and has five other children from China in her class. Furthermore, Caroline has worked long and hard to convince the Chinese government that she should be allowed to adopt a second daughter from the same city as her first. She anticipates the adoption to take place in the near future of this writing.

"I wrote government officials that what I share with my sisters and they share with theirs is not what I can give my daughters; I can't give them shared genes. But I can give them a shared story.

"What now exhausts, thrills, and scares me is that ability to love and care unconditionally for a child more than anyone else. Without it there would be a big hole in my life. Being a mother is taking your coat off and wrapping it around your chilled daughter only to have her say, 'but now you're cold Mommy.' It's the simplest acts that count."

Lesbian Daughters, Straight Moms

Most of the available information confirms that for a woman who is a lesbian, the most difficult personal task she faces is admitting that she is gay to herself and then her family—particularly her mother. The fear of rejection and loss of approval is uppermost in her mind. Anne F. Caron, Ed.D., and author of *Mothers and Daughters* (Henry Holt and Company, 1998), found that it is a circle of lesbian friends that finally helps a daughter gain the courage she needs to tell her mother.

Knowing when and how to tell their mothers, to lessen her pain and avoid her self-blame, is also of extreme concern to daughters. However, most parents do not think they contributed to their son or daughter's homosexual preferences. A national study reported in *Homosexuality and the Family* in 1989 found that the vast majority—87 percent of parents—thought their gay or lesbian son or daughter was born that way.

Woman to Woman

The number of women who are self-ascribed lesbians is small in comparison to the total number of gay men. A 1992 survey of women, conducted by the University of Chicago, revealed that 0.9 percent of the female population is lesbian and 0.5 percent is bisexual. Other reports say that nearly 4 percent of the female population is lesbian and 10 percent of the male population is gay. More conservative studies put the male gay population at 2 to 6 percent. A 1994 study mentioned in *Newsday* (August 18, 1994) cited figures of gays as 6.2 percent for men and 3.6 percent for women.

Mothers should be aware that most lesbian daughters deeply want to maintain a close tie with them, Carson maintains. Although that bond may have been strained or weakened during previous years under the stress of concealment, your daughter is not deliberately trying to be defiant when she confides her sexual preference to you. On the contrary, Carson sees this as an authentic attempt to reconnect and express her love by being truthful.

Accepting a Daughter's Sexual Preference

Studies by Sarah F. Pearlman, reported in the *Journal of Feminist Family Therapy* in 1992, describe how moms generally react to the disclosure that their daughter is a lesbian. Pearlman discovered that ...

1. Mothers worked through a specific sequence of emotions—infusion, devastation, loss, struggle with coming to terms, increased tolerance, complete acceptance, residual sorrow, and regret.

2. Mothers who adapted most easily to the discovery (the author notes but always with that residual sense of sorrow) were college educated, socially and politically active, working women.

3. The discovery was most difficult and painful for women who had no college experience, were not involved in social or political causes, and did not work. They were deeply wounded by the idea of not having a traditional daughter.

Woman to Woman

There are several well-received books currently on the market that deal with lesbians and their parents that you may want to consider reading. They are *Beyond Acceptance: Parents of Lesbian and Gays Talk About Their Experiences* (St. Martin's Press, 1997), *Straight Parents, Gay Children* (Thunder's Mouth Press, 1999), and *My Child Is Gay* (Allen and Union, 1998).

Coming to Terms, One Mother's Personal Story

"I had been wondering for several years if my daughter might be gay, although she had a boyfriend in high school and college. I never bothered asking her. I didn't want to hear the answer. It's like if you ignore it, it will go away," admitted Margaret, a middle-aged mom and teacher.

Margaret's daughter told her right out of college 11 years ago that she was gay. "When it first hits, its like a big lump in you," Margaret explained. "The first couple of years it took a little time getting used to. I wasn't ashamed but I didn't discuss it with my friends or family, just my husband and a professional. I am a very private person. When I would get down, then I liked reading a book I found by mothers of other lesbians. It helped to know I wasn't alone and to read about their situations."

Both Margaret and her daughter went through a period of adjustment. "The first time she came to visit with a girlfriend she wouldn't stay at our house. She went to a motel down the street. I allowed it the first time but told her after that it was asinine and not to come home if she didn't want to stay with us."

"The hardest part then and now is dealing with the fact that we won't have grandchildren.

"The best advice I can give to other mothers is to be thankful you have a daughter and look at her carefully. So she is gay. What's the difference as long as she is a good and kind person? She is a human being. I had to look at it like this: Everybody has different problems with their kids. Some parents lose a child through death, others have children who are sick or on drugs. Seeing all these kids who commit suicide, many of them because they are gay, is sad. Yes, it is hurtful because she isn't like a traditional daughter, what you would expect. But in this day and age what do you expect, anyway?

"I think talking is the most important thing. Of course, my husband and I told her she could come to us for anything, any time. It isn't the easiest life. I know it took a while for her to find herself. I think some of our problems during her high school years had to do with it, too. I wish I had known then so I could have helped her.

"It sounds funny when she says she is going out on a date. It's just not the norm or what you would expect to come out of her mouth. You get used to it. We are both comfortable when she comes home and brings a new female friend. Her women friends are nice to be around and bright.

"I made up my mind to look at the positives. My daughter is probably more fun to be with now than when she was a teenager. And she appreciates me even more now, too. Some of her gay friends have not been as fortunate in their relationships with their mothers."

Advice for Mothers and Daughters

This is a smidgen of advice to begin the process of reconnecting for all moms and daughters, adopted, lesbian, or challenged. Moms, confront your feelings head on. Get professional help if you need to, but acknowledge what is in your heart and head.

Woman to Woman

A terrific parental resource that provides help dealing with feelings, disseminating useful information, and dispelling falsehoods is the organization, Parents and Friends of Lesbians and Gays. Their Web site is www.pflag.org. Take a look in the privacy of your home if you have been uncomfortable seeking out others for support and understanding.

Then acknowledge it to other vis-à-vis a support group or close friend until you can be completely honest and free with your discovery.

Mothers and daughters, keep communicating. One-on-one conversations, letter writing, exchanging books are all worthwhile avenues to try. Don't try to change one another. You will be more successful working on accepting one another. And, keep loving each other. Life is short. A mother and a daughter are too precious to cast aside.

The Least You Need to Know

➤ Regardless of a mother's handicap, a daughter is likely to be more touched by her mother's ability to demonstrate love, support, and pride for her.

➤ The current climate surrounding adoption is starting to move in a positive direction, but attitudes still prevail that could adversely affect the adoptive mother and even her adopted daughter.

➤ Adoptive mothers need to be particularly empathetic and aware of their adopted daughters deep feelings. Perception may be stronger than love in some cases.

➤ An adoptive mom needs to extend her view and be accepting and appreciative of her daughter's differences to provide a secure and comfortable home.

➤ Some things are more important than others. When it comes to daughters, being a lesbian isn't one of them. Being your child, and loving and respecting her, is.

Part 5

Sharing Revelations, Making Adjustments

The time has come to take our investigation into mother-daughter relationships and personalize it. We will use elements that we have discussed thus far to evaluate whether or not your emotional attachment to your mother or daughter is a healthy one, bring your expectations—met and unmet—out into the open, and uncover those turbulent currents that run beneath the surface of your relationship.

However, before you jump feet first into trying to fix whatever is wrong or improve the slightest flaws, you will be well-served to learn how to talk with your intergenerational partner. Ample tips, explanations, and cautionary warnings are provided for you in Chapter 20, "It's Time to Learn How to Talk."

Once you have learned your lessons well, you will be ready to make repairs and improvements in your mother-daughter relationship. Specific thoughts on how to await your inspection in Chapter 21, "Improve and Repair Exercises for Mothers and Daughters." Specific and succinct directions for adopting a better mind set, meeting the prerequisites of a mature relationship, and climbing out from under the gloom of the blame-game will move you closer to becoming a harmonious, understanding, and fun mother-daughter duo.

Finally, if you have problems that are beyond the scope of this book, you will be given instructions how to select a therapist in Chapter 22, "Calling the Doctor."

Chapter 19

Assessing Your Mother-Daughter Relationship

In This Chapter

➤ Laying all cards on the table and out in the open

➤ Mothers and daughters, connected and disconnected

➤ Deciding if you make a healthy pair

➤ Knowing the signs of individual ill-health

➤ Facing turbulent undercurrents

➤ Shining the light on intrusive mothers

In order to complete all of the questions you will personally be asked in this chapter, you need to rely on information and explanations that have preceded these pages. To get the most out of this examination of your mother-daughter relationship, do not hesitate to refer to earlier passages to gain clarity of issues.

This chapter is critical in illuminating specific interaction between pairs of mothers and daughters. The results of this probing will be applied to the next chapter's discussion in which we address how to improve feelings, responses, and one's overall mother-daughter relationship. That will set us firmly on the course of reaching this book's goal—understanding, celebrating, and enjoying this special bond and relationship that is for mothers and daughters only.

If you are sincere in wanting the best from your mom, your daughter, or yourself, proceed thoughtfully.

Pearls of Wisdom

"... My mother talks about how she and I are more like sisters than mother and daughter .... I feel strong when she says those things, like I am much older and wiser than I really am. It's just that the strength doesn't allow for weakness. Being my mother's sister doesn't allow me to be her daughter."

—Writer Rebecca Walker, born in 1969, daughter of Alice Walker, author of *The Color Purple*

Understanding the Levels of Emotional Attachment in a Mother–Daughter Relationship

There are several ways to go about measuring the state of the emotional attachment or closeness in a mother-daughter relationship. Research by Alexis J. Walker found among pairs of mothers and daughters, those that exhibited the highest level of attachment toward one another also had the highest level of reciprocal interactions and mutual assistance.

Those who appeared to have the lowest level of attachment were found among dependent daughters in younger pairs of mothers and daughters. Walker cites two facts that she feels contribute to this:

1. The mother-daughter relationship is not usually highly reciprocal at this point in time.
2. A daughter's dependency threatens her realization of those important feelings of autonomy.

One can safely assume, therefore, from this and previous information, that feelings of closeness should most easily be realized by mothers and daughters who are intergenerational equals.

Pearls of Wisdom

There is something to be learned in this statement made by an 80–year-old mother. "The connection I feel with each of my three daughters is dependent upon their personality, how busy they are, whether or not they are sensitive to my feelings, and how trite they consider my interests to be."

The Health of Your Mother–Daughter Connection

Before we begin, remember that the mother-daughter relationship is not a static one. The health of your attachment fluctuates over time and with circumstances. However, it is safe to say that you can discern an overall pattern that distinguishes the vast majority of your interactions and enables you to more closely align yourself with one of the patterns below.

Marilyn Irwin Boynton and Mary Dell, authors of *Goodbye to Mother Hello Woman* (New Harbinger Publication, Inc., 1995), have divided mother and daughter connections into five categories that form a continuum of behaviors—not iron clad boxes. An adapted version of their classifications of "connections" appears in the diagram.

Note that those individuals who replace the word "attachment" with "connection" are making a very important distinction. Attachment infers dependency. Connection allows more for a position of self in a relationship. It implies a mutual understanding and acceptance of differences and preferences, according to Rose R. Oliver, Ph.D., professor of psychology and women and gender studies at Amherst College.

Building Blocks

Individuation is taking full responsibility for one's adult self and actions; it means shifting from being mothered to mothering one's self.

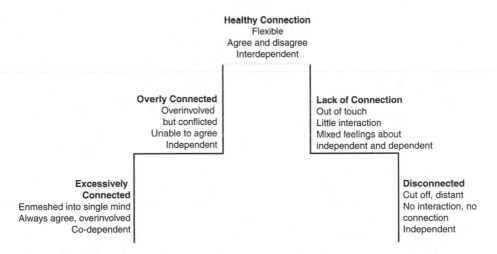

Healthy Connection
Flexible
Agree and disagree
Interdependent

Overly Connected
Overinvolved
but conflicted
Unable to agree
Independent

Lack of Connection
Out of touch
Little interaction
Mixed feelings about
independent and dependent

Excessively Connected
Enmeshed into single mind
Always agree, overinvolved
Co-dependent

Disconnected
Cut off, distant
No interaction, no
connection
Independent

This figure is an adapted and amended version of five relationship styles presented by Marilyn Boynton and Mary Dell in their book Goodbye Mother Hello Woman. *The type of connection is what we are after.*

Individual Health

We know in romantic love relationships that the durability, health, and satisfaction of a couple depend greatly on their individual emotional health. The same is true for mothers and daughters. Consequently, it is valid and important to measure attitudes with emotional overtones that might prevent or enhance satisfying interaction between mother and daughters and a daughter's achieving *individuation*. Here's a short quiz to help you rate your level and expression of critical factors. Choose the response that best reflects how the characteristic applies to you.

1. *Overly sensitive.*
   Never   Hardly Ever   Sometimes   Always

2. Sometimes lack self-esteem or self-confidence.
   Never   Hardly Ever   Sometimes   Always

3. Blame others for my problems.
   Never   Hardly Ever   Sometimes   Always

4. Concentrate on faults of others.
   Never   Hardly Ever   Sometimes   Always

5. Do not take responsibility for your own action.
   Never   Hardly Ever   Sometimes   Always

6. Lack feelings of strength and independence.
   Never   Hardly Ever   Sometimes   Always

7. Easily feel rejected.
   Never   Hardly Ever   Sometimes   Always

8. Unable to set limits and convey these to others.
   Never   Hardly Ever   Sometimes   Always

9. Resent or envy other people's success.
   Never   Hardly Ever   Sometimes   Always

10. Find yourself in a state of *loneliness*.
    Never   Hardly Ever   Sometimes   Always

Each of the characteristics in this quiz is an important measure of one's individual health. A steady stream of "Always" answers signals serious personal health issues. Trying to maintain a good relationship with a mother or daughter who falls squarely into this category would be exceptionally difficult. On the other hand, unanimous "Never" answers could very well indicate a mother or daughter who is so assertive, strong, and self-assured that her intergenerational partner finds her unapproachable or daunting.

However, because each of these characteristics implies a state of health that affects all relationships, the best position to find oneself in is a strong showing of "Hardly Ever" answers. Deviating from these positions of health is normal now and then.

Sample Health Problems

Forms of resentment, jealousy, and envy can be generated by both mother and daughter. Examples of this health problem were admitted by two different women from separate mother-daughter pairs.

A daughter of an attractive supermom who managed several children, her legal career, and her husband all to perfection, deliberately tried to find fault with her mother. To appease herself in this race (she thought she was losing) and topple the stature of her mother, the daughter throughout her teens and twenties would consciously and frequently tell her mother what was wrong with her. This certainly isn't a sign of health or a way to an endearing relationship.

Similarly, a mother of grown women felt diminished by and resentful of the achievements of her oldest daughter. All was well when Mom was in the lead and felt there were reasons for her daughter to look up to her. Now that her offspring has accomplished things she herself doesn't feel capable of, she is less assured and takes an uncomfortable backseat in the presence of this daughter. She admitted, "I feel inferior and am probably not as secure as she is. If I had my own accomplishment, I might not feel this way."

In both cases, much of the health of the mother-daughter relationship is usurped by a lack of individual health, confidence, and self-esteem.

Building Blocks

An **overly sensitive person** feels rejection and pain that is unwarranted and prolonged because of someone else's actions—perceived slights or critical comments, cancelled dates, and even invitations that never arrive.

Building Blocks

Loneliness is an internal sensation of feeling alone, out-of-place, or disconnected even when in a crowd of people.

Bringing Expectations Out in the Open

In light of all you have read in this book, there should be no doubt in your mind that both mothers and daughters may inadvertently set unrealistic expectations for one another that sabotage the overall satisfaction of their relationship. Your job here is to record and evaluate whether your expectations and those of your intergenerational partner have been met or not, and whether they have positively or negatively impacted your relationship.

Woman to Woman

Penn State University researcher Karen L. Fingerman found that frequency of interaction between mothers and daughters does not appear to be related to relationship quality. Factors that Fingerman and others find more important in a good relationship in adult years are degree of intimacy, support, understanding and acceptance, and the absence of residual conflicts and resentments are likely to offer a greater chance for harmonious, enjoyable relationships between mothers and daughters.

Here is the space for you to list and evaluate your top 10 expectations. However, if you feel other expectations are just as important, keep going. Be cautious, on the other hand, that a lengthy list doesn't indicate that you are placing too many specific conditions and restrictions on either your mother or your daughter. After each expectation, indicate whether it is met, mostly met, or mostly unmet. Also identify the expectation's potential negative impact and potential positive impact.

1. _____

   _____

2. _____

   _____

3. _____

   _____

4. _____

   _____

5. _____

   _____

6. _____

   _____

7. _____

   _____

8. _____

   _____

9. _____

   _____

10. _____

    _____

Keep this list handy. You will need it for the next chapter. In the meantime, how your checkmarks stack up will tell you a lot. If your expectations are being met relatively well, then chances are you are on the road to a pretty decent mother-daughter relationship. Conversely, if your expectations are not usually being met, your mother-daughter relationship is probably in the dumps.

Last, determine the validity of your expectations. If expectations add to the reciprocity of your relationship, increase understanding, promote equality, consider how realistic it is for the other party to fulfill them, and outline how many have the true potential to be met. They can have a positive impact on your relationship. But, if your expectations do not meet these qualifications, most likely they are having a negative impact on your relationship.

Explosives

Ladies—mothers and daughters—if you keep expecting something to happen that past history has proven never will, stop dwelling on it. Engage yourself in positive expectations that have the potential to be met. Otherwise, the finger of blame just might start shifting in your direction.

Expecting Perfection

If you are expecting perfection in your mother or daughter, you won't find it. There is good and bad in everyone. What you must determine is if you are allowing your critical eye to taint the positive potential of your relationship.

Perhaps you are focusing only on or allowing the unlikable qualities in one another to overshadow the likeable. Here is an opportunity to restore some balance. List the five things you like most and the least about your mother or daughter.

Likes	Dislikes
1. _____	1. _____
2. _____	2. _____
3. _____	3. _____
4. _____	4. _____
5. _____	5. _____

After filling in the "dislikes," ask yourself if you are being fair and tolerant. Then apply a little more understanding and acceptance to your perspective.

Exposing Turbulent Undercurrents

The following list identifies some of the troublesome undercurrents to check for. Each has already been thoroughly described to you. Now it's time to see if they are present and affecting your mother-daughter relationship.

Daughters, circle the undercurrents that are present in your relationship. This will clearly demonstrate where the weaknesses lie in your relationship with your mother and what you must work on fixing. Do you still …

➤ Feel a lack of acceptance?

➤ Harbor old grudges?

➤ Remain resentful of your position in the family?

➤ Look for approval?

➤ Resent your mom's mothering style?

➤ Blame Mom for your unmet dreams and goals?

➤ Feel controlled by a maternal introject?

Two other factors that lie beneath the surface and can wreak havoc on mothers and daughters need to be looked at separately. Their undercurrents can cause massive tidal waves of disaffection.

Pearls of Wisdom

"Mothers and daughters and daughters and sisters may recognize each others faults, but they should be big enough to realize that there is more to their relationship and tolerate those faults in order to bring themselves closer together."

—Lillian Kanter, age 80, mother of three adult daughters

Recognizing the Intrusive Mom

Not only can an *intrusive* mom be a pain, but also she breeds ill will and harmful qualities in her daughters. Intrusive moms …

➤ Habitually give unsolicited advice.

➤ Have no respect for their daughter's privacy and barge into her room or go through cabinets in her home.

➤ Show unwanted concern in their daughters' weight and appearance.

➤ Ask too many personal questions.

➤ Try to influence personal decisions.

Pearls of Wisdom

"It's not what I say to my daughter, it's what I don't say that is important."

—Georgia Cheses, mid-50s, mother and grandmother

Start ➔   ➔   ➔   ➔   ➔   ➔   ➔ Finish

Intrusions   Decreased autonomy   Increased reliance and dependence on others

Charting the path of intrusive behavior.

A Bird's-Eye-View of the Cycle of Intrusion

So what's so bad about these moms you may ask? Nothing if you are strong enough not to pay attention or be affected by their intrusiveness. However, that is not always easily accomplished. Rose R. Oliver, Ph.D., professor of psychology and women and gender studies at Amherst College, describes a cycle that is put into motion by the intrusive mom. This diagram shows how it goes.

The Effects of Intrusive Mothering

One only need look at the general traits associated with daughters who have been raised by intrusive mothers to understand the damage. Daughters who have lived with intrusive moms often tend to ...

➤ Regularly defer their own interests to those of others.

➤ Experience feelings of vulnerability.

➤ Rely on the judgments of others rather than their own.

➤ Be uneasy with disagreement.

➤ Require the opinions of others to formulate their own ideas.

➤ Need approval to feel secure.

➤ Feel as if they are being judged.

It is clear from this list of traits how intrusive moms could rob their daughters of autonomy. Without autonomy, the mother-daughter relationship is in trouble.

Building Blocks

To be **intrusive** is to intrude or to force oneself or one's opinion where it is not wanted, invited, or welcome.

Pearls of Wisdom

"Respecting each other's privacy is paramount in a friendship between adults and should be primary in the friendship between mother and daughter."

—Ann F. Caron, Ed.D., *Mothers and Daughters*

Determining If You're Caught in the Wheel of Mother–Blame

Before you answer the question, you might want to go back and review Chapter 12, "The Mother-Daughter Dilemma in a Nutshell." Daughters are the ones who do the blaming and, therefore, the ones who should answer this quiz. However, Mom, if you want to know whether your daughter is perpetuating a cycle of blame, consider if she engages in these actions.

1. Do you harbor ill feelings toward your mom regarding past events?

2. Are you angry that Mom does not anticipate, meet, or understand most of your needs?

3. Are you angered by your mother's inability to protect or lead you out of harms way and unhappiness?

4. If you are dissatisfied with your life, do you think it has a great deal to do with the way you were nurtured?

5. Are you thoroughly frustrated and upset by your mother's inability to understand you, your dreams, and your professional aspirations?

6. Have you allowed all of the above to cast a negative cloud over your relationship with your mother?

7. Because of your perceptions in the questions 1 through 4, do you dislike your mother as a person?

All you are allowed on the negative side of things are two "sometimes" before you fall into the chasm of mother-blame. Answering "no" to all the questions signifies you have not been tainted by the cycle.

Drawing Conclusions

How you have answered and pondered the questions put forth in this chapter should indicate where the trouble zones in your mother-daughter relationship lie. Don't stew in this information. Start reading the next chapter and begin addressing the weaknesses between the two of you. There is plenty of guidance ahead on just how to accomplish this daunting task.

The Least You Need to Know

➤ A mother–daughter relationship in which there is an excessive degree of attachment does not leave room for individuation and harmony.

➤ It takes an emotionally healthy mother and healthy daughter to have a mutually satisfying and fulfilling relationship.

➤ Expectations have both a positive and negative side. Only reasonable expectations fall into the former.

➤ Troublesome undercurrents flow from several different wells—mother's, daughter's, or both. Before you can subdue the troubled water, the source of origin must be revealed.

➤ Moms who are nosey, controlling, or unselfishly caring can have a seriously negative impact on their daughters and their daughters' relationships if their intrusive behavior is excessive and out of control.

Chapter 20

It's Time to Learn How to Talk

> **In This Chapter**
>
> ➤ Arriving at intimate junctures
>
> ➤ Measuring the intelligence of your emotional responses
>
> ➤ Talking in a way that mom or daughter listens
>
> ➤ Knowing when to open or close one's mouth
>
> ➤ Getting through to your teenage daughter

As long as you are talking, why not do it in a way that promotes closeness, love, and caring as well as lessens the chance for creating conflict?

That is precisely what this chapter will help mother and daughter do. Too often issues are blown out of proportion by the innocent choice of wrong words or ill-timed conversations. Among the most important lessons are learning how to listen and respond with empathy, knowing what to say, and learning when not to give that advice that is ready to roll off your tongue.

Who's Talking?

According to a study by Karen Fingerman, assistant professor at Pennsylvania State University, mothers and daughters are in frequent contact. Ninety percent of younger sets of moms and daughters talk on the phone two to three times a week, and 99 percent of older moms and daughters speak to one another on the phone every other week.

At any age, there seems to be pleasure in those phone conversations with Mom. In fact, many women who had already lost their mothers made comments to me similar to the one by Carolyn Weingberg of Oregon. "I miss talking to my mother on the phone the most. She was a dear!" It isn't any wonder then that Carolyn keeps up via the telephone and email with her three married daughters scattered around the world.

What Are They Saying?

The whole point of communicating is to share, discuss, and advise. A large amount of communication with our mothers and daughters deals with daily matters or mundane chitchat. Fingerman's study of 182 mothers and daughters showed that younger moms and their daughters particularly enjoy talking about the latter. Older moms and daughters focus a great deal of their conversation on the daughter's children and other family members. They converse as if they were talking to a friend.

Talking, of course, is also an important way of resolving issues. However, experts advise mothers and daughters not to view communication as a confessional. No matter what the topic, communication is best viewed as an opportunity to develop a real intimacy between mother and daughter.

Woman to Woman

Talking on the phone or conversing face to face aren't the only meaningful ways that mothers and daughters communicate. For others, sharing a book or article and writing letters express thoughts they are unable to verbalize and creates understanding.

Building Blocks

Rapport is a natural harmony between two people that enables them to feel comfort and pleasure in one another's company.

Understanding Intimacy, the Real Bonus of Communication

Whether you are aware of it or not, the conversations with your mom or daughter open a door for the growth and formulation of intimacy—familiarity with another person's private emotional and physical well-being. In my opinion, intimacy is the real cornerstone of *rapport* and closeness between mother and daughter. For that reason it is important for you to understand how this develops; only then can you consciously try to reel in those bonus points.

The first step is to engage in self-disclosure, commonly referred to as revealing one's personal and innermost feelings. Examples are dreams, fears, goals, insecurities, and joys. Sharing these private realms of oneself does make the individual vulnerable to the reactions of someone else. However, Shauna L. Smith, author of

Making Peace with your Adult Daughters (Perseus, 1991), says it makes you more human—and I believe, more approachable! The big qualifier is that self-disclosure has to be a two-way street to lead to real intimacy and understanding.

From this expression of self-disclosure comes intimacy that enhances closeness between mother and daughter. And along with mutual disclosure and understanding there develops a mature level of *interdependence* that is the cornerstone of a healthy relationship.

The following diagram provides you with a visual model of how this marvelous cycle begins, continues, and grows on its own volition once set into motion.

Building Blocks

Interdependence is the mutual intermingling of independence and dependency that affects caring, support, and interaction.

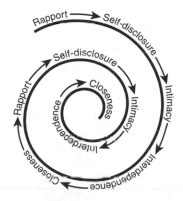

The cycle of rapport and closeness.

Emotional Intelligence and How It Affects Your Mother–Daughter Communication

Emotions play a major role in our lives. They guide us as well as influence our decisions and style of communication. How well one interprets and is appropriately influenced into action by emotions determines their *emotional intelligence*.

This is a quality separate from one's intelligent quotient or IQ. In fact, since the mid-1990s scientists have begun to argue that emotional intelligence, as opposed to one's IQ, is a greater determinant of success because it affects skills like empathy, social responsibility, assertiveness, problem-solving, stress, tolerance, optimism, persistence, and warmth.

It is believed that emotional intelligence is partly shaped by genetics. Nonetheless, there are experts who think that an individual can be taught to understand feelings and their effect on themselves and others.

How your mother or daughter reacts or speaks to you reveals, to a large extent, her level of empathy—the ability to be aware of other's feelings and take those into account. Whether or not she is cognizant of the impact of her emotional message and is concerned with this is a key to the success of your conversations, discussions, or arguments. Recognizing the underlying emotions of how a message is delivered and received directly influences whether a response will be positive or negative.

Building Blocks

Emotional intelligence is a collection of mental abilities that help an individual recognize and understand their own feelings or emotions, those of others, and then act or react appropriately. This term was coined by Dr. John Mayer, Ph.D., and Dr. Peter Salovey, Ph.D., in 1989 and popularized by the 1995 release of *Emotional Intelligence: Why It Can Matter More Than IQ* by Daniel Goleman (Bantam Books, 1997).

Explosives

A mother's stage of life has a great deal to do with how well she listens. During periods when she is distracted or stressed and is perhaps a poor listener, daughters tend to feel unloved, rejected, and unworthy.

Unfortunately if either mother or daughter has a flawed level of emotional intelligence and they are unwilling or unable to empathize with one another, their communication can be seriously marred.

Mastering the Art of Verbal Communication

How you communicate affects all of your relationships. A good conversationalist needs to know when to talk, when to listen, how to talk, what to say, and what not to say. It is helpful in this endeavor to get the fundamentals down first. Keep these points in mind the next time you sit down for a chat:

➤ Respect the other person's right to privacy and their boundaries.

➤ Make a concerted, conscious effort to listen objectively and understand thoroughly.

➤ Try to partake in an equal exchange; a conversation is a dialogue not a monologue.

➤ Do not interrupt and allow the other person to finish speaking.

➤ Do not use words that are accusatory, threatening, demanding, critical, or full of blame.

➤ Be aware of how your mother or daughter listens and adjust your style.

➤ Use humor to break the tension.

➤ Control you facial expressions.

➤ Listen to yourself; you don't want to sound intrusive.

➤ Don't lecture or chastise.

➤ Sound positive.

➤ Determine the best time and place to talk; consider a relaxed atmosphere like a special lunch, outing, walk, or drive in the car.

➤ Remember that it's not necessary to draw everything out into a full-blown discussion; unless you sort out the inconsequential issues, you may dilute the importance of the big ones.

How to Refine Your Listening Skills

You can't partake in the art of conversing unless you also know how to listen. So, let's make sure that we all know what it means to be a good listener. A good listener …

➤ Walks away with new information.

➤ Doesn't do all of the talking.

➤ Speaks when the other person stops talking.

➤ Asks questions pertinent to the other person's remarks.

Woman to Woman

Robert Provine, professor of neurobiology and psychology at the University of Maryland says that laughter is really about communicating. "Laughter is part of the universal human vocabulary …." A laugh may help smooth things out in a conversation as a punctuation or cover an awkward moment. Furthermore, women tend to laugh more with women and men more with men.

Pearls of Wisdom

"My relationship with both my daughters is harmonious. The older one is easier as we have developed a short hand to keep things in perspective. The younger is seeking her independence so I have to be careful to listen and suggest."

—Susan Neumer, Chicago, daughters aged 30 and 24

➤ Opens her mind.

➤ Puts herself in the other person's shoes.

➤ Doesn't listen defensively.

➤ Demonstrates to the speaker she has heard what has been said.

➤ Discerns from the content of the conversation, their mother's or daughter's *emotional intent*.

Building Blocks

Emotional intent is the unspoken emotion behind spoken words. Because they are unvoiced, it is easy to misread them. For example, Mom may ask whether a daughter is happy—not to imply that she is incompetent in her marriage—but to assuage her worry over her daughter's well-being. The same is true for a mother of a teenage daughter who questions her about the guy who is taking her out Saturday night. She may not be attacking her daughter's judgment, just easing her own fears.

The Special Art of Talking to Teenagers

The following suggestions are from the book, *"I'm not mad, I just hate you!"* They were written expressly with teenagers in mind. The authors call upon moms to engage in responsible communication with their adolescent daughters by adhering to these eight points before they start talking:

1. **"Check Your Emotional Temperature."** Emotions can get in the way of good communication.

2. **"If Necessary, Cool Down."** Use whatever works to defuse your raging anger or emotions.

3. **"Think Through Your Goal."** Determine what you want to accomplish by bringing up a topic.

4. **"Choose a Good Time."** Timing in communication is everything. Consider when your teenager will be most receptive to what you have to say.

5. **"Talk Directly to Her."** That means within the same breathing space.

6. **"Boost Your Chance of Being Heard."** Employ all the polite, sincere charm you would use when speaking to a friend.

7. **"Be Aware of Your Body Language."** Speaking softly but looking like you are ready to pounce on your teenager will subvert your message.

8. **"Keep an Argument from Becoming a Fight."** Do not be drawn into a fight when what you want to have is a discussion.

Do not dismiss these eight points until you have tried them, nor give up in frustration. It will take time to master this technique. You might also find some other pointers in a useful book titled *Keep Talking* (Andrews McMeel Publishers, 1999) by family therapist Lynda Madison. You may want to try a few of Madison's suggestions in conjunction with the eight points above.

Talking Your Way Through Tenuous Times

Communication skills can get mother and daughter through tenuous times if they are creative in their thinking. For instance, if you keep annoying your mother or daughter by saying something the same old way and keep getting the same old response, ask her how you might express things better. You might also want to ask her what you say that pleases her the most. Be sure to interject a few of these into your conversations.

Once you have the vocabulary and the skills of communicating down, you will be able to …

➤ Express your hopes for your relationship.

➤ Jointly develop goals for your relationship.

➤ Identify what is important to both of you.

➤ Discuss your met and unmet expectations.

➤ Find solutions to conflicts by discovering and responding to common ground.

Pearls of Wisdom

"We always talk things out when things aren't going well. After a really bad argument, I always make her come into my bed at night before she goes to sleep. We never go to bed mad at each other."

—Mary Ellen Cohen, 47, daughter age 18, Ft. Lauderdale, Florida

Explosives

Here is a word of warning from a mother of four children. She advises not to talk in a way that will cause divisiveness among family members. This can interrupt the harmony and goodwill among the entire family unit. She is particularly careful not to discuss her beefs about one daughter with another, nor will she allow herself to carry tales from one to the other.

Woman to Woman

Studies show that psychologically healthy families are open and forthright with one another and aren't prone to keeping family secrets, holding back feelings, or failing to discuss and disclose troubling or important events. This includes the details of why parents divorced, a sibling's drug problem, or a grandparent's serious illness.

Pearls of Wisdom

"I never discuss marital issues or fights with my mother, I try to do what she thinks is right, make her think that she is right, and compliment her."

—Jill, Buenos Aires, mother of two sons, in her mid-30s

Appropriately, the latter technique is part of the "Friendship Model for Resolving Conflicts" described by Shauna L. Smith, author of *Making Peace with Your Adult Children* (HarperPerennial, 1993). This model is based upon finding the common ground between mother and daughter. The idea is great, but without good communication skills that common ground can stay buried a long time.

Playing the Avoidance Game Two Can Play

There are subjects wise mothers and daughters avoid discussing with one another. At times, that is prudent. On the flip side, a steady practice of avoidance allows unexpressed troublesome issues that ought to be aired to fester. Failing to discuss personal thoughts and feelings prevents the growth of true intimacy.

When Mom Cannot Tell You How She Feels

It is particularly difficult for moms, age 60 and over, to discuss their feelings, says, author Ann F. Caron. This "silent generation" she notes is different than the younger generation that has been taught to more readily express and share their inner feelings.

Indeed, an 80-year-old mom told me, "I don't feel I can talk as openly to my daughters as I would like to because I am afraid it will start an argument." Yet this same mother added, "I think we would have a healthier relationship if we did communicate but it takes two people. I could never start it."

What she would like to tell her daughters is that she doesn't feel as independent as they think she is and that there are many times she would like their assistance. "They accept my independence too much," lamented this unhappy mother.

When Talking Makes Up for Lost Time

Georgia is a 50-something mom of a 34-year-old daughter who admitted that she was too young and immature when motherhood was thrust upon her. From age four on, her daughter lived with her father. "It was not a time in my life I am really proud of," Georgia revealed.

Although Georgia describes her earlier relationship with her daughter as close, they never really spoke intimately with one another. Their conversations were more about "the nuts and bolts of daily life" as opposed to their personal lives. "There was never really an opportunity for me to share certain parts of my life with her."

However, finding herself alone after the death of her second husband to whom she was married for 19 years changed much of that. "I am more needy and discuss many things with my daughter that before I would have discussed with my husband. I think she has reacted to this intimacy in a way that she feels she has gotten her mom back. There is an open invitation to be a part of each other's lives, and a road has opened to share feelings that we didn't before."

> "My daughter was confused over her second pregnancy (she already had a 14-year-old daughter and had been married to her second husband for 7 years). We discussed what it would mean to have a baby now. Still, I don't think we share enough. After talking to you I think I will ask her how she sees herself in 5 years, 10 years, and ask her what her future hopes and dreams are and share mine with her.

> "I don't think I ever gave a thought to the idea that my mother had hopes and dreams. I loved her dearly but we did not have much common ground. I can't remember sharing any intimate moments with her."

Fortunately Georgia's willingness to open up has ensured that the future holds a different story for her and her daughter.

Giving and Getting Advice

A number of studies indicate that throughout their lives daughters seek a mother's advice; however, giving that advice is tricky! Frequently, it sounds like these women are calling to solicit a mother's advice when what they really want is for Mom to be is an "innocent listener" or "sounding board."

"It took a long time before I caught on, gave my opinion and had it trounced on," admitted one mom. "My daughter wasn't really calling for my opinion. She just called to hear herself talk."

Pearls of Wisdom

"One thing many mothers like to give freely is advice, and those mothers with Controlling Styles give it especially freely."

—Nancy Cocola and Arlene Matthews, *How to Manage Your Mother*

Mom, It's None of Your Business

Considering the findings by Dr. Fingerman, moms best opt for caution when wanting to hand out unsolicited advice! "Daughters seem to view their spouses and offspring as constituting a family unit unto itself, distinct from their relationships with their mothers," Fingerman said.

However, mothers don't perceive it the same way and see themselves as a more integral part of their daughter's family life. "As a result, mothers may feel free to offer advice or direct affairs in their daughters' lives in a manner that daughters experience as intrusion."

When It's Safe for Advice Givers

Most moms find it much safer to give advice when …

➤ They are specifically asked for it.

➤ There is a matter that is of great importance.

➤ They see consequences their daughters may not be aware of.

➤ They ask their daughters if they can give their opinions.

➤ They use phrases that ask questions like, "Have you considered this?" instead of giving advice that is opinionated and dogmatic.

Paying attention to how advice might be given could ensure a smoother ride for mothers and daughters. More suggestions to reach this goal follow in the next chapter.

The Least You Need to Know

➤ How you say something may be more important than what you say.

➤ Chances are you will miss an important message and fail to give an appropriate response if you don't use emotional intelligence to interpret the words of your mother or daughter.

➤ Teen talk requires forethought and readiness before words are uttered.

➤ Every mom needs a reality check of where she fits into her daughters life and what advice it is proper to give.

Chapter 21

Improve and Repair Exercises for Mothers and Daughters

In This Chapter

➤ Determining whose job it is to make relationship repairs—mother or daughter

➤ Building a new belief system

➤ Getting rid of the blame factor

➤ Taking steps toward a mature relationship

➤ Putting all cards out on the table

➤ Resolving divisive issues together

Hopefully your mother-daughter relationship isn't in shambles, or even terribly stressed for that matter. However, whether you are in need of major repairs or small fixes to make things better, renew your love, or promote greater understanding, you have come to the right chapter. In long-term relationships, there is the tendency to get lazy, gloss over trouble spots, and coast. That isn't permitted here.

In this chapter, we will deal with the data you collected in Chapter 19, "Assessing Your Mother-Daughter Relationship," that should have clearly assessed your relationship, delineated its weaknesses, and heralded its strengths. For those areas that need reworking, renewal, or repair, there are plenty of suggestions and exercises for you and your mother to improve on together. Now is the time to begin dealing with and changing what stands in the way of a more satisfying, loving mother-daughter relationship.

Making Repairs and Improvements Takes Two

There are those therapists who think that mothers must take the initiative to set repair in motion. For instance, Dr. Charney Herst says, "The relationship you have with your daughters is one you create, by who you are and what you want from each other. You have to negotiate, confront, mediate, and since a mother is older and often wiser, if she wants change, she should initiate the process."

In my opinion, Herst is only half right when talking about the adult mother-daughter relationship. Some daughters may not be older, but that doesn't preclude them from being wiser. Secondly, whoever is the big enough person to make the first step, I applaud her.

However, what is equally important is that once either mother or daughter expresses a desire to improve upon their relationship, both mother and daughter need to take an active, committed role if any improvements or changes are to take hold.

> **Pearls of Wisdom**
>
> "In managing our mother today, past hurts should be used as warning lights for areas of our relationship to be changed, rather than emotional triggers to condemn us to suffering the same fate over and over again."
>
> —Alyce Faye Cleese, *How to Manage Your Mother*

Don't Block the Attempt for Repairs

A daughter may block a mom's attempt to make repairs or improve their relationship if she …

➤ Is steeped in denial and does not allow herself to confront the pain and anger of her relationship.

➤ Refuses to stop playing the blame game.

➤ Wishes to make her mother feel guilty.

➤ Tries to fan the flames of *conflict*.

➤ Perceives attacks that aren't real.

No mom is a match for a daughter who is waving these flags.

> **Pearls of Wisdom**
>
> "'I did my best,' I was finally able to say, 'and still I hurt you. I am sorry.' My daughter is compassionate and forgiving. More than that she is understanding. We sit, sipping out tea, and talk frankly about 'the old days' of her growing up and my inadequate, perhaps, but still fierce-hearted mothering."
>
> —Writer Alice Walker, *Essence Magazine*, 1995

No One Should Beg for Forgiveness

Forgiveness has an element of a catch-22. Mothers and daughters feel they are magnanimous in granting forgiveness, and the recipient is gratified to receive a pardon. On the other hand, the underlying fundamental concept of forgiveness is hazardous to your relationship.

Some psychologists assert that forgiveness is much more about guilt and blame. Dwelling on either won't get you anywhere. Asking for forgiveness and working hard to obtain it isn't taking the relationship forward. Rather it signifies focusing on something that was already done and cannot be taken back. A better option would be to look ahead and employ the understanding and judgment that will prevent a reoccurrence of offenses.

Devising a New Belief System

If your old way of thinking hasn't produced the most harmonious, loving feelings between mother and daughter that you can each summons, it is time to toss out that old belief system full of misconceptions, misunderstandings, and leftover ill feelings, and come up with a new one. However, the new belief system must be founded on pertinent, reliable facts that will affect positive change in your mother-daughter relationship. I have provided 10 worthy points that should formulate for you a sound basis for a new and improved *belief system:*

1. Any emotional stress caused by your mother-daughter relationship to either party, no matter how slight, is worth fixing!

2. An older mother who is tired of mothering has the right to retire, but not withdraw, from the job.

3. There is a difference between trying to understand a mother or daughter's behavior and trying to sanction it.

4. Confrontation does not have to be combative. It's all in the way you handle it.

5. It can be beneficial to discuss the issues that drive a wedge between mothers and daughters.

6. In a healthy mother-daughter relationship, each adult takes responsibility for her own actions and for the relationship. There is no passing the buck.

Building Blocks

It is time to hand over a more sophisticated definition of conflict as it occurs between mothers and daughters. **Conflict** is the eruption of mental tension born out of desires, needs, and forces that are in opposition among two or more individuals.

Building Blocks

A **belief system** is composed of fundamental ideas that affect how an individual looks at and evaluates a set of circumstances, experiences, or individuals. Indeed it colors the overall way in which one looks at and approaches the world around them.

7. Mothers and daughters cannot solve each other's problems. They can support, guide, and assist. However, each party owns her own problems.

8. Intimacy is achieved through self-disclosure, love, and mutual dependency; it is not determined by dependency.

9. Not all mothers or daughters have the capacity to change. In this instance, someone is going to have to do more than her share of accepting.

10. Mothers and daughters are human beings who are fallible and make mistakes.

Building Blocks

Egocentric individuals focus on themselves, their own interests, and how everything relates specifically to them. Their focal point is so preoccupied with self that it may exclude anyone else's interests, points of view, or feelings.

Finding the Right Tools to Make Improvements and Repairs

The most basic tool in your chest is also one that is imperative to improving, reviewing, and resolving any mother-daughter issue. It is called objective thinking. Objective thinking must incorporate having a neutral mindset, stepping back, relying on the facts, and divorcing reason from emotion.

Objectivity promotes clarity. It encourages thinking that will benefit mother-daughter relationships, and will help those who are seeking repairs and improvements.

Subjectivity, Not a Worthy Tool

The opposite of objectivity is subjectivity. It does not benefit your pursuit of making improvements and repairs. An excessive subjective mindset indicates an *egocentric individual* or mom. Subjective thinking relies on personal emotions, preconceived notions, one point of view, personal interests, a lack of empathy, narrow vision, and egocentric observations.

If you are unable to leave subjectivity behind and to achieve objectivity on your own or discern fact from fiction, it may be time to make an appointment with someone who can be an impartial participant in the process. (For those who are considering enlisting face-to-face and personalized counseling, refer to Chapter 22, "Calling the Doctor.")

Necessary Add-Ons to Your Normal Behavior

Before you can hope to improve your mother-daughter relationship, there are significant attitudes that need to be put into play on a regular and ongoing basis. Put a check mark by the ones you need to improve upon:

____ Showing tolerance

____ Being open as opposed to secretive

____ Practicing humility

____ Abandoning a defensive mindset

____ Employing a giving mode

Woman to Woman

It has been called to my attention and now to yours that a pleasing mode is different from a giving mode. It is thought that one does things to please others in order to gain approval and obtain an emotional repayment. Adopting a giving mode, however, implies action out of one's own need and for one's own pleasure without needing or expecting anything in return. That is an important distinction to remember.

Studying the Anatomy of an Argument

You may have just stormed out of your daughter's house or hung up the phone furious at your mother. Yet you can't really figure out why the disagreement or conversation you were having resulted in a *reactive problem* or escalated into a major conflict.

Consequently, I think it is worthwhile to stop and take a look at how arguments arise. The model I like is described by Andrew Christensen, Ph.D., and Neil J. Jacobson, Ph.D., authors of *Reconcilable Differences* (Guildford Press, 2000). Although this model was designed to explain conflicts in love relationships it easily makes the transition into mother-daughter conflicts as well.

Christensen and Jacobson's anatomy of an argument involves three stages. A modified presentation of their anatomy is provided in the illustration.

Building Blocks

A **reactive problem** is one that arises as a result of another individual's actions or behavior to the initial or first problem that arose.

Stage 1	Stage 2	Stage 3
An Initial Provocative	**Unsuccessful Coping**	**Reactive Problem**
Actions or inactions that trigger significant differences, vulnerabilities, and emotional upset	Blame, accusation, coercion, anger, overreaction, minimizing, and avoidance	Escalation that creates a new or intensified problem and rigid and extreme positions that can result in alienation or disconnection

How a problem can escalate into alienation or disconnection.

How to Prevent Escalation

Along with all of the information given to you beforehand that described problems that may nudge their way into the mother-daughter relationships, you are armed with the knowledge of how conflicts escalate. This plethora of information would be useless unless you were committed to seeing the necessity to circumvent this natural progression of initial problems into bigger and more explosive reactive ones.

Ways to accomplish just that include ...

➤ Dropping emotions that ignite further conflict.

➤ Finding an option that empowers you to influence a more positive outcome.

➤ Staying calm and not exploding or allowing anger to overtake you.

➤ Making your feelings known in a constructive fashion.

➤ Taking time out and postponing your reaction.

➤ Making invitations for resolution without putting all the blame on your mother or daughter.

Pearls of Wisdom

"Give as much as you expect to receive back and be as considerate of your mother as she is to you."

—Roberta Davis, mother and grandmother

How to Extend Verbal Invitations for Resolutions

Verbal initiations require your thoughtful consideration. They can initiate success or failure in your attempts to communicate. Examples of these types of statements are ...

"I am feeling angry by what was said. I would like to cool off and then talk about it later."

"This is the way I just interpreted what you said. Perhaps you don't realize how that sounds to me or how it makes me feel."

"I think you have overstepped your bounds. I am not comfortable discussing that with you.

I appreciate your concern. Perhaps there is another way I can make you feel more at ease with my decision."

"I think we both have to realize that each of us has to make some concessions here."

"I appreciate your opinion. I will consider it. Does that make you feel better?"

These are noncombative statements that demonstrate you have boundaries you expect your intergenerational partner to respect. At the same time, you are expressing your opinion without being so presumptuous as to express your partner's. These sentences invite your mother or daughter to make other statements to clarify her points and to understand that her words have great affect on you.

Building Blocks

Resolution means coming to terms with a situation, making changes, solving a problem, finding a solution, and determining future action.

How to Arrive at a Resolution

The best road to finding a *resolution* to a problem, small or large, is to …

➤ Step back for an objective view.

➤ Be specific in your own mind about what will improve the situation.

➤ Don't be stubborn and resist change.

➤ Prioritize what bothers you the most, don't attempt to work on everything at once.

➤ Acknowledge and praise one another's attempts to resolve problems.

➤ Use diplomacy.

➤ Address conflicts and don't allow them to fester into major battles.

➤ Stop fearing loss of love and begin believing in the power of it.

Pearls of Wisdom

"Blame is a trap: As long as we can pin the rap of our misery on Mom, we keep her strong, and we keep ourselves weak."

—Victoria Secunda, *When You and Your Mother Can't Be Friends* (Dell, 1991)

Getting out from Under the Gloom of Blame

Mother-blame can be harmful and crippling, particularly the kind that blames Mother for the things we don't like in ourselves that remind us of her. Paula J. Caplan, Ph.D., said, "Mother-blame limits your freedom: You can't be an adult who freely considers all of life's possibilities. You restrict yourself to certain activities, interest, and friends to prove how different from Mother you are." (In the event you need a refresher course or want to refer to your scores on two earlier mother-blame quizzes, turn back to Chapters 12, 15, and 19.)

Pearls of Wisdom

"It is helpful to realize that be-cause children do not usually fully appreciate adult sacrifice on their behalf, it is not surprising that some mothers are tempted to complain about the struggles they are having in order to at-tract some attention, approval, and support."

—Alyce Cleese, *How to Manage Your Mother*

It is a wise mother or daughter that can move beyond all forms of blame and say, "I'm sorry if I've hurt you, but let's move on from here."

They know that blame …

➤ Keeps you a victim.

➤ Doesn't allow you to move forward toward something better.

➤ Keeps you stuck in a dead end.

➤ Usurps the power of the individual.

➤ Gives someone else the right to decide your happiness.

All of the ill effects of blame ought to point out how important it is to rid ourselves of it. The only way to fully achieve this is to grow up, take responsibility for ourselves, give up the subordinate role as children, and stop blaming each other for failing to fulfill all of our expectations. I can't help you do the first three things in this last list. I can, however, help guide you to have a fruitful discussion on expectations that will help eradicate the fourth point.

The Matter of Expectations

You already have a list of expectations that are either met, mostly met, or mostly unmet, and that have either a negative or positive potential to affect your relation-ship. Now is the time to refer to it, re-evaluate it, and have a heart-to-heart talk with your mother or daughter.

It isn't fair to assume that your mom or daughter knows what your expectations are or that they are being stubborn about meeting them. And, it isn't right not to tell them how great you think they are for fulfilling the legitimate expectations you have of them. Furthermore, it is unfair to think that a mother can raise a child without ex-pectations, dreams, wishes, or thoughts about her well-being. However, it is when those expectations intrude into a daughter's life and become burdensome that they become problematic and need to be addressed.

So here are my suggestions:

1. Get two pads of paper and two pencils. Sit down with your intergenerational partner and explain that you have a serious game to play that has the potential to make your relationship even better. Both of you write out five expectations the other fulfills and five that you don't.

2. Do not use your original list for this exercise. It is important for you to each be working on this at the same time. Be sure to emphasize the good along with the bad, be open-minded, and listen carefully.

3. Before you begin your discussion, consider sharing significant parts of Chapter 15, "Daughters, Inside and Out," with your partner. Knowing where the idea came from and having an objective bystander explain what constitutes legitimate or unfair expectations should prevent defensive posturing.

4. Have an honest and open discussion, defend your position, and ask for change.

5. Work out a list of expectations that each of you wants to try to meet.

6. Set a time to further your discussion so that you will be sure to report whether each of you is living up to your bargain, whether fulfilling each other's expectations felt good, and if not, what difficulty you are having meeting them.

Explosives

Experts claim that most mothers expect their adult daughters to share their values and tastes as well as emotional components of their personality.

Questions for Reluctant Participants of the Expectations Exercise

Some expectations, according to Dr. Charney Herst, author of *For Mothers of Difficult Daughters,* that may not be on your list but which need to be addressed are …

1. How you expected your daughter might honor you or give you pleasure.

2. Whether or not you expected your daughter to express criticisms directed at you if you were able to accept them.

Pearls of Wisdom

"Until we eradicate sexism, most women will lack self-confidence, and this makes our mothers' approval especially important to us."

—Paula J. Caplan, Ph.D., *The New Don't Blame Mother*

Learning the Prerequisites for a Mature Relationship

Daughters, this one is for you. Here are your assignments for reaching a mature, intergenerational relationship.

Assignment #1

1. Break the approval cycle.
2. Make sure that your maternal introject is in check.
3. Recognize and accept that you are an adult.
4. Be secure in your personal identity within the mother-daughter relationship.
5. Take responsibility for your behavior.
6. Learn to respect and accept the differences between you and your mother.
7. Be strong enough to set personal boundaries, limits on your mother's intervention, and be able to express your honest opinion.
8. Learn to be a participant in an interdependent relationship.
9. Speak up about what matters to you.

Assignment #2

In order to accomplish many of the above points, you should take time to conduct a self-examination that will differentiate you from your mother. Fill in the blanks.

	Mom's	Yours
Temperament	_____	_____
Work	_____	_____
Dreams	_____	_____
Values	_____	_____
Personal Style	_____	_____
Relationship Style	_____	_____

Feel free to add to this list any qualities you wish to explore. The goal of this exercise is to demonstrate that you are two authentic individuals. Now share the results of your homework with your mother.

Clearing the Air and Starting Over

There is still some work to be done to clear the air and make a fresh or better start. Daughters still need to expose and discuss Mom's emotional hooks or the buttons she pushes that set you off. And moms must be able to come clean with their gripes, hurts, and concerns. There is no blaming allowed here!

When you feel brave and confident enough, equipped with all the aids that have been supplied for you, wander through the pages of this book together to continue your discussions and gain greater understanding.

Together, verbalize the vision that you have for your relationship. Give consideration to the role models, magic moments, and mother-daughter friendships celebrated in Part 6, "A Celebration of Mothers and Daughters."

Woman to Woman

There is sufficient research to suggest that when daughters become moms they forgive their mothers for previous inadequacies.

The Least You Need to Know

➤ Mothers and daughters can repair their relationship and strengthen their bond of love together.

➤ Mothers and daughters must be willing to take the first step to make important adjustments that will serve their relationship better.

➤ Blame, intolerance, and a lack confidence in one's individuality sabotage the chances of building a healthy and satisfying relationship.

➤ A willingness to address, empathize with, and accept your mother's or daughter's point of view is essential.

Chapter 22

Calling the Doctor

In This Chapter

➤ Determining what to do when your mother and husband are at odds

➤ Deciding when snooping is absolutely necessary

➤ Spotting serious problems

➤ Recognizing when it's time to intervene and call in the therapist

---

Don't panic yet. If you have failed at your attempts to make peace with your adult daughter or curb your teenager's unruly behavior, there is more help out there for you.

Before turning to therapy or the when, hows, and whys for intervention, there may still be a few unturned stones. Some of the most common problems not yet touched upon, but mentioned by mothers and daughters, have been singled out for you. They are problematic pebbles that a variety of therapists and researchers have been called upon to address.

On the other hand, if after reviewing the entire chapter these unturned stones turn out to be immovable boulders or you find that your daughter has a severe problem such as an *oppositional defiant disorder,* do not delay in seeking additional help!

"Why Won't My Stepdaughter Let Me Be Her Mother?"

Stepfamily advocate and president of the Stepfamilies Association of America, Dr. Margorie Engel's reply to the question is, "That's not the right expectation to place on either the stepmother or the stepdaughter. If the stepmother's intent is to replace the mother, she is going to create a lot of friction between herself, her stepdaughter, and her husband. The most you should hope for is to become friends. A stepparent functions like an adult friend and confidante."

Building Blocks

Behavior that is uncooperative, defiant, and hostile toward parents or other authority figures to the extent that it interferes with daily functioning is called an **oppositional defiant disorder.**

Woman to Woman

You may also want to check out two good resource books, *The Enlightened Stepmother: Revolutionizing the Role* by Perdita Norwood and Teri Wingender (Avon Books, 1999) and *The Complete Idiot's Guide to Stepparenting* by Ericka Lutz (Alpha Books, 1998).

"No one should expect a perfect relationship," Engel continued in her interview. Reality is somewhere between what you read in the tabloids about the wicked stepmother and what you see in idealized programs like *The Brady Bunch*. She cites the confusion over roles as one of the major issues that face stepfamilies.

Engel does think that stepmothers who don't have biological children of their own deserve a special hug. "They have the hardest job of all, pour in all that attention but will never be their stepdaughter's mother. They have built up this fantasy over the years that simply can't come true."

What you can expect out of step-mothering and how to succeed at it is clearly outlined in Chapter 24, "Role Models for One and All."

"What's a Gal to Do If Her Mother and Husband Don't Get Along?"

Dr. Judy Kuriansky—New York clinical psychologist, media personality, and author of *The Complete Idiot's Guide to a Healthy Relationship* and *The Complete Idiot's Guide to Dating,* gives us her answer to this question. First of all it is really important to recognize that there is nothing wrong with you. Dr. Judy empathizes with you; "It is a sad situation when your mother and your husband do not get along and it is wonderful when they do."

What you may have to do when things are less than perfect is …

➤ Adjust to the fact that you do not have one big happy family and accept that as your reality.

➤ Consider these two people as you do your friends and view them as separate individuals in your life who you can understand but not control.

➤ Spend time with each of them separately.

➤ Talk to each of them and let them know that you are not getting in the middle of them to play peacemaker.

These are the preliminary steps to take. You still have two more important points to consider: what puts them at odds and how you divide yourself between the two of them.

"Why Don't Your Mother and Husband Get Along?"

It could be they simply aren't a natural, good fit or that your husband merely never won your mother's approval or there is a rivalry and competition for your time and affection, Kuriansky explains. On a deeper level, Dr. Judy recognizes that there may be other dynamics at work here. Their relationship could have triggered other family dynamics that revive earlier feelings of being left out or transfer a son's disdain of his mother to his mother-in-law. Whatever you uncover, Kuriansky warns, "Don't try to play the therapist."

Rather, she suggests that a therapist move your mother or husband forward to remove this angry element that affects their relationship.

Woman to Woman

Not even Sigmund Freud, the father of psychoanalysis, got along with his mother-in-law right off the bat. It took three years to arrive at a friendly relationship. Without referring to his own life, Freud later wrote that husbands resent a wife's attachment to her mother. Likewise, he said, mothers are jealous of their daughter's love for someone else.

Pearls of Wisdom

"Everybody has to be understanding in a relationship." (That includes your mother, your husband, and you.)

—Dr. Judy Kuriansky

In the Meantime, Who Should Get Top Billing, Your Mother or Your Spouse?

Dr. Judy answers this part of the question by explaining that both your mother and your husband have equally important places in your life, although generally one's husband has the bigger allegiance. However, there are times and circumstances when one of them has to take center stage—particularly in cases of a mother's illness. It is up to you to evaluate who that will be, and communicate to the other why he or she has to take the backseat at the moment.

Of course it helps if your mother understands that her role and priority in your life is different from your husband's!

"Will a Daughter Necessarily Be Negatively Affected If She Lives with One Parent and Not with Two?"

Psychologist Susan Jeffers, Ph.D., author of numerous books—most recently *I'm Okay … You're a Brat: Freeing Ourselves from the Mad Myths of Parenthood* (Renaissance Book, 1999)—has both professional and firsthand knowledge with which she can answer this question.

When Jeffers' daughter was 10 (28 years ago), she divorced her husband and gave him physical custody of their two children. "My ex was a wonderful nurturer. He loved the details of raising children. He adored it. My attention was always drawn more to the academic world," she explained. "My daughter would never say I 'left' her. That is a strange word. It is a responsibility of a parent to be involved whether they are or aren't living with their children. My relationship improved 100 percent when I wasn't living with mine. Everything was special then; we didn't take anything for granted."

> "I feel sorry for parents today that are destroying their peace of mind and have lost their sense of humor rather than finding ways to fulfill their own lives and at the same time the needs of their children."

Woman to Woman

At age nine, Jenny Ryer, daughter of Dr. Margorie Engel, lived with her dad for four or five years after her parents divorced. During that time she saw her mother everyday. That was the critical point, noted Jenny, now an adult. "It wasn't problematic for our relationship that we didn't live in the same house. I didn't mind and it wasn't awkward when I did eventually go to live with her. We are very close." (A more in-depth look at this story can be found in Chapter 24, "Role Models for One and All.")

Jeffers says unfortunately for women, the issue is fraught with misinformation that contributes to an erroneous public conception, criticism of the mother, a premature determination that a daughter will be maladjusted, and the assumption that a good parental relationship is not likely.

Jeffers and her daughter Leslie, now age 38, disprove the latter point. That is clear by the close relationship the two women have today and have had in the past. Leslie wrote in a letter to her mother, "I am learning so much about myself and love itself through my relationship with you. How lucky I am to have your undying love and support ... I thank you by doing my best to take the risks and chances to become the most I can be, You showed I, too, have this strength and ability."

Facts, Not Fiction About Raising Children

What Jeffers thinks one needs to be aware of when answering how a child will be affected by living with one parent and not two is ...

➤ Giving residential custody to a father does not mean a mother abandoned her children, but simply that the children sleep at his house.

➤ Awarding custody and determining who raises the children should not be based on gender; men can raise children as well as women.

➤ It's insulting to men to say they shouldn't have equality in the home while women are fighting for equality in the workplace.

➤ Giving up residential custody of children at the conclusion of a divorce is becoming more common for women than in the past.

➤ Maintaining the intensity of either relationship is possible, despite which parent a child is living with.

➤ Tying a child's adjustment to one facet of his or her life is impossible because there are so many factors that affect the child's growth.

➤ Planting the victim mentality into the child's mind is more detrimental.

Jeffers is passionate about all of the points above that make a case that primary parenting by Dad should not and need not be viewed negatively. Where she sees a real potential for harm, is in the pervasive "victimhood epidemic."

The Victimhood Epidemic

Single women and their children who have an absentee, uninvolved father have been particularly prone to the victim mentality that has been perpetuated by society and problems in psychology, stressed Dr. Jeffers.

"It is very unfortunate and prevents individuals from taking responsibility for their lives," Jeffers says. "I truly believe that people left as a single parent do the victim routine for themselves and pass that along to their children rather than saying, 'I am strong and you are strong and we are going to have a great life together.'"

"It does not have to be a disaster. Thank God one parent is there. Stuff happens. Kids have to learn that you can handle whatever happens in life. That's the message!"

"My Daughter Is Hanging Out with the Wrong Crowd. What Should I Do?"

Dr. Mary Lou Johns, Ed.D., CPCC, and a retired Chicago, Illinois, middle school principal, is currently a life coach and can be reached at www.blueskycoaching.com. She has several hints to help moms address this problem.

"Changing a friendship group" could signal trouble in a child's life, Johns says. It is an appropriate time for Mom to step in. However, before doing so, she should try to decipher what motivated her daughter's actions. This could be a daunting task if a mother has failed beforehand to get to know her daughter and develop a relationship. "Moms have to be proactive. I have seen mothers who think everything is fine, but her daughter is considered an outcast."

Hopefully Mom's insight will be clear enough to make an initial determination whether …

1. Her daughter is not being accepted by other girls.

2. This is part of her daughter's experimental phase—"Kids are poised to rebel so that they can make choices."

3. Her daughter has crossed the line and this is really a cry for help.

4. She must simply endure and know that this phase with her daughter shall pass.

Once you have made that determination it is time to state your concerns.

Explosives

Dr. Johns has a warning: Mothers have to be careful not to overdo their involvement if the situation isn't serious. Smothering a daughter prevents her from finding and feeling capable of devising her own solution. On the other hand, Mom is underdoing it if she doesn't find out what's going on.

Determining the Best Way to Approach Your Daughter

Moms need to be up front and approach their daughters if they are concerned about a new newfound friendship group or boyfriend. The trick is in how you say it. One slip of the tongue and these kids won't listen to a thing you have to say.

To keep the lines of communication open, follow these tips from the educator:

➤ Listen without being judgmental.

➤ Maybe share something from your past that may be similar.

➤ Get your daughter to talk about her feelings, especially if she feels she doesn't fit in.

➤ Use a neutral subject like a movie to open the door to a conversation, and then, ask her how she thinks the girl in the film felt and ask if that ever happened in her school.

➤ Make her see that she can be understood.

➤ Tell her, "I think you are making the wrong choice here but I will love and support you no matter what."

Building Blocks

Superego is the term given by Sigmund Freud to that part of an individual's mental functions that pertain to the expression of conscience, guilt, and moral attitudes.

If the last point is particularly pertinent to your situation, a lesson in values may be in order.

Taking Time Out for a Lesson in Values

There is nothing wrong with telling a daughter, "We don't do that in our family!" It is, however, a lot easier laying the groundwork for values and a healthy *superego* before she arrives at your doorstep with friends of whom you totally disapprove.

Johns understands that it is difficult for busy, working moms to get into those deep conversations about values. Still, they are essential. Children will generally abide by rules and values that are strongly enforced, especially if they understand the consequences of breaking them.

Pointing out how a new friendship group or boyfriend breaks with your family's values, if this is a rebellious maneuver, won't be nearly as convincing if this is the first time the subject of values has been broached.

"Am I Right or Wrong to Snoop into My Daughter's Private Affairs?"

Pediatric and clinical social worker Margey Cheses, M.S.W. and L.I.S.W., has a definite opinion on the subject. "It is a risk versus boundary issue. It is always best to try and avoid intrusive behavior by keeping the door open so a daughter will share issues with you. That is not always possible to do. If you suspect that it is a question of personal safety, notice risk factors, or observe changes in behavior that appear suspicious then it is time to intervene," Cheses says.

Building Blocks

Excessive behavior that is socially destructive and characterized by fighting, stealing, arson, truancy, and leaving home is called a **conduct disorder.**

Building Blocks

Anorexia nervosa is a potentially life threatening eating disorder characterized by loss of weight that falls 20 percent or more below the normal standards.

"If you are in doubt, put down your defenses as a mother. Observe your daughter and listen carefully. There may have been times you haven't heard things because you didn't want to. Children are a wealth of knowledge if you listen and take in their perspective."

Try Talking Before You Snoop

If you suspect your daughter is taking drugs, engaging in unsafe sex, showing signs of *anorexia nervosa,* or participating in any other dangerous behaviors, come right out and ask. Don't allow a *conduct disorder* to go unchecked. "Asking her won't give her ideas," Cheses stresses. "What it will do is give her permission to talk about it. Talking also helps to build trust in a relationship and should be pursued before you begin to snoop."

Cheses recommends you …

➤ Ask open-ended questions.

➤ Look at your child while she is talking and observe her behavior.

➤ Ideally keep a dialogue open so you won't have to be intrusive.

➤ Believe in your daughter and give her confidence and support.

If you cannot get the information you need by talking and think your daughter is in danger, then Cheses says it may be time to check her private space.

Knowing What to Look For

Common high-risk behaviors that pardon your snooping are eating disorders, substance abuse, dangerous sex practices, and potential suicide. Sometimes the only way to confirm your suspicions is to invade your daughter's privacy.

Eating Disorders

"An eating disorder can be a tremendous risk to your daughter's health," Cheses explains. "The longer it continues the more difficult it is to stop it. You can look for diet pills or bags of vomit in the trash or hidden in her room. It is also a good idea to eat with your child.

Substance Abuse

"If you think your daughter has a drug problem, you don't want to hold back. Look for dilated eyes and notice if she is tending to distance herself from you, emotionally and physically," says Cheses.

Once again if you have to check her dresser drawers, count her cash, or read her locked diary, crossing the boundary line is secondary to the potential risk factors and your daughter's safety.

Dangerous Sexual Practices

A mother needs to know if a daughter is being victimized sexually, practicing unsafe sex at a young age, or making up for some emotional deficiency by reaching out sexually. If the only way you can confirm your hunch that one of the above is happening is by invading her privacy, then you should check her Internet chat rooms and look for secret letters or notes to friends.

The Potential for Suicide

If you suspect that your child is suicidal, do not take any chances. Do not delay gathering all the information you can, talking to them, and initiating *intervention* immediately!

Building Blocks

Intervention is confronting an individual over a situation with the goal of making them face up to what they are doing and seeing how their actions are affecting him or herself and those around him or her. Intervention could entail anything from conversation to physically moving the person to another location.

Learning More Telltale Signs of Significant Trouble

Depression among teenagers and young women is a matter of great concern today. It is something for which moms should be on the lookout. Indications that your daughter is suffering a normal bout of depression that lasts approximately two weeks includes symptoms such as sadness, despair, loss of interest in usual activities, and lethargy.

Major depression is much more serious. A specialist should be consulted if your daughter neglects her daily functions and stays in bed, is prone to crying, or expresses that she feels like a failure or does not like herself.

Agitated depression is at the other end of the spectrum and is characterized by hyperactivity, nonstop activity, sleeplessness, avoidance of others, and the inability to find pleasure. It, too, may necessitate calling the doctor.

Determining What's Next

If you have confirmed that your daughter is having significant and serious problems, it is time to be up front, Cheses says. Intervention is necessary. Start by telling your daughter you snooped. Give her the reasons why. Tell her what you found and then figure out a plan to help her. That could very well include therapy with an objective, trained professional.

How and where to find appropriate therapy is covered at the end of this chapter in the section titled, "Finding the Right Help."

Building Blocks

Narcissism is an extreme interest in and preoccupation with one-self. The narcissistic individual often looks at the world only from their point of view and how external factors reflect upon or affect them.

"Who Else Should Seriously Consider Therapy?"

Victoria Secunda, author of *When You and Your Mother Can't Be Friends,* lists other cases of daughters who most likely are in need of therapy. They include women …

➤ Who were abused, had a childhood that was very hurtful, or have lingering pain over childhood trauma.

➤ Who, as a result of being smothered and spoiled children, turned into extremely *narcissistic* adults ridden with anxiety and indecisive behavior.

➤ Whose mother shows signs of illness, cruel behavior, enjoying their daughter's unhappiness, feigning death, exhibiting controlling behavior, thriving on discord.

➤ Whose mother may have had a personality disorder or a substance abuse problem.

➤ Who were deserted by their mothers.

Pearls of Wisdom

"Therapy offers you a safe place to go through the process of healing and growth." Nonetheless some individuals who need therapy are put off by it because they don't trust a therapist or value self-sufficiency which they think precludes therapy.

—Shauna L. Smith, M.S.W., *Making Peace with Your Adult Children*

Secunda concludes that it is important women who find themselves in one of the above categories realize it is their mother who failed them, rather than look at themselves as the failure.

"How Do I Find the Right Help?"

With so many treatment options and professionals today, selecting the right help can be confusing. Here is a handy guide to help clarify credentials and therapies.

A *clinical social worker* is a social worker trained to apply the theories of social work as a treatment to psychological dysfunction.

A *life coach* helps an individual to formulate and carry out individual goals that will assist them in achieving success in the present and the future; a coach is not trained to act as a therapist.

A *professional counselor* has specialized graduate training in counseling.

A *psychiatrist* is a practitioner who has completed medical school and has received specialized training in psychiatry; uses therapy and medication to treat patients.

Psychoanalysis is a specific technique of analysis that pays particular attention to the interpretation of unconscious thoughts and feelings.

A *psychoanalyst* is an individual with specialized training in psychoanalysis.

A *psychotherapist* engages in treatment of patients by using the principles and goals of psychotherapy.

Psychotherapy is the treatment of emotional problems directed to bring about change in behavior, improve relationships, and reduce stress.

A *social worker* is an individual trained to help clients meet basic human needs and ensure individual well-being.

The Least You Need to Know

➤ Any relationship is the responsibility of two people not just one.

➤ Step-moms, like biological moms, must rely on realistic expectations if they want to create a harmonious mother-daughter relationship.

➤ The best prevention for teenage trouble is a communicative mother-daughter relationship. It is harder to create this after the fact.

➤ Mom, it's okay to snoop whenever there is a real risk of harm to your daughter.

➤ Be judicial in selecting the best type of help or therapy for you or your daughter by knowing all of the options.

Part 6

A Celebration of Mothers and Daughters

Congratulations. You have just arrived at the best part of the book, the part that holds all the rewards and tender stories. I have called this final section of the book a celebration because it focuses on a job well done and the bounties of good mothering and daughtering.

If you have not already arrived at this destination in your personal lives, you will be privy to glimpses of coveted friendships between mothers and daughters, role models who are to be applauded, grandmothers who delight in their granddaughters, and other treasured moments to which you can look forward.

Chapter 23

Alas, Mothers and Daughters as Friends

In This Chapter

➤ Whether it's possible for Mom to be a true friend and still be Mom

➤ How to negotiate a friendship with Mom

➤ Why some mothers and daughters cannot be friends

➤ More than one best friend

➤ A mother-daughter friendship quiz

Arriving at the stage when a true friendship between mother and daughter is finally possible is like finishing a box of Cracker Jack after breaking your tooth on a tough nut and finding the grand prize.

Not all mothers and daughters glide into the friendship phase. It may take a little work and some extra understanding to achieve this valuable reward, but it is worth every bit of added effort.

Is Friendship the Pot of Gold at the End of the Rainbow?

Childhood rebellion has come to an end and the maturity that comes with age takes over. In fact, age is the primary factor that generally signals an end to childhood dependency and produces just the right setting in which mothers and daughters can become true friends.

What you have to look forward to as friends is a relationship in which you ...

➤ Celebrate, enjoy, and respect one another's differences.

➤ Communicate confidently with honesty and understanding.

➤ Can be yourself.

➤ Have someone to laugh and cry with.

➤ Give and get support, companionship, and love.

➤ Have someone in your corner on whom you can rely.

➤ Tolerate less than desirable qualities and revel in the good ones.

➤ Experience a rare, almost indescribable, connection of spirit and soul.

➤ Have a genuine, unselfish concern for one another.

Part and parcel of all of these qualities is an equitable coming together to mother and daughter.

Pearls of Wisdom

"A friend may well be reckoned the masterpiece of nature."

—Ralph Waldo Emerson

Can You Divorce the Mother-Daughter Bit from Your Friendship?

It is the general consensus among professionals that moms will always be moms and daughters will always be daughters; moms will forever lay claim to the parental role and daughters will forever be assigned to the role of child. Despite this caveat, Washington, D.C., psychologist Susan Gordon, Ph.D., agrees with colleagues and researchers who further note: "Mothers and daughters can have a wonderful, loving friendship."

There are, however, differences that distinguish the mother-daughter friendship but do not diminish it in any way. Gordon contends:

Pearls of Wisdom

"There is something basic, primitive, and powerful about mothers and daughters that implies, 'Where else but with a mother can you be safe in this world?' I have worked with a lot of women who need their mothers to still be mothers."

—Susan Gordon, Ph.D., Washington, D.C., psychologist and mother

➤ There may be certain areas for discussion that are off-limits and uncomfortable for mother or daughter to broach about their personal lives that aren't there with a woman friend who is not their mother.

➤ There is a part of daughters that need to know that this person is still "Mom," despite their ability to act like adult peers and friends.

➤ Even middle-age, autonomous daughters do not want to relinquish the sense that Mom is like a sanctuary although there is a shift in roles in later life and the daughter becomes Mom's sanctuary.

Can Mothers and Daughters Be True Friends, or Just Peers?

Some mothers and daughters have a perfectly fine peer relationship, but they never quite advance to the level of real friends that is differentiated by a genuine affinity for one another and a sharing of spirit and soul.

Dr. Lucy Rose Fisher, who studied successful peer-like mother-daughter relationships, identifies five qualities that are characteristic of this type of friendship. These pairs of mothers and daughters ...

1. Are realistic and objective with respect to one another.

2. Are significantly involved in one another's life.

3. Are able to maintain their separate boundaries.

4. Value their own independence and are respectful of the other's.

5. Are conscious of not being too dependent on one another.

Candidates for Heartfelt Friendships

Researcher, Karen L. Fingerman, Ph.D., makes a valid point when she says that mothers and daughters will never be at the same stage at the same time. While this affects aspects of their relationship

Pearls of Wisdom

The mother-daughter friendship is "an affectionate relationship that is based on mutual likes, and respect—sometimes even admiration—for each other's differences as adults."

—Victoria Secunda, *When You and Your Mother Can't Be Friends*

Pearls of Wisdom

"One of the best aspects of sharing a real friendship with your mother is knowing that she'll always give you an honest answer or opinion. Even your closest girlfriends might not want to cross certain boundaries that moms and daughters who are friends do not have."

—Sara Jane Harris, age 31, mother of a 2-year-old son in Bethesda, Maryland

and distinguishes intergenerational pairs from friends who are chronological contemporaries, there are many women who have significant, true, and meaningful friendships with older and younger women. In that respect friendship defies the boundaries of age.

Woman to Woman

Now here is an interesting discovery. While we noted that daughters who became mothers suddenly reconnected with their moms in a way that daughters without children didn't, we must also note that parenthood does not appear to be a significant factor in mothers and daughters forming adult friendships with each other. In fact, some say that the arrival of children actually dilutes the importance of a daughter's mother in her life because her own system of support has widened.

Furthermore, there are a number of other factors that effectively bridge the generation gap. Other researchers believe that mothers and daughters have a natural affinity to become friends because they share the same history and biology, know each other very well, and overwhelmingly express the desire to become friends. These pairs have the luxury of being their naked selves in a relationship without having to be concerned with social pretense or chatter just to fill spaces of silence.

Pearls of Wisdom

"When I became a mom, my friendship with my own mother rose to a new level and we became even closer. I now know firsthand how much of her went into raising me."

—Abbey Gleicher, age 30, mother of a toddler son in Rockville, Maryland

But the women who have the best capacity to be friends with their mom, according to a study by Jane B. Abramson, author of *Mothermania, a Psychological Study of Mother-Daughter Conflicts* (Lexington Books, 1987), have been well-mothered, lead rich lives, have self-esteem, are successful, and express psychological well-being.

Friendship Blockers

Elements that block the formation of friendships between some mothers and daughters include …

➤ The inability by daughters to tolerate or accept Mom's bad, as well as her good, qualities.

➤ Their inability to give up the rigid confines of mother-daughter roles.

➤ A lack of natural affinity or love that encourages true intimacy.

➤ The unwillingness or inability to give up old gripes or poor legacies, create better patterns of interaction, or change.

➤ A lack of emotional and supportive reciprocity.

➤ The absence of mutual interest in all aspects of each other's lives.

These are the most prominent blockers. Significant others reside with pairs of mothers and daughters who have not yet reached a level of autonomy and equity.

Is It Possible to Negotiate a Friendship?

Don't worry if you and your daughter aren't friends now. Therapist Dr. Susan Gordon works mostly with women trying to negotiate relationships with important people in their lives, and she says, "Any relationship can be negotiated if you have the skills." That includes friendships with other women, a spouse, your mother, or your daughter.

What this process involves, Gordon feels, is …

1. Loving and accepting one another.

2. Respecting each other's boundaries.

3. Discussing and negotiating boundaries.

4. Showing respect for boundaries.

5. Not intruding upon private areas that are not comfortable to share.

6. Accepting that you have the option to stand back when either mother or daughter wants you to be closer or more revealing and you don't want to.

7. Finding a degree of closeness as friends that is comfortable for both.

8. Allowing the space that each other needs.

9. Providing room for others to enter one another's life.

While all of these nine points are equally important, the final one requires further explanation.

Pearls of Wisdom

"There is plenty of room in our hearts for best friends and good friends. You don't compromise your mother-daughter friendship by bringing in other people."

—Susan Gordon, Ph.D.

Making Room for Other Friendships

One of the primary tenants of friendship, Gordon notes, is allowing each other the freedom to broaden their circle of friends. Demanding exclusivity can damage an otherwise satisfying friendship. This is particularly critical for mother and daughter.

Their friendship is too tight and too close if there isn't room for anyone else, says Dr. Gordon. "A mother or a daughter should not feel threatened by the other bringing new people into their lives who create loving relationships."

This includes a daughter's spouse, her in-laws, or Mom's new husband.

Woman to Woman

Moms beware. It seems that one of the ways your mother-daughter friendship can disintegrate before your eyes is in a dressing room on a shopping excursion together. Nothing arouses those old feelings of being mothered, smothered, and criticized or resurrects old clashes quite like giving your honest opinion on a dress that—in your opinion—is too sexy, an unbecoming color, or tight in all the wrong places. This is one place to use the polite, prudent restraint of friends who are not related.

Recognizing the Look of Friendship

Here are two perspectives, one from a daughter and another from a mom.

A Daughter's Image of Friendship

"There were many times growing up that Mom set aside her role and we just went out and had fun. It might have been something as simple as going out to lunch and talking like girlfriends or as elaborate as camping with me in the outback of Australia when I was 20.

"A couple of years ago when I took all my belongings and moved to Boston for graduate school, my mother and I drove the 800 miles together in a Ryder's truck. That's when we adopted the names of Thelma and Louise. We had a ball talking all the way. We each have a picture of us standing in the back of the truck, sweaty in our jeans with muscles flexed after unloading the whole thing and carrying it up one and a half flights of stairs.

"I know that our friendship is important to my mother so when I am discussing something with her that takes a friend's viewpoint, not a mom's, I tell her if she sounds too mother-like. We can be very honest with each other.

"Our friendship goes both ways. I am interested in what she is doing and ask her lots of questions. She knows that I am there for her. I am still less mature and more defensive than her so she probably has to work a little harder at our friendship than I do."

A Mom's Image of Friendship

"I always knew that I was my daughters' friend. It wasn't until more recently that I knew these adult women were and wanted to be my true friends. That realization came after I began to feel their sincere support and interest in my work along with an accurate realization of my innermost feelings, aspirations, and frustrations.

"I feel as if our friendship is mature and reciprocal now. It is much more than enjoying one another, which we do, and sharing interests, which we do. My daughters extend their groups of friends to me and invite me to be part of their lives outside of what one might expect for women who stick to just their mother-daughter roles and habits.

"I can say with full confidence that I respect and admire the two women who are my daughters. I learn from them and grow with them. Their company is a source of constant joy. I know they work hard at being a friend. I know that I do the same. I don't think friends could possibly be anything more than what we have together."

Pearls of Wisdom

"Daughters have great need for their mothers to be their friends and love them down to their toes no matter what. She needs to feel loved by her mother when she feels the most unloved and the least desirable."

—Mary Lou Johns, Ed.D.

Do You Pass the Friendship Test?

How good of friends are you with your mother or your daughter? This little test will give you the answer and let you know in what areas you are deficient. Simply put a checkmark in the appropriate column.

	Most of the Time	Hardly Ever
1. Do your know what the other is thinking?	_____	_____
2. Are you able to anticipate ways to make life more pleasant and pleasurable for the other?	_____	_____
3. Do you act on this information?	_____	_____
4. Do you enjoy doing things together?	_____	_____
5. Do you find pleasure in talking and sharing life with each other?	_____	_____
6. Do you feel free to be yourself?	_____	_____
7. Do you think your mother or daughter feels free to be herself with you?	_____	_____
8. Can you laugh and have fun together?	_____	_____
9. Can you each be the teacher?	_____	_____
10. Do you find gratification and pleasure in showing interest in the other person's life and accomplishments?	_____	_____

If you are wise and lucky enough to have achieved a friendship that rated 10 checks in the left-hand column, you have something very special to celebrate and savor. If, on the other hand, your checkmarks are lined up unanimously in the right-hand column, you have not yet found the prize package at the bottom of your Cracker Jack box.

The Least You Need to Know

➤ There are differences between mother–daughter friendships and two non-related girlfriends.

➤ Not all mother–daughter friendships extend beyond the limits of peer-like friendships.

➤ Accomplished, well-mothered women have the greatest capacity to become friends with their moms.

➤ A quality friendship is hallmarked by two individuals who possess maturity and autonomy.

➤ Mother–daughter friendships do not exist at the exclusion of other friendships.

Role Models for One and All

Role models provide important life lessons that all mothers and daughters can benefit from. These models come cloaked in the trappings of the famous, professional, and stay-at-home moms. Success at what they do or did and how they have influenced others is what qualifies them for this chapter.

There is no value judgment applied to which mom has done the best job or whose viewpoint is right or wrong. There is no endorsement of feminism, divorce, single moms, or unwed motherhood here. What there is and what is called for is open-minded thinking and recognition of valuable decisions and actions.

Daughters Give Credit to Mom

How rewarding to find *Fortune* magazine's October 25, 1999, issue reported that the women on its Power 50 list gave a lot of credit to their moms. Daughters who attribute much of their success to Mom's influence paint a lovely picture that all of us would like to hang on our wall.

"We never had a box drawn around us like most kids do," Debby Hopkins, CFO of Boeing, told *Fortune*. Evidently her mother, a newspaper columnist, still helps to break down barriers and provides an example of encouragement for Hopkins. A picture of her mom riding an alligator sits on her desk. Hopkins said, "Whenever I feel like I'm up to my ass in alligators, I look at that picture and think, 'Just go for it.'"

The popular writer, Carol Higgins Clark, said in a May 1999 *Good Housekeeping* article that, "In spite of all the hardships, my mother always made sure there was a lot of laughter in our home. That's why, when I started writing mystery novels, I decided to use a humorous angle; it seemed to flow naturally from the way I was raised."

Building Blocks

A **role model** is someone who provides an example of behavior which one chooses to emulate and fashion themselves after.

Terry McMillan, author of the novel turned movie *How Stella Got Her Groove Back,* told *Good Housekeeping* in May 1999 that her mother advised, "Say what you mean and mean it, and be willing to deal with the consequences. It'll make you strong." Although her mother has passed away, her influence has not waned. "... hardly a day that passes that I don't hear her voice, telling me what I know I should do," McMillan said.

You don't have to be on anyone's "list," nor does your mom, to find a perfectly solid and invigorating role model right in your own backyard.

Explosives

According to an opinion poll published in the June 22, 2000, *Wall Street Journal,* then First Lady Hillary Rodham Clinton was the most admired woman in politics by democratic and feminist voters and second to Elizabeth Dole by one percentage point among all categories of women voters. However, she is not likely to be a primary role model for a majority of married women, say the pollsters.

A Model Mom Inspires Both a Daughter and a Granddaughter

"I always admired my mom for her tenacious, hard working, never ending work habits," began 35-year-old Stacey Royer, mother of three daughters under age 8 and part-time professional fundraiser for the Children's Defense Fund.

Her mother, an educator and president of her own philanthropic consulting firm, recently won The Women of Achievement Award given by the YWCA. Stacey is the one who nominated her mother for this impressive local honor.

"Hannah once asked, 'Who invented milk?' I said God. She wanted to know who invented God and then answered the question herself by saying, 'I know, his wife.'"

"I think my daughter is like this thanks to the great role model she has in her life. She is strong and confident."

Pearls of Wisdom

"... Because my mother is an artist and makes an effort to meet other artists everywhere we go, and because we are people of color who take the time to learn as much as we can about the culture we are visiting, and because we treat the people we meet as if the are human beings and not objects, ... we are embraced by people ..."

—Rebecca Walker, daughter of writer Alice Walker and author of *Black White and Jewish; Autobiography of a Shifting Self* (Riverhead Books, 2001).

Beating the Odds with a Model of Love and Wisdom

Thirty-nine-year-old Monique Forte was raised in New York City with her nine siblings by a single mother, Ollie Forte. Although Ollie recently passed away at the age of 60, Monique says she continues to be her role model.

"We grew up in the projects," Monique explained. "It wasn't a very good area. My mother said just because we lived in that environment, we didn't have to be a part of that environment. She showed us how to live with integrity in the midst of all this negativity. Each of my sisters and brothers is leading a beautiful life. No one got shot, did drugs, or went to jail."

"Mom was a strong woman and definitely was a woman of wisdom and knowledge. She taught us how to look at people and love them—not judge them. She allowed us to see the consequences of our own actions. She always said, 'If you are right, you are right, if you are wrong you are wrong, no matter how much I love you.'

"What she taught, she lived by her whole life. She was an evangelist who ministered the word of God, life, and hope. There was a way out of things if one could find ways to change, she said. All ten of us minister that message in some way."

Monique has not only tried to emulate her mother's values and incorporate them into her daily life, but as a single mom herself, has relied upon her technique to raise her 13- and 16-year-old sons. "My mother used reverse psychology on us by holding us responsible for our friends. She said, 'I won't choose your friends for you but if they do something wrong in our house or in the neighborhood you are accountable for them because you brought them there.' It made you very conscious of the friends you chose. I told my 16-year-old son the same thing about a boy I didn't feel good about."

When this boy got Monique's son in trouble she handled it just like her mom did. "He was crying and upset and said he didn't do anything wrong, that it was his friend and he didn't know he was going to steal something," Monique said. "I told him he would have to do better at choosing his friends and get to know them better. He is pretty cautious now."

"Mom always had a way of keeping a smile on her face that said everything will be okay," Monique recounted. "Words cannot describe what this woman did for us and how much of herself she deposited in each and everyone of us."

Pearls of Wisdom

Seventeen-year-old Meagan Ross of Detroit, Michigan, has followed her mother's example when it comes to interacting with others. "My mom taught me how to correctly deal with people, the good and the bad; never let the bad ones get you down and always be able to let go. I also try to give to other people and care about them the way she does."

Step-Moms Can Learn by Margorie's Example

The stepmother-stepdaughter combination is the most difficult one that results from two families joining households. So can you imagine being the mother and step-mom of a total of five young women ranging in age from 14 to 21? That is precisely the position Margorie Engel, at the time a practicing Boston attorney, found herself in after marrying her second husband. Not all of the girls lived with Engel, but she has come to know them well and 15 years later she says, "I love all the kids."

Engel has managed to maintain a friendly relationship with each of these young women, but she is not oblivious to the unique problems that challenge stepfamilies.

Consequently, she became an advocate and spokesperson for stepfamilies, developed an expertise in legal issues that affect stepfamilies, authored two books on related topics, and currently serves as president of the Stepfamily Association of America.

Whether or not a step-mom is able to carve out a successful relationship with her stepdaughter is sometimes beyond her control, particularly if a biological mom is not supportive of the friendship. Even when a mother is deceased, her idealized ghost competes with the step-mom and prevents acceptance, Engel explains.

Engel attributes her own success to …

➤ The fact that she had biological daughters and was already aware "that the mother-daughter relationship is fraught with a lot of tough terrain in the best situations."

➤ Understanding that the most she should expect was to become friends with her stepdaughters, not replace their biological mother. "It really comes to expecting to be a friends."

➤ Realizing that "trying to blend a family sets up a mythical situation."

➤ Allowing the biological parent to deal with issues of visitation, finances, and discipline.

➤ Helping out in areas in which there was some common ground, such as their careers.

➤ Trying to understand and respect the position of her stepdaughter's mother.

➤ Not making a major deal when the girls' biological mother did not want her to attend a special function such as a bridal luncheon, even though she felt awful inside.

➤ Not engaging her stepdaughters in conversation about their private relationship with their biological mother.

➤ The fact that her husband too had children of similar ages as her own, and that as stepparents they had no disparity in tolerance, and that both of their families balanced out the time and commitment they had to other individuals.

Engel isn't blowing her own horn. There are conversations she wished she had engaged in with her stepdaughters when she married their father and things that should not have been said when times heated up with her girls' stepmother and their

Pearls of Wisdom

"I have always felt that there is enough room in your life for everybody and for many different kinds of relationships. You don't need to put everybody in their own separate box and expect them to act according to the same mold."

—Jenny Ryer, 29-year-old daughter and stepdaughter

father. Nonetheless, part of Margorie's empathy to everyone involved—her stepdaughters and their mother—has to do with her own daughters' inheriting a stepmom, too.

Explosives

Here are some facts and figures that will make you get your attention. Sixty-five percent of all remarriages result in the formation of stepfamilies. Roughly 67 percent of all women and 30 percent of all children will spend some time with a stepfamily that is inclusive of cohabiting couples. A large number of remarriages fail because of complications surrounding stepchildren and stepparents.

For more lessons in reality thinking for step-moms, turn back to Chapter 22, "Calling the Doctor." A good resource for step-moms of stepdaughters is the Web site of the Stepfamilies Association of America (www.saafamilies.org). The association helps individuals deal with the legal, family, and psychological issues and dynamics unique to stepfamilies, and provides suggested reading material.

Tight Spots, a Role Model Mom Shares Her Survival Tips

Differences in outlook, values, goals, and ages create a disparity of expectations or "tight spot" that is often more troublesome for Mom than her daughter. What makes a woman caught in a tight spot a role model is how she manages to control her own disappointment and put the lid on her pain and anger in order to maintain a loving, communicative connection with her daughter. That takes real soul-searching, courage, and a more than healthy dose of what every daughter is looking for—acceptance.

Sally's Surprise Tight Spot

When I initially called to ask Sally, a multi-degreed Ph.D. liberal thinker with traditional values and a conventional, long-term marriage to a professional man, if she would be willing to talk about the tight spots she had encountered with her children, she laughed and asked which spot was I referring to. She had already been through her son's divorce five years after an elaborate traditional wedding and the interfaith marriage of one daughter.

I explained I was interested in how she had managed to appear unscathed to the observer's eyes, after fulfilling her seven-month-pregnant daughter's request to throw a small family wedding for her, ASAP. "Oh that one," she replied with laughter.

Of course what the casual bystander did not see was all the "self-talk" that Sally had engaged in for some time. "I am at the point where I know myself well. I know I will get to the state where these horrible feelings will pass and that things will get better. I have faith in myself and my ability to adapt."

"When Beth told us about the pregnancy, I was so shocked at first. I'm sure I must have asked her if she was going to get married, and she said eventually but not now. I had waves of sadness and happiness. I was scared and worried for her. I must have come around really quickly, because I remember going to Beth's doctor appointment with her two days later and cried when I saw the ultrasound. It helped that Beth kept telling me that she knew this was a shock and that it was rough for her, too."

Acting the part of the reassuring mother who said all the right things like, "It will be fine and we love you, we're here for you," actually made those feelings more genuine, Sally said. Still, six months later when Beth said she wanted to get married, Sally admits, "I was surprised and delighted."

Pearls of Wisdom

"The mother-daughter relationship provides a sanctuary throughout our lives. The sanctity and importance of that relationship calls for it to be treated with honor and respect by two people."

—Dr. Susan Gordon

Sally's Self-Talks

Sally has no problem describing what she does or what she tells herself when a tight spot erupts between herself and either of her daughters. Her method has moved her from "catastrophizing" a situation by saying something like, "I'll never be able to see my grandchildren again," to a point of confidence, grounded in the mutual need between mother and daughter, that will move them to the other side of a tight spot.

Nonetheless, when trouble starts Sally deliberately calls up key phrases to remind herself that there are tons of ways to handle the situation besides what she learned from her family of origin.

Woman to Woman

Like many women, Sally has found that some friends are better at helping you get over tight spots than others. "I protect my mental health and have friends who can laugh with me and share honestly. I find it is rare that anyone has this Pollyanna relationship with their daughters. I have had to let go of long-time friends I found made me explain myself and were judgmental. They made me feel bad about myself. I guess the people who really matter to me aren't going to be sarcastic or hurtful."

"My key phrases are, *if your standards are low enough you won't be disappointed*. At first blush that sounds pretty negative, but what it means is that if we get down to basics and your standards are more humble, you will be less likely to get bent out of shape. I also try to remind myself that *life is not a contest.* I grew up driven by high expectations and external standards of achievement. I am constantly trying to draw my psyche back to center and the basics of what is important. I tell myself that *it's just a different world now* and try to focus on the positive things in my life that, years ago I would not have thought possible for me.

"Another thing I tell myself is—*get off the committee before you are kicked off.* For Beth, it was the pregnancy committee, for my other daughter it could have been the preschool or finance committee. This helps to remove myself from their actions. It's a constant challenge to disengage yourself. I am still learning to let go because you want to feel included and needed. This really never gets resolved. As a mother you just have to know where the line is."

Free to Be Me, Free to Be You

The beauty of Sally's hard-fought journey is that she has arrived at an understanding that allows her to enjoy the friendship afforded mothers and daughters who successfully navigate tight spots. Furthermore, she has learned that her focus at this stage of life should be on herself and her husband.

"It felt selfish at first," Sally admitted, because she was used to wanting to please her kids before pleasing herself. Currently she is writing a series of professional management books, expanding her business, and traveling.

Nonetheless, she does confess, "A large part of me and us as a couple has to do with our children because we enjoy being with them."

Pearls of Wisdom

"When I was a rebellious teenager, my mother put up with a lot! I had weird clothes, weird hair, and my room must have smelled bad because I *never* cleaned it. But she let me do all that crazy stuff, so I learned it was okay to express myself. She encouraged me to go to an unusual college where I really flourished ... and low and behold in my adult years, I discovered what an amazing, courageous woman my mother can be."

—Hilari Lipton, age 33, Albuquerque, New Mexico

Single Moms, Proof of Success Is in the Pudding

The single mom in this saga is a role model of strength, dedication, and commitment, with a strong vision of moving ahead.

Before they were out of cribs, Rita's daughters Penny and Polly could be counted among the large contingency of children being raised by single moms. By the time they were seven and eight, their father, a playful and present participant in their lives, remarried, severing all but a minute amount of contact with his daughters. Despite his absence and the emotional toll that might have overwhelmed other impressionable little girls, Polly and Penny managed to get through school as top students, participate in all kinds of extracurricular activities, and develop friendships with boys and girls. Currently they are college grads with budding careers. Marriage is on the horizon for Polly.

A great deal of their success rests with their mother Rita, a 50-year-old educator who has never remarried. "My kids came first. Everything I did I chose to do. I was 100 percent there for them, just as I would be if I were married. They had quality of time, my undivided attention, and physical and emotional support. I must admit that when I got divorced I thought being single would be temporary. But with the men who entered my life, it would have been hard for me to watch them parent my kids. That wasn't martyrdom; it was simply my choice, as was not having men sleep over. There was just a real respect among the three of us for each other."

"You cannot compensate for the lack of a father. I felt my time and energy would best be spent in supporting them, being open to listening to them without poking around and intruding on feelings they did not want to share. We were very up front and forthcoming with each other. I wasn't looking for anyone to take the place of their father, and I didn't try to replace him either. Even though our family had a missing link, I could provide the girls with the example of a work ethic,

Pearls of Wisdom

"My mother and I have a unique bond because I am single and she is widowed. We really support each other. I listen to her and she listens to me. I will always be eternally grateful to her for showing me how to be a mother and for her support."

—Karen Robins, age 50 whose mother is 80, Phoenix, Arizona

Pearls of Wisdom

"I want to move in a fashion that helps me through the transition of letting go of motherhood and moving into my womanhood .... To teach and learn and accomplish things."

—Goldie Hawn, actress, *Redbook*, July 2000

how to deal with people, and how to be a strong female. I presented myself as a very real person with flaws who had achieved a healthy balance.

"I think they would agree that they came through as unscathed as one can under the circumstances, although not having a father in their lives will always affect them, partly because I didn't allow them to use that as an excuse. I knew that factored into the equation and I validated those feelings, but they knew that they were expected to move on as I had and become lifelong learners about the world and themselves."

The Least You Need to Know

➤ Daughters find role models in mothers who teach them how to live life to the fullest with integrity and conviction.

➤ Step-moms rarely, if ever, take the place of biological moms and need to create a different role for themselves.

➤ Mothers manage to successfully survive "tight spots" if they evaluate what is really important in their lives and in their daughter's.

➤ Single moms looking for role models should select women who know how to move ahead without looking back.

Chapter 25

The Icing on the Cake: Grandmothers and Granddaughters

In This Chapter

➤ A grandmother's special love

➤ Grandma's many roles

➤ Long–distance grandmothering

➤ Precious memories

➤ Make room for grandsons

The relationship between grandmother and grandchild is a natural one that proves to be a most delectable and delicious treat. Indeed, there are plenty of jokes that refer to throwing out their parents and keeping the grandchildren. A grandchild provides so much pleasure for grandparents that all attention shifts to them. I know this personally, because my daughter has to repeatedly remind me to give her a kiss once I come up for air from embracing my grandchild after stepping off the plane.

This chapter attempts to describe the indescribable emotions of grandparents, shed light on their many roles, and reveal the precious moments spent with grandchildren.

Looking at Things from a Daughter's and Grandmother's Point of View

No matter what sex the baby, there is something warm and wonderful seeing your mother with a child you have produced. There is a sense of pride and gift-giving.

Explosives

Victoria Secunda, author of *Why You and Your Mother Can't Be Friends,* believes that daughters should be on the lookout when it comes to grandmothers because your child presents a situation in which she thinks she may have another chance to parent. "If she cannot have you-as-child, at least she can rekindle her mothering authority as a grand-mother, telling you how best to do your parenting job," warns Secunda. "And that's when the trouble often starts, when there may have been little, or none, before."

Presenting a Granddaughter

Joanne McCoy is one of eight children. Her mother—Marian, who lives in Dallas—was amazing, Joanne said. "She showed so much love to all of us. She really made each one in my family feel special."

Consequently when Joanne had a little girl, she decided to name her Marian after her mother. "It was wonderful for me to be able to name my daughter after such a wonderful mom and be able to pass along that name as a legacy. I know it made my mother feel very special."

Presenting a Grandson

"It makes me feel more proud than ever of being able to give my mom two wonderful grandsons," said Jill Abolt, an ex-patriot living in Buenos Aires with her husband. "I get so excited each time my mom walks off the plane and see how big she can smile from just seeing Josh and Alex. It feels like the best grade I ever got! It means the world to me that my mom has made such efforts to come and visit the boys no matter how far away we are."

Becoming a Grandmother

"You enjoy your grandchildren more than your own. You have the opportunity to look at a very different world through their eyes as girls today. It is very

Pearls of Wisdom

"A mother becomes a true grand-mother the day she stops noticing the terrible things her children do because she is so enchanted with the wonderful things her grand-children do."

—Lois Wyse, *Funny You Don't Look Like a Grandmother* (Avon Books, 1990)

interesting. I find myself trying to hold them back and keep them young. They are influenced so early by a sexual culture," remarked Barbara Brandt, mother of two daughters and one son, and grandmother of three granddaughters and two grandsons.

"I think it is very natural for a grandmother and granddaughter to bond and to look more to the fun side of things with them. If you daughter feels she has been loved, she is happy to see this closeness develop between her mother and her daughter."

Uncovering Grandma's Many Talents

There is no doubt that a mother's love for her daughter's little one, whether boy or girl, is a reflection of her love for her daughter, adds to a daughter's feelings of acceptance, and is deeply gratifying for both women. But that is just the tip of the iceberg!

Grandma's Unique Mixture

A grandmother is a unique blend of essential and nonessential elements. She ...

➤ Enriches her grandchild's life with love, affection, support, and a connection to a family history.

➤ Is a playful companion, baby-sitter, friend, and confidante.

➤ Can act as an intermediary between mother and daughter during difficult times.

➤ Can give guidance and advice that sometimes parents are not able to.

➤ Has the luxury of spoiling a child without dealing with the consequences.

➤ Is often a role model and a figure of female power.

➤ Is able to experience the sheer delight of her grandchildren and provide unequivocal acceptance because she is not responsible for them.

➤ May have to assume a parent's role by proxy or fulfill emotional and security needs in her granddaughter's life.

➤ Can be more concerned about the grandchild's individual needs because there is not that same concern expressed by parents that their children's behavior reflects upon them.

Woman to Woman

Ann F. Caron, Ed.D., author of *Mothers to Daughters: Searching for New Connections* (Owl Books, 1999), says that grandmothers can be particularly useful and helpful to mothers because the older woman can balance the younger one's concerns by offering a viewpoint that spans a much longer period of time.

➤ Has fewer expectations of her grandchildren than their mother, which makes it easier for the grandkids to feel fully accepted and experience less pressure.

➤ Is able to see and evaluate things more clearly.

Proximity, economic considerations, health factors, a daughter and her mother's marital status, and personality traits often determine which of the above roles a grandmother plays in her granddaughter's life. However, as statistics prove, many more grandmothers today are finding themselves fitting into the role as primary caregiver.

Grandma, Acting as a Backup

Hope Edelman, author of *Mother of My Mother* (Random House 1999), explains that, "Dependable, predictable adults are the foundation of a child's world. In the child's mind, grandparents serve as backup parents, the nest that will break the family's fall."

Pearls of Wisdom

"White hair that melts into gray, softly framing flawless ivory skin and delicate blue eyes. Her elegance is easily visible and after a few words so is her wisdom. She is more than a grandmother. She is a matriarch, nurturer, second mother and friend. My grandmother is all of these things and more to me. She has given me strength, advice, and unconditional love, for this, I will always be grateful."

—Jamie Robins, age 23, Virginia

According to figures reported by Generations United, a national coalition organization, in 2000 nearly 2.5 million grandparents have become backup parents, raising 3.9 million of the children not living with parents. The primary causes they cite for the broken nest and subsequent grandparent role are: divorce, substance abuse, parental death, abuse, neglect, poverty, family violence, unemployment, incarceration, abandonment, mental health problems, AIDS, and teenage pregnancy.

A grandmother must, nonetheless, protect herself when she is called upon too often, said Mamie McCamey. Her daughter came to live with her when she was pregnant and about due to deliver a girl. These three generations of women lived together until Mamie's granddaughter was grown.

Ensuring Emotional Closeness

Determining whether or not a grandmother or granddaughter will be close depends on several factors, Edelman says. She found in her study that in cases where the mother and younger daughter are close, then the grandmother takes on a more supplemental role. Secondly, Edelman factors in the proximity of the grandmother and says that it is easier to develop an emotionally close relationship with a grandmother who is not separated by distance. Third, she points to how compatible grandmother and granddaughter are.

Maintaining Close Connection Despite the Distance

However, this doesn't tell the entire story. Sixty million grandparents in the United States live in a separate city from at least one grandchild. These grandmothers are working hard to create an emotional closeness with grandchildren. In order to accomplish this, they visit or call often, write letters, and include self-addressed envelopes, send pictures, tape message, communicate via e-mail, and show as much concern, interest, and love as possible.

Maternal grandmothers may have an edge on long-distance grandparenting. A mother is the parent who most often gives or denies access to her children. Therefore, sociologists Andrew J. Cherlin and Frank F. Furstenberg Jr., co-authors of *The New American Grandparent* (Harvard University Press, 1992), advise grandparents to be careful to develop and maintain a good relationship with their grandchildren's mom.

Pearls of Wisdom

When asked what is it like to be a great-grandmother, 86-year-old Ida Rosen replied, "Need I tell you? It is seventh heaven!"

Woman to Woman

Grandparents are eventually relegated to a "ceremonial position" that replaces their younger, more interactive days. That's why it is important to build a relationship that will reach well into their adulthood. One realistic grandma who planned trips and all kinds of fun when the grandkids were young said, "I know what will eventually happen. Our grandchildren won't always be so available and we will become less important to them. But their memories will be good."

289

Making Every Visit Count

Whether you are around the block or halfway around the world, grandmas should work on ensuring that their visits go smoothly. Take time to be alone with your granddaughter, and show interest in her activities. Don't interrupt her normal activities, and don't overstay your welcome. Do fun things and leave behind good memories. Be helpful to your granddaughter and her mother. And bring surprise packages—everybody loves them! As delicious and delightful as grandmothering is, make no mistake that there is thoughtful effort involved in the best relationships.

Enjoying Precious Moments and Memories

Grandmothers make a lasting, loving impression. There is no better way to express this than through beautiful memories shared by granddaughters.

Hearing a Different Kind of Bedtime Story

"The most precious moments with my grandma are spent listening to her recount the stories of her life. Sitting in her bedroom, we share hours talking and reminiscing. When she begins telling a story or anecdote I see her return to times past. Her narrative is vivid and complete, evoking emotions that she felt; happiness, joy, wonder, and at times, sadness. This time with my grandmother not only furthers my understanding of her, but enables me to apply the lessons of her life to my own," said Jody Robins, 22, of Los Angeles.

Pearls of Wisdom

"When my grandmother finally dies ... I know it is mainly experience which binds us, memory, and not blood. Now, only I hold the memories of our time together. Only I nurture our relationship, massaging it to yield sustenance, a sense of being connected through time and space and culture."

—Rebecca Walker, author of *Black White and Jewish: Autobiography of Shifting Self*

Wearing a Name with Pride

"I am actually named for both of my grandmothers, Eleanor Reilly Ackley. On October 22, 1970, they may have felt honored to have this new baby named for both of them, but it was I who was given the honors that day.

"My two grandmothers could not have been more different, but I had a loving relationship with each of them. I have never tired of people telling me, upon learning my name, how they knew the original Eleanor Ackley for years and what a wonderful woman she was and is. My other grandmother suffered a debilitating stroke when I was four. I didn't realize what an influence she had on me until around the time of my wedding when my mother and I would wonder what she would think, how she would word something, or what she would order as we made all of the wedding arrangements. We kept her in mind a lot, and I think she would have approved of it all (including the groom)!"

Celebrating Holidays with Grandma

Whenever I set a holiday table, my mind wanders over the trails of my youth. Invariably I picture my sisters and I huddled in the backseat of our yellow convertible for the four-hour ride to our grandmother's house. We were content to sit quietly, awaiting the affection and attention that my Grandma Raab would shower upon us when we arrived. I sense again how grand the dining room in her house appeared before my youthful eyes—lead glass window, velvet upholstered high back chairs, elegant touches of china and crystal made me feel like a princess.

Upon dismantling her home more than 20 years ago, my grandmother gave me some of the china and silver pieces I was accustomed to seeing on her meticulously arranged, oversized holiday tables. It was with pure joy that first holiday in my own home with my grandmother at my table beaming at the familiar serving pieces and place settings.

Each holiday table is a potpourri of tears as well as laughter. Before I knew it, my holiday table was changing, the number around it in flux. Grandma was right, using her beautiful heirlooms warmly reminds me of her presence now that she is gone. The opportunity to reflect on our special relationship is soothing.

Woman to Woman

How actively helpful a grand-daughter becomes during the years in which her grandmother is aging or infirm depends on several factors. The most notable take into account her mother's involvement, the quality of the grandmother–granddaughter relationship, and proximity.

Bonding with Your Grandsons Is Just as Easy

There is a new man in my life. I am completely love-struck and starved for his presence, despite the age difference that spans half a century. Missing him can send me into an ice cream binge that won't begin to squelch my desire just for him.

We fell in love one night as he lay on my shoulder shortly after his birth, in the darkness and solitude of my daughter's home while Andrew's parents slept. I was at liberty to endlessly walk around the house and brush my face against his for a week, rock him in whatever direction I deemed best, and whisper into his ear any words I wished.

Planting kisses on his little head I said, "Ma Ro is here Andrew. Ma Ro loves you." I knew Andrew loved me, too. And so began our night-long talks. For the most part, his big eyes were open and attentive to the story characters I made up just for him, the plans I revealed for our future, and tales of his mother's childhood.

Woman to Woman

For issues and answers pertaining to grandparenting try logging onto www.grandparenting.org, the Foundation for Grandparenting, a nonprofit educational and re-source organization.

I know it won't be a public love affair and that giving him garbage truck rides and rolling him over my head to land softly on the couch or make whirring noises with me and his fire trucks, which I keep at my house, will soon be traded in for big guy friends who play ball. But this little fellow has opened up a whole new world for me—not just the marvels and wonders of grandmothering—but of having a boy in my life after only raising girls.

It might be a challenge for me to find ways to continue to relate as he grows. I may have to improve my pitching arm, learn the intricacies of soccer, or brush up on rocket science. But there is no doubt I will! Just hearing his long-distance voice or a garbled, 22-month-old's rushed, "Hi Ma Ro" add a gleam to my face and ignites a flame in my heart that isn't reserved for granddaughters only.

The Least You Need to Know

➤ Grandmothers add an important, loving, and helpful dimension to a child's life.

➤ Grandmothers create different relationships with their granddaughters than they did with their daughters.

➤ Grandmothers must take the initiative to forge out relationships with their granddaughters and make themselves available to them.

➤ Moments between grandmothers and granddaughters form precious moments that last for a lifetime.

Chapter 26

Savored Moments and Memories

In This Chapter

➤ Creating cherished moments

➤ Polishing the sparkle of memories

➤ Sharing a unique way to honor Mom

➤ Hats off to daughters

➤ Making toasts to moms

This chapter is one of sheer pleasure and joy. It should result in smiles and tears of recognition. It is the calm after the storm of adolescence, the struggle for autonomy, the bouts of mother-blame, the pre-wedding arguments, and innumerable arguments and makeups. It is your pot of gold at the end of your rainbow!

Beginning the Celebration

We are through analyzing the complicated intricacies of the mother-daughter relationship. It is time to celebrate and share our savored moments and fondest memories. These are, after all, the precise goals that all of us as mothers and daughters should have in mind.

The best joys of motherhood and daughterhood are simple. They evolve from the pleasures of being together, learning from one another, understanding each other, and uniting in friendship and womanhood. The seeds for such rewards can be sown intentionally or arise inadvertently out of the most ordinary moments. However they bloom, they leave their marks on each of our lives.

In celebration of the journey we have taken together, the one you have taken individually within your family circle, or the one you are about to embark upon, I offer a collection of savored moments and memories from childhood to old age. They are an inspiration for all that mothers and daughters can be.

Creating Memories and Moments to Last a Lifetime

If you wish to purposefully sow the seeds of a savored moment, I have some recommendations on how to begin. Although complete clarity of the meaning and emotion of these moments will not be possible until you have indulged yourself in reading the entire chapter.

Nonetheless, for moms and daughters seeking a beginning, what you are looking for is an atmosphere that …

➤ Encourages you to talk.

➤ Allows you to be silent.

➤ Fosters discoveries.

➤ Reinforces the mutual security and safety you feel in one another's presence.

A quiet walk, new adventure, intimate lunch, or any number of shared activities can act as a catalyst. To make the most of the proper atmosphere, use what you have learned in this book. So much of what happens between mother and daughter is automatic. However, so much of really good mothering and daughtering is intentional and necessary.

It's All in How You Read It—Together

Book clubs for adults foster intimacy, growth, intellectual insight, understanding, and friendship among close participants. They can do the same for mothers and daughters.

Leigh Merinoff and her daughter Leslie, age 13, had been involved in a mother-daughter book club for almost 4 years. "It gives us a commitment together once a month," Leigh explained. "It started out as something that Leslie and I did that her brother wasn't included in. It was a way to feel more sophisticated. She went in her PJs and it was fun. It is something she and I do together, something that doesn't involve her friends or mine. The book club is like this little secret activity that no one else shares. We are able to sidestep everything else in our family, enjoy ourselves, and pass the gift of literature to our daughters. It had helped created a bond when others are having problems."

I think the most telling of all the things Leigh shared with me about this marvelous experience was this: "Three years ago when we started the group, the daughters would choose to sit across from all of the moms and when we would speak they laughed and squirmed. They all complained like crazy but went anyway. Now Leslie sits next to me."

Some Fresh Air Might Do You and Your Relationship Some Good

Every now and then it is important to breathe fresh air into our mother-daughter relationships. That was what Susan Neumer from Chicago had in mind when she took her 24-year-old daughter, Alison, to Vail for morning hikes and nighttime talks. It turned out to be the optimal, idyllic spot in which they could reawaken their closeness and carry on important talks and decision making without interruption.

"The trip wasn't just one of those special moments," Susan said. "It was one of those fantastic times together. The kind of time you can't have

Pearls of Wisdom

"I am beyond grateful for the times we (Hillary and Chelsea) have circled the globe together. And if those travels have changed minds in countries where daughters are not as prized as sons—well, all the better."

—Hillary Rodham Clinton, former First Lady and now a New York senator, in *People* magazine, February 15, 1999

with a grown child unless you are in a setting separate and apart from all of the normal pressures one deals with in regular life."

Susan set the scene. "Alison was at a crossroads in her life: She had broken up with her boyfriend and was thinking about changing jobs. She had moved away from home and we lost the opportunity to talk and be intimate in a way that we used to."

Pearls of Wisdom

"I always remind Meagan that we all make mistakes and I will not always be the perfect mother, or she, the perfect daughter. But in my heart, I will always try to understand her needs and her dreams, and will be there for her always."

—Elizabeth Ross, Bloomfield Hills, Michigan

Pearls of Wisdom

When a mother passes away prematurely, there will always be a void at special times. "I really missed my mother at my wedding and the birth of my kids. I don't know how she would have been with her grandchildren."

—Eliana Abbema, mother of three, Nairobi, Kenya

"We hiked separately since Alison was more advanced than I and at night we got into bed and talked. The hotel only had a room with a king-size bed available. Our talks were very important because we were having communication problems. We needed an atmosphere where no one could intrude on our lives and there would be real freedom to explore each other. We needed a place that would help conversation flow rather than force our lines of communication open.

"Alison really opened up, and I think I learned to respect her independence on that trip. I could see her coming together in front of my eyes. She was beautiful in every respect and it made me feel good inside. There were so many warm and cozy moments. In many ways it was like having a small child again. There was just us, isolated from everyone and everything else, including adult burdens that confronted us both."

The trip, five days and six nights in total, left a lingering affect on Susan and Alison. "I think our communication has been far better and we are kinder to each other and have more of a tendency to give us each greater latitude."

Building a Tribute to Our Mothers: The Chair Project

Each of us finds a way to express ourselves. Some are more original than others. An 8-month project by 12 intergenerational women in Columbus, Ohio, titled "Stories of Sacred Thrones: Commemorating Our Mothers" is certainly among the most unique and touching tributes to mothers. The project culminated with an art exhibition bearing the title, "Chairs Always to Have So your Mom Can Sit Beside You." Ermajean MacDonald Tucker, Lucinda's 79-year-old mother flew in for the show.

The Thoughts Behind Chairs for Our Mothers

"It started by writing about our mothers and imagining them sitting somewhere," said Lucinda Kirk, leader and group originator. "One person's memory triggered another person's memory. Doing the project was a wonderful way to revisit and settle some of those earlier, rebellious times."

Woman to Woman

When Blair Schroeder was 17, she used money from an after-school job to buy her mother a diamond bracelet. Her mother graciously accepted the gift, returned it, and then told Blair that all she wanted was a sweater and put the balance back into her daughter's savings account. Unfortunately, Blair's mother, Gladys, passed away when her daughter was in her early 20s. Nonetheless, Blair remembers her mother's kindness to this day.

In the process of decorating chairs that were meant to describe and identify their mothers, each of the women made significant revelations. The pasted photographs, favorite objects, packs of cigarettes, letters, and other odd scraps of memorabilia depicted Mom—as did the daughters' written descriptions. All had a surprising impact on the creator.

Rediscovered Memories

"We were amazed at who our mothers were, beyond being our mothers. We were looking for all of their identities. We found that decorating our chairs was a way of making peace and honoring them. Decor-ating my chair was a reminder that my mother had always been creating art in her decoupage, needlepoint, and sewing. It gave me greater understanding that she is a person," Lucinda explained.

Pearls of Wisdom

"When my three girls were growing up, one was smart, one was sweet, and one was pretty. Now they are all grown up and every one of the is smart, sweet and pretty."

—Betty Schiff, Sarasota, Florida

"My mother loved her chair. She was pleased and amused at the way I had represented her. I wanted her to come up from Florida so that I could talk her through what I had put on it. I meant it to really honor her. Our mothers were not really honored in the generation in which they grew up. I thought that it must be the first time in her life something was all about her, not my father or his business and their public life. I think for her it was something quite extraordinary to have your daughter honor you in that way. She was surprised at how much time and thought it had taken to create the project and the chair. I know she liked seeing me in my professional role." In conjunction with the project, Lucinda, an English instructor at Ohio State University, presented a paper to academic folklorists.

Lucinda's involvement in the chair project spanned three generations. Carmen, her college-age daughter participated as well and did not allow her mother to see her chair until she could unveil the completed object. When she did Lucinda said, "I was honored and surprised by what she had written and the images she had used. There was a tree with branches and I saw how intertwined the things were that she had gotten from me. There were things I had given her that I thought she had forgotten about. It was a beautiful chair."

Celebrating Mothers Everywhere and the Spirit That Unites Us

As mothers, each of us is unique. Nonetheless, the spirit of motherhood unites us worldwide, and I realized this when I went to visit my daughter in the Peace Corps in East Africa. Even before I had arrived I had tried to take consolation and find comfort in the protection my daughter, Halley, insisted the Kenyan women, whom she referred to as "the mamas," afforded her.

"Don't worry so much," she wrote. "Mamas are everywhere. When I ride the *matatu* (a local bus), I sit next to a mama or rest my head on her back if I am standing. It's okay. Mamas are like that."

Once I arrived in Kenya I wanted to see this selfless brigade that dotted the hillsides, tending crops and standing watch as my daughter wound her way through their small farms. At the mention of Mama Hannah, the woman Halley lived with for three months during training, I felt a twinge of jealousy. After all, the title represented a sacred relationship I thought should be reserved for me.

There could be no denying, however, that Mama Hannah extended the same concern and care to my daughter that she did to her five children, the oldest of whom was named Hannah. When I finally climbed the steep dirt road to Mama Hannah's small wooden home and was greeted by this small woman with a scarf wrapped around her head, tears streamed down my face. That defied the barrier of our languages and expressed my appreciation for serving Halley double portions of food, carefully boiling her water, and watching over her when she became ill.

Later in our journey I, too, was called Mama by those African men and women younger than I. The label made me proud of my age, my maternal accomplishments, and my daughter. By the time we arrived at Halley's cozy four-room home in a rural city named Machakos, I was comfortable sharing Halley with the other mamas, particularly Mama Joanne. Halley had had the good fortune of renting from Mama Joanne Madanguda, living within snoring distance of her home, and being warmly invited to be a part of her family. This remarkable woman found time for everything, including making sure that her fair-skinned American daughter wore sun block, learned how to cook on paraffin burners, and was neatly dressed in public.

When I walked in our daughter's home, I sensed that Mama Joanne also had something to do with the fact that this was the neatest, cleanest, most acceptable place Halley had lived in since leaving for college in Wisconsin five years ago.

We accepted an invitation for lunch at Mama's. I immediately became at ease in her kitchen, helping her prepare *chapati* (fried bread) while our daughters sat back and laughed as we mamas explored each other's lives. We talked about women's issues, the absence of chickens outside my back door, and the fact that I owned a washing machine and dryer. When we pulled out of Mama Joanne's compound two days later, she waved vigorously with both arms.

I thought of Mama on the day I was scheduled to fly home and leave Halley in Kenya. The thought of parting made Halley and I sad and silent. The only remedy that occurred to me to ease the pain was to call Mama Joanne. Halley, red-eyed but steady, dialed the number from our hotel in Nairobi. Mama answered and, with her usual enthusiasm, laughter, and insight began by saying, "Halley we can't wait for you to come home. We miss you." A smile quickly spread over our daughter's face.

Pearls of Wisdom

"A mother understands what a child does not say."

—Unattributed

Proposing a Toast to My Daughters and All of Yours

Here's to surviving me, loving me, and becoming the marvelous women you are!

Watching you become women, mothers, professionals, and compassionate citizens is a marvel and a joy. You are full of talents as well as understanding, forgiveness, humor, and empathy that make you special individuals. Your intellect and curiosity propels you constantly to new heights and I relish sharing in your discoveries and learning from you. Your rich lives have turned you into my teachers and role models. The desire to remain a source of information and inspiration to you demands my own daily growth.

Pearls of Wisdom

"I loved my mother so much ... she wasn't remarkable or anything ... just a good mom. People would say to me all the time that I had become my mother's mother ... 'No, no; I am her daughter. I am still learning from her.' To the very end she had the ability, by sheer presence, to change the way I felt about the world."

—Gaye Dunn about her mother who suffered with Alzheimer's (*Mothers and Daughters*, a pictorial book by Lauren Cowen and Jayne Wexler, 1997, Courage Books)

I look forward to the future and appreciate the past that has so generously unfolded a history of love, respect, and friendship. I count myself among the luckiest women on the planet who have had the opportunity and good fortune to experience the joy of daughters. The bond between us as mother and daughter, and as woman and woman, is a gift not to be taken for granted. It must be celebrated and cherished.

Pearls of Wisdom

Goldie Hawn told *Redbook* in July 2000, that she stopped working for a period after her mom became terminally ill: "My mother was a big part of my life and it was a joy to be able to take care of her till the end. I've made choices not to work, choices not to go out of town, choices in terms of my priorities ... but there's nothing I would call a sacrifice."

To my girls, Sara Jane and Halley, and to all daughters, this is a toast to you—the light and love of your mothers' lives!

Proposing a Toast to Our Moms

To my mother and all moms who have loved us unfailingly, worried about us without reprieve, taught us repeatedly, and put all of their energies, dreams, and wisdom into raising us—your daughters, I toast and thank you. Your fortitude, foresight, and forgiveness is of such huge magnitude that only other mothers can comprehend it.

However, never think that your daughters have not reaped the benefit of your endless time and careful, thoughtful nurturing. Just look at the women who stand before you—those who have joined the circle of womanhood, offered their friendship, and expressed their love and concern. Hopefully we are proof that we have been worthy of your endless mothering.

What can we offer as a gift in return? The best we have to give is our love, compassion, empathy, understanding, forgiveness, respect, and friendship. My hope is that as daughters, I, and all the rest of us, Mom, can be a source of your joy, pride, and comfort as the years continue to unfold.

The Least You Need to Know

➤ Taking time to share moments as mother and daughter is a gift worth giving.

➤ Celebrating our mothers, our daughters, and our relationships is a reminder to each of us of their value.

➤ Realizing that there is nothing quite like a mother.

➤ Realizing that there is nothing that can compare to a daughter.

Suggested Reference Books on Early Childhood Development

The early years of your child's development are critical to his or her well-being. Therefore moms and dads should take time to educate themselves for the task of childrearing. The list of books in this appendix has been compiled to help you understand and enjoy the process. The reward of your diligence will be happy, healthy parents and children.

Allen, Eileen K., and Lynn R. Allen. *By the Ages: Behavior and Development of Children Prebirth Through 8*. Marotz, Delmar Publishers, 2000.

Eisenberg, Arlene, Heidi E. Murkoff, and Sandee E. Hathaway, B.S.N. *What to Expect the First Year*. Workman Publishing Company, 1996.

Faber, Adele, and Elaine Mazlish. *How to Talk So Kids Will Listen and Listen So Kids Will Talk*. Avon Books, 1999.

Farber, Betty, ed. *Guiding Young Children's Behavior: Helpful Ideas for Parents and Teachers from 28 Early Childhood Experts*. Preschool Publishers, 1998.

Lovine, Vicki. *The Girlfriend's Guide to Surviving the First Year of Motherhood*. Berkeley Publishing, 1997.

Mack, Alison. *Toilet Learning: The Picture Book Technique for Children and Parents*. Little Brown and Company, 1978.

Pruett, Kyle D., M.D. *Me, Myself and I: How Children Build Their Sense of Self: 18 to 36 Months*. Goddard Press, 1999.

Pruitt, David B., M.D., Editor-in-Chief. *Your Child: Emotional, Behavioral, and Cognitive Development from Birth through Preadolescence.* Harper Resource, 1999.

Spock, Benjamin, M.D., and Steven Parker, M.D. *Dr. Spock's Baby and Childcare: A Handbook for Parents of the Developing Child from Birth Through Adolescence Revised and Updated.* Penguin Putnam, 1998.

Vocabulary Words

anorexia nervosa   A potentially life-threatening eating disorder.

authentic individual   Includes all of the experiences, emotions, and thoughts of a person that contribute to her complete and true identity.

belief system   A composite of fundamental ideas that affect how an individual looks at and evaluates circumstances, experiences, or people.

bias filters   Factors that affect an individual's perception of the work around them.

bonding   The attachment mothers rapidly form with their infants after birth.

co-dependency   A serious personality disorder in which there is a loss of self, where other peoples' needs become more important than one's own.

conduct disorder   A behavioral problem that is characterized by excessive and destructive actions.

conflict   The eruption of mental tension born out of differing desires, needs, and forces.

co-parenting   Two parents sharing in responsibilities and decision making, and providing for the physical and emotional care of children.

defectors   Daughters who leave their childhood home and sever all contact with their mothers.

diversity   A variety of individual differences (in the contemporary sociological sense).

dysfunctional family   A unit that functions abnormally or inadequately and is, therefore, considered impaired.

egocentric   To focus on oneself and the relationship of all external factors to themselves.

emotional intelligence A collection of mental abilities that help an individual recognize and understand feelings and emotions.

emotional intent The unspoken emotion behind words.

empathy The ability to project one's own intellect and feelings into another person's life, situation, or experience.

evolution The scientific study of the development of a physical organ or organism over time.

evolutionary psychology The study and reconstruction of the past and how it has influenced contemporary behavior.

family Two or more people who not only share a common residence, but an economy and affection.

family alliance A bond between two family members that affects the structure and functioning of the entire unit.

filial anxiety Worry expressed (during a time period in which a mother is in good health) by middle-aged daughters about their mothers' future need for assistance.

filial responsibility The perceived level of responsibility by a son or daughter toward their parents.

financial independence To be economically self-sufficient.

genes The matter within the male and female chromosome that determine inherited characteristics in a new life.

guilt The legal or ethical acceptance of having done something that is wrong.

imitation theories Theories that describe a child's early identification with and desire to model after the same sex parent.

individuation To take responsibility for one's adult self and actions.

interdependence The mutual intermingling of independence and dependence that affect caring, support, and interaction.

intergenerational independence Individuals who belong to different generations and live autonomous, independent lives.

intervention The process of confronting an individual with regard to serious and potentially damaging actions.

intrudress A woman who intrudes and thrusts herself upon others without being welcome and enters into conversations and places where she has no right to be.

intrusive To intrude or to force oneself or one's opinion where not wanted, invited, or welcome.

loneliness An internal sensation or feeling of being alone, out-of-place, or disconnected.

martyr mother A mother who holds onto the sacrifices made for her children and tries to extract guilt and gratitude from them.

maternal introject A psychological term referring to that part of a mother's voice or messages that live within her child's psyche.

matrophobia The fear of becoming like one's mother and emulating her basic characteristics.

menarche A girl's first menstrual cycle.

micromanager An individual who oversees and takes responsibility for the smaller details.

narcissism An extreme interest and preoccupation with oneself.

oppositional defiant disorder A malady that is characterized by uncooperative, defiant, and hostile behavior towards authority figures and interferes with daily functioning.

overly sensitive To feel rejection and pain that is unwarranted.

parental anxiety The concern parents have for their future needs and whether or not their daughter will be willing to care for them as they age.

psychological edge To have a greater ability to think logically and systematically than another individual or individuals.

rapport The natural harmony between two people that enables them to feel comfort and pleasure in one another's company.

reaction formation The act of thwarting or rejecting the maternal introject.

reactive problem A problem that arises as a result of another person's actions or behavior.

repressed memories Past events buried in the unconscious mind.

resiliency The ability to rebound or recover and regain emotional or physical strength after confronting a situation that compromised one's normal state of being.

resolution Coming to terms with a situation or finding a solution.

reverse mortgage A home equity loan that converts equity in a home for cash and is paid in allotments to the lender.

rite of passage A formal custom, ceremony, or event that marks the transition of an individual into adulthood or an organization.

role model Someone who provides an example of behavior which one chooses to emulate and fashion themselves after.

self-esteem   The expression of how much an individual values him or herself.

self-reflective   The ongoing thought process in which an individual stands back and evaluates his or her own behavior.

self-supporting   The ability to financially support oneself.

sibling rivalry   The rivalry felt between children in a family for the affection and attention of their parents.

sociology   The study of human behavior based on how relationships come into being, what social forces maintain and change them, and why they dissolve.

superego   The individual's mental makeup that is the expression of conscience, guilt, and moral attitudes.

temperament   The constitution of innate qualities at birth that determine one's reaction to his or her environment.

testosterone   A chemical found in larger quantities in males and attributed with primary gender differences.

vibrancy   A state of mental health that denotes acceptance of self and is not dependent upon outside acceptance.

young-old   Individuals over 65 who maintain active, vital lives and have up-to-date interest in the larger world.

Index

C